Pilgrim Spy

Pilgrim Spy

My Secret War Against Putin,
the KGB and the Stasi

TOM SHORE

CORONET

First published in Great Britain in 2018 by Coronet
An Imprint of Hodder & Stoughton
An Hachette UK Company

1

A CIP catalogue record for this title is
available from the British Library

Hardback ISBN 9781473696754
Trade paperback ISBN 9781473696761
eBook ISBN 9781473696785

Typeset in Bembo MT Pro by Palimpsest Book Production Ltd,
Falkirk, Stirlingshire

Printed and bound in Great Britain by Clays Ltd, Elcograf S.p.A.

Hodder & Stoughton policy is to use papers that are natural, renewable
and recyclable products and made from wood grown in sustainable forests.
The logging and manufacturing processes are expected to conform to the
environmental regulations of the country of origin.

Hodder & Stoughton Ltd
Carmelite House
50 Victoria Embankment
London EC4Y 0DZ

www.hodder.co.uk

The words 'Always a Little Further' are engraved on the stone-work of Ascension at Hereford Cathedral and on the Regimental Clock Tower, which stands in Stirling Lines, Hereford, and carries the names of those who were killed in action and therefore failed to 'beat the clock'. The words are from the 1913 poem *The Golden Journey to Samarkand* by James Elroy Flecker, and were adopted by the SAS in the 1960s.

We are the Pilgrims, master; we shall go
Always a little further: it may be
Beyond that last blue mountain barred with snow
Across that angry or that glimmering sea . . .

The most potent weapon in the hands of the oppressor is the mind of the oppressed.

Steve Biko

In memory of Boss Andy (Andrew) Massey,
the most gifted officer I've ever known.

And for my darling wife who up until now never knew and,
God bless her soul, never asked.

Prologue

Prologue

W HAT YOU ARE about to read is a true story. A story that has never been told or shared. Not with my closest friends. Not my wife. No one.

It is not a story that glorifies war. It is a factual first-hand account of events that took place behind the Iron Curtain during the final months of the Cold War between August and November 1989. As the year drew to a close, the world quietly looked on, as it had for over twenty-eight years, while a nation did its best to drag itself from beneath the heel of a brutal oppressor through peaceful protest. But as the size of the demonstrations grew, and the East German state responded with violence, intimidation and imprisonment, behind the scenes, secretly, something else was being planned. Europe's history in the second half of the twentieth century and beyond would have been very different if it had succeeded.

This is the story of a man who, through no fault of his own, found himself in the right place at the wrong time. Or, as I now like to think of it, the wrong place at the right time. A career soldier who found himself in circumstances of extreme danger and driven by a need to survive, while at the same time trying to protect those he considered his friends and comrades. Some will say that what was expected of me at the time was totally unreasonable, but I like to believe that any Special Forces soldier would have done much the same as I did in the same extraordinary situation I found myself in during those final months of the Cold War.

As I say, I have never talked to anyone about what happened during those dark days, not even my wife – although she has had to deal with the aftermath: the long silences, the mood swings and me just wanting to be alone, all brought on by enormous feelings of personal guilt and regret.

There are those who will ask, 'So why tell the story now, after all these years?' the short answer is because now, thirty years on, the people who were involved are nearly all dead or long retired. No operational secrets are being revealed and no lives are being put at risk. Although the fact that a British soldier was operating behind the Iron Curtain, alone and for close to four months, might still raise a few eyebrows. But I believe this is an important episode that needs to be made public. And without me to tell it, the story of what really happened during those final months of 1989 would probably never be known. Also, like many stories worth listening to, it comes with an underlying message that, if ignored, could have grave consequences.

Thirty years ago, European dictatorships were a grim reality for much of Eastern Europe and their immediate neighbours in the West. Today there is a generation who remember this and their fear now is that with Russia on the march again, trying to regain many of its former territories, the work of liberating these peoples could be undone and the horror of living under such authoritarian governments could return.

I am proud to have played a small part in the liberation of a nation, but the events leading up to, and immediately after, the fall of the Berlin Wall changed me for the worse and for ever. The things I saw, the decisions I made, the actions I was forced to take at the time, turned me into a person that I struggle to live with, even today. For many years, these events totally destroyed my faith in human nature, reducing any notions of friendship to nothing more than a hollow gesture. I had been six years old when social services branded me a problem child, something that I eventually overcame. But following the events of 1989 everything was different for me. Now I was an angry, suspicious loner who not only avoided forming relationships, but did his best to drive people away. Why? Because, to quote the lawyer Kobayashi (Pete Postlethwaite) in the film *The Usual Suspects*, 'One cannot be betrayed if one has no people.'

Pre-Op (Pre-Operational) Briefing

A S MOST OF you will know, and those of you who have no first-hand military experience will probably have guessed, the intelligence relating to the geography of the combat area – the calibre of the enemy, its strength (numbers), location and weaponry – all need to be of the highest quality if your mission is to stand any chance of success. To this end, if reading this book is to be a worthwhile experience, there are certain things you should be aware of before you begin your journey.

The characters you will meet here are/were all real people. I have done my best to describe them, their personality, role and actions in the months leading up to the fall of the Berlin Wall. However, as you would expect, the names have been changed to protect both the innocent and, far less deservedly, the guilty.

The locations, their names and descriptions were all authentic at the time. But following the fall of the Wall, the dissolution of the German Democratic Republic (the old East Germany), the withdrawal of Soviet forces from Eastern Europe and the apparent demise of communism, many have now changed their names. Also, in an attempt to erase the painful memories of the previous forty-one years – between 1948 and 1989 – others have disappeared entirely.

Unlike most stories that appear in books, the cinema or on TV, the life of an operator, or field agent for want of a better term, is usually somewhat uneventful. In fact, I would even go as far as to say boring. And although at the time in East Germany the threat of betrayal and capture by the likes of the Stasi and KGB were genuine, most of an operator's time was and is spent sitting, watching and waiting for something to happen, or for someone to appear. So, to avoid this book becoming something of a boring 'Guard Report', I have concentrated on times when things *were* happening.

All the dates are accurate, but the times of day are only as accurate as memory allows and are put there partly to help the reader keep track of the story. The only other things I have taken licence with are the conversations that took place in a foreign language. However, their content, the decisions made, and the resulting actions – those that were taken either during or following these conversations – are, to the best of my memory, accurate. Furthermore, although the ability to recall actions and events in great detail is vital for the likes of bobsleigh, luge and Formula One drivers as it enables them to pre-adjust their position on the track and begin to drive a curve long before it arrives, it can be a curse to a highly trained soldier or operator as it enables our memory to drag up past events, then play them back in high definition, bringing back all the sights, tastes, smells and memories that, for the sake of our ongoing sanity, we would far rather forget.

May 1985

Stirling Lines, Hereford

I CROSSED THE road that ran from the guardroom to the Squash Court gate, an emergency exit from the camp, and out on to Hoarwithy Road, stepping over the grass verge, and turning left on to a narrow tarmac path. As I drew level with the Regimental Clock Tower, I paused as I often did. It wasn't the clock or the time of day that interested me. It was the names inscribed on the tower that made me stop and think of those who were no longer around. Members of the Regiment killed in action, so 'failed to beat the clock'. Like Sergeant Talaiasi Labalaba – the Fijian SAS legend, killed in July 1972 while single-handedly manning a 25-pounder Howitzer at the Battle of Mirbat, enabling his small team to fight off over 250 terrorists. The eighteen men who lost their lives when their helicopter went down in the freezing waters of the South Atlantic during a ship-to-ship transfer on the night of 19 May 1982. Captain Gavin (John) Hamilton MC (Military Cross), who died on 10 June of that same year while operating behind enemy lines on West Falkland, and far too many more to mention here. Some, like Talaiasi Labalaba, had been killed before I reached the Regiment, but there were others I knew personally, and whose loss greatly affected us all.

I turned away from the clock and as I continued along the path towards the building that housed the Ministry of Defence Police – what we called the 'MOD Plod's lodge' – I spotted a man who can only be described as one of the shadiest individuals the Regiment had to offer.

Dawson.

He was tall and wiry, fit, and the only thing that gave any hint of his advancing years was his greying hair. He was dressed from head to foot in DPM (Disruptive Pattern Material), which most civilians refer to as camouflage kit, a pair of combat trousers and a Special Forces windproof. Beneath the windproof he wore an olive-green shirt, and on his feet a pair of dark green jungle boots.

That was one of the unique things about the Regiment: at the time, there appeared to be no definite dress code. The SP (Special Projects) team who were on immediate standby twenty-four hours a day travelled in civilian clothes so, as you would expect, unless they were involved in training they wore civilian kit and their hair long. As you walked around the lines you would see a mixture of trousers, shirts and footwear, all of it British, but designed for use in a variety of theatres: jungle, desert and North European.

Unlike some of us, who would look like a bag of shit even when dressed in a £2,000 Savile Row suit, Dawson was one of those rare individuals who didn't just wear his uniform; it hung on him like a second skin, as if he'd been born wearing it. The type of guy who could make a black bin bag look chic.

He was a senior officer, a colonel I think, although I don't remember him ever wearing any rank. That was not unusual. Very few Regiment officers wore rank on their windproofs. A windproof has no epaulettes – so there was nowhere to stitch on pips or a crown.

He wasn't part of a squadron, or RHQ (Regimental Headquarters – the Head Shed). He was what was known as a free runner. He floated in and out and was there only when he needed to be, when there was a job that needed doing.

The gap between us narrowed, and I saw him smile.

'Morning, Tom.'

It was a part of the Regimental culture that officers who knew you would call you by your first name, but the tradition only went one way.

'Morning, Boss.'

As we came together, he stopped. 'What are you doing after NAAFI break this morning?'

The last person I wanted to get involved with that morning was Dawson. He was what the military refer to as the perfect manager, someone who possessed the 'three F's'. He was 'fair, firm and friendly', but with Dawson there was always an agenda. The fact that he was approachable and softly spoken also made him the perfect interrogator and, as such, a very dangerous animal. He was the type of man who could get you to tell him your darkest, most damaging secrets. I wracked my brain, but nothing sprang to mind. 'Nothing, Boss.'

'Good. Do you know where my office is?'

I did. Dawson's office was in a single-storey building that ran off the back of the MOD Plod's Lodge, directly behind the Squadron Armouries. 'Boss.'

He laid his hand on my shoulder and squeezed it as he continued down the path. 'Good man. Shall we say eleven thirty then?'

My heart sank. The softening-up process was already in motion. 'Boss.'

It was 11:25 when I knocked on Dawson's door. A good soldier always arrives five minutes before a parade or appointment, and even today bad timekeeping is one of my pet hates. Turning up late for a meeting, or even a pint with a mate, does nothing more than tell the other person that you consider their time far less important than your own.

A shout came from the other side of the door. 'Come in.'

It was the first time I had been in Dawson's office. A grey industrial carpet covered the floor, and the room was bare to say the least. As if it had no permanent resident. There was a desk, which Dawson was currently sitting behind, scribbling on an A4 notepad; a narrow table pushed up against the wall directly behind him and a visitor's chair on my side of the desk, but there was nothing of a personal nature, no pictures, not even a calendar.

The other thing I remember about it was the smell. The room felt damp. Like a storage locker that had been closed up for a week or two.

He lifted his head and smiled. 'Take a seat; I'll be right with you.' He then went back to his writing. My apparent discomfort evidently amused him as a few seconds later, without raising his head, he said, 'No need to look so worried. This is an informal chat. I just need to find out a little bit more about you – for the records.'

I forced a smile. I knew what was about to happen. When you first join the army, you sign the Official Secrets Act. Then, later, if you progressed to the Special Forces or any other unit where you might have access to sensitive material, like the Missile Regiment (a Royal Artillery Regiment which handled Britain's battlefield nukes), or the Intelligence Corps, you were what they call Negative Vetted (NV'd): a cursory look was taken of you and your immediate family. However, I'd already been through both of those processes, so what was about to happen to me was probably going to be much more severe. I guessed I was about to be Positive Vetted (PV'd) and, regardless of what Dawson said, I had every reason to be worried.

My personal life, and that of my entire family, past and present, was about to be put under the microscope. Everything about every one of us, living or dead, was about to be scrutinised. But what worried me most was the past I never discussed, not even with my closest friends.

But then passing the PV process would most likely open a multitude of doors, not all of them good, but they were doors that could lead to opportunities most soldiers can only dream of. Doors that would give me access to the type of information that only a privileged few ever saw or knew about. It could turn me from being someone who was currently trained to carry out the most difficult of tasks in places that can only be described as third world shit houses, into someone who finally got to know 'why'. While failing the PV process wouldn't bring about an immediate end to my career in the Regiment, it would significantly reduce my chances of further promotion, and the knowledge that new challenges and opportunities would be well beyond my reach would be a constant irritation throughout the remainder of my military career. It was a day that I had hoped would eventually come but, now it was here, it was enough to put a frown on my face.

The thing that frightened me most about the process was knowing that, once this informal chat was over and I returned to my daily routine, Dawson would begin sifting his way through the information I was about to provide, selecting the pieces that interested him. These could well be the pieces that did the most damage, and in the process systematically tear my dysfunctional family's past apart; scrutinise every minor indiscretion; dig up every dirty little secret my family had; highlight any flaws in my character, my background and associations; find anything that made me vulnerable to blackmail or manipulation by criminal organisations or foreign intelligence agencies. Then, when he was done digging, he would decide if any of what he'd found made me a security risk.

However, in the end, whether I passed or failed, I wouldn't know one way or the other. Not unless the powers that be deemed it necessary.

It was a good four minutes before Dawson lifted his head again, but the pad that sat on the desk in front of him was still open and the pen remained in his hand. Four minutes, during which I had become more and more uneasy.

He leant back in his chair and smiled.

'Why don't we start with you telling me a little bit about yourself?'

'Starting when?'

'How about at the very beginning, when, and where you were born?'

Dawson was starting with the simple questions he already knew the answers to; the information he had gleaned from my personal file; a technique routinely used by interrogators. The process was simple; put the subject at ease and establish a rapport before getting down to the important stuff, the pieces of information that really interested him.

'March 'fifty-two, The London Hospital, Whitechapel, East London.'

'Your parents?'

'Both British. Born in the East End. Within the sound of Bow Bells. True cockneys.'

Dawson smiled. 'And your grandparents?'

Now we were getting down to it. 'On my father's side, both British – East Enders.'

He lifted his eyes from the notepad and raised his eyebrows. 'And your mother's parents?'

There was no point in trying to soften the blow. 'My grandmother was Prussian, from what is now part of Poland. My grandfather was Italian – from Naples.'

'When did they arrive here? In the UK?'

'I don't know the exact dates. All I know is that it was before the start of the Second World War, around 1935 to 1936.'

He had begun writing again. 'Were they interned, during the war?'

'No.'

He lifted his head and I saw him raise his eyebrows again. Such an outcome was unusual to say the least. Most of those who had immigrated to Britain from Germany and the Axis countries (those countries who would eventually side with Hitler's Nazi Germany) before the war had found themselves quickly interned as possible spies or saboteurs in purpose-built camps, such as the one on the Isle of Man.

'All still living?'

'They're all dead.'

'And your parents, are they both still alive?'

'As far as I know. My mother suffers from MS and is currently at a Cheshire home outside Chippenham, Wiltshire.'

'And your father?'

'The last I heard, he was kicking around Australia somewhere. Sydney, I think.'

'You're not close then?'

'No. He left when I was five. I've only seen him a few times since.'

Dawson smiled. It was one of those smiles that say, I know it goes deeper than that, a lot deeper. 'Did you have a happy childhood?'

I settled back in my chair. 'Not really. A year after my father left, my mother, no longer able to cope with three kids under six, contacted social services and I was institutionalised for the next nine years.' I smiled. 'And there are some that say I should still be there.'

Dawson had stopped smiling. 'That must have been a pretty harrowing experience for a six-year-old?'

'It wasn't all bad; I learned some crucial lessons during those first couple of years.'

'Like what?'

'Like that there's no point trying to reason with some people. Once they stop listening and the conversation moves on to the shouting and screaming stage, there's no longer any point in arguing. So, why not just miss out the non-productive stages and go straight to violence?'

Dawson's eyes widened. 'That's a risky strategy for one so young, and I suspect not that big, probably one of the smaller kids in the facility?'

'Not really. A chair is a great leveller when it comes to both size and strength. Wallop a bigger kid across the hips or knees with a metal-framed chair and, if you're quick, you can do more than enough damage to stop him getting back up again.'

A grin crept across Dawson's face. 'So what made you join the army?'

'To cut a long story short, three weeks after leaving boarding school I was homeless, living on the streets. Joining the army wasn't so much a career choice as an act of desperation.'

Dawson had stopped writing again. 'Some of your colleagues say that at times you're not the friendliest person in the world. That you don't form relationships easily.'

I smiled. I wasn't about to tell him anything he didn't already know. 'Given my childhood and life during my teens, I suppose some would say I now have serious "trust issues".'

He opened a buff-coloured file sitting on the desk beside him. 'In fact, on your first confidential report as a sergeant, your CO at the Parachute Regiment wrote, "This man would do well to learn the art of diplomacy."'

I smiled. 'He did. But it didn't stop him from giving me an "O" – "Outstanding Grade" – that year, or for the two following.'

Dawson flicked over the pages and confirmed what I had just said. 'True.' He then lifted his head and stared at me. 'But, given what he's written, would it be fair to say that you don't suffer fools gladly?'

Our eyes were locked. 'I don't suffer fools at all. A soldier's life is complicated enough. I see no point in making mine any harder or getting myself killed in order to keep some idiot happy.'

Dawson changed tack. 'So, are there any skeletons in the cupboard I should know about?'

'Like what?'

'Shall we say, members of the family that have strayed from the path, taken to crime; associated with foreign powers; terrorists?'

I couldn't control myself and burst out laughing. 'My whole family are cockney. Both my father and his brother went to school with the Krays. In fact, my uncle Alfie did three years in Parkhurst for his "association" with the Twins. Turning to crime comes with the territory. It's in the genes, and reinforced with mother's milk.'

His expression had now become serious. 'Does that also apply to you?'

'No. But who knows what might have happened if I hadn't joined the army.'

The conversation about me and mine continued for another thirty minutes, sometimes backtracking, going over the same ground again and again, making sure I gave the same answer the second and sometimes the third time around. He then said, 'Tell me about your wife and her family.'

Shit.

Don't get me wrong, they were, and still are, good people, but coming from where they did, well.

'They're all from Belfast.'

'Right or left footers?'

Political correctness wasn't a big thing in those days, well, not where the army was concerned.

'Right. A Protestant, loyalist family.'

Dawson had begun making notes again, but under his breath I heard him say, 'Well, that's handy.'

Our 'informal' chat ended forty minutes later and, as I walked down the path that led past the MOD plods, through the main gate and on towards the sergeants' mess, I had no idea how I had fared.

December 1985

Stirling Lines, Hereford

I T WAS JUST after ten in the morning. I grabbed my Bergen (the airborne forces' term for a large rucksack) off the floor and was halfway out of the door when the phone rang. I dropped the Bergen at my feet and picked up the phone.

'Shore.'

'Tom, it's the CO. I understand the SP (Special Projects) team are working down at the Embassy today?' It was Colonel Thompson, the Regiment's commanding officer.

Following the massacre of Israeli athletes at the 1972 Munich Olympics, the Regiment's colonel at the time, Peter de la Billière, later to become general, had suggested that the Regiment would need to provide a fast response solution to any such events that happened on UK soil in the future. De la Billière tasked Thompson, who was a troop captain at the time, with conducting a feasibility study and drawing up the blueprint for a new Counter Terrorism (CT) unit or, as they later became known, the Special Projects (SP) team. As a result, Thompson had always taken a keen interest in what they were doing. The Embassy Thompson was referring to was a large purpose-built building on the edge of the Regiment's training area thirteen miles west of Hereford. It was here that the SP team carried out training exercises and developed new anti-siege techniques.

'Yes, Boss.'

'Well, when you're ready to set off, come around to RHQ, we'll travel down together – in the staff car. We need to have a chat.'

No matter how you dress it up, even though it had been presented as a friendly request, this was an order.

'Roger that, Boss.'

I had no idea what Thompson had on his mind, but the prospect of a private chat with the CO in the back of his staff car had

13

immediately spiked my curiosity, and as I rounded the corner of RHQ I spotted him making his way down the path towards his car.

Gavin Thompson was a reasonably big man, not overweight by any stretch of the imagination, just well-proportioned. He had dark, slightly wavy hair and, like Dawson, looked smart no matter what he was wearing or what he was doing at the time. He had a presence about him, quiet but at the same time commanding, another one of those who was fair, firm and friendly. He was also without doubt the most gifted officer I have ever known and privately I thought of him as Captain Hurricane after the comic book character from the sixties.

In those days staff cars, the vehicles that normally ferried about the commanding officers of the British Army's line regiments and the generals who commanded its major formations – those that were referred to by Special Forces' soldiers as part of the 'Green Army' – were traditionally large Fords or Vauxhalls sprayed dark green or black. They displayed the occupant's regimental or formation crest on the bonnet and carried military-style number plates in a two-figure/two-letter/two-figure configuration, but Thompson's staff car was different. In keeping with the Regiment's more secretive and fast response traditions, it was a dark blue, top of the range Volvo saloon with a beefed-up engine, which meant that if the need arose it could accelerate down the road like a scalded cat. It also sported the very best in run-flat tyres and displayed normal civilian number plates that, when run through a PNC (Police National Computer) check by an inquisitive traffic officer, would come back as 'blocked'; Home Office speak for 'mind your own business'.

At the end of Bullingham Lane we turned right on to Ross Road and headed for the Belmont Roundabout where Thompson handed me a file.

I looked first at the file, and then at Thompson. The pink file jacket said it all and, although not a word had crossed my lips, he knew the question I was asking.

'It's OK, you can read it. Your PV status came through last month.'

Given my uncle Alfie's association with the Krays, along with my multinational background and the fact that my wife was from Northern Ireland, nobody was more surprised than me that I had passed. However, apart from Thompson, myself, Dawson, of course, and a handful of selected individuals – those who needed to know – no one else would ever know what they had discovered about me.

As we passed Belmont Abbey I closed the file and handed it back to Thompson.

He pushed it into his briefcase and without looking at me said, 'I understand you're about to head off for a few weeks' leave.'

'Yes, Boss. I've always fancied a crack at the luge . . .' Next to being involved in a live contact, sliding feet first down a bobsleigh track at over seventy miles an hour, less than four inches above the ice and without brakes is, in my view, the ultimate adrenaline rush.

I was never going to make the national team, not at thirty-four – like the gymnasts and swimmers at the time I was already considered too old – but I was still keen to try it. The Forces traditionally supplied a number of the British teams' athletes for these types of sports, not least as they gave you the time and the financial support to go and practise abroad.

'I've managed to secure a place on an introductory week being run by the GBLA [Great Britain Luge Association] at Igls in Austria,' I continued. 'If everything works out, and I can demonstrate that I have an aptitude for the sport, it will be followed by a second, more demanding week in Yugoslavia.'

Thompson smiled. 'Good. It's that second week in Yugoslavia that I want to talk about.'

My heart sank a little. Yugoslavia, although it was not an official member of the Warsaw Pact, it was one of those countries allied to the Soviet Union. Following the end of the Second World War, Stalin had allowed it to retain its independence from Russia, which at times had led to a rather shaky and sometimes tumultuous relationship with Moscow. But, it was still a communist country, and to all intents and purposes situated behind the Iron Curtain. As well as the 1.2 million Soviet troops that were stationed in the countries that bordered Yugoslavia, Moscow also maintained a military presence within the country.

Although I had obtained prior permission for my luge trip, that didn't mean that it was a sure thing. Back in those days a Special Forces soldier – in fact any soldier – travelling behind the Iron Curtain was not only rare, it was also seen as something of an issue.

It always raised questions to the suspicious-minded people whose job it is to worry about these things. Was I going there for a reason other than the luge? And, even if my reason for visiting was innocent, might I be compromised and blackmailed?

'Is there a problem with the trip, Boss?'

Thompson leaned forward and tapped his driver on the shoulder. 'Turn the radio on, Brian, and raise the volume.'

I suspect that it was not an unusual request, because the driver immediately did as he was asked.

Turning to me, Thompson lowered his voice.

'Not at all. It will still go ahead. However, while you're in Yugoslavia I have something I'd like you to do and, as always, what I'm about to tell you is strictly need to know' – which is Regimental speak for 'keep it to yourself'.

'Understood, Boss.'

Now, the press and film industry would have you believe that Special Forces' soldiers are superhuman killing machines. Rambo-type individuals who operate without feelings or emotion and are capable of overcoming insurmountable odds while working alone, deep undercover behind enemy lines. Conversely, it is also said that truth can be stranger than fiction and it's true that, when put to the test, especially when the lives of innocent hostages are at risk, Special Forces' soldiers are more than capable of killing and are no strangers to doing what needs to be done, regardless of how unpleasant it is.

It was during the Princes Gate siege (the Iranian Embassy) that Maggie Thatcher reportedly told the CO at the time, 'Everybody dies. Nobody comes out alive. It causes too many problems further down the line.' She was, of course, talking about the terrorists.

In general, though, for most of the time, *British* Special Forces' soldiers would rather operate on stealth: working silently, remaining hidden from view, as we complete the task we have been set; normally gathering intelligence for an upcoming operation. As for working alone, well, even when working in plain clothes 'across the water' – as we called it, in Northern Ireland – you were never really alone. Backup was never that far away and, even if you couldn't see it, you knew it was there, and you never went anywhere unarmed. But all that was about to change for me.

Friday, 10 January 1986

Sarajevo, Yugoslavia

I T WAS ELEVEN thirty in the morning. The sky was clear, a vivid blue in colour. I was deep inside Soviet Occupied Yugoslavia.

I was standing beside the 1984 Winter Olympic bobsleigh and luge track, a kilometre below the summit of Mount Trebević, looking down on the medieval city of Sarajevo.

When I had arrived at the track the city was hidden beneath a blanket of thick fog but now, an hour and a half later, it had lifted, leaving it bathed in bright sunshine, and from up here it was a picture of peace and tranquillity.

If you had told me then that this beautiful city would one day soon be turned into a living hell then, given the tranquil scene before me right now, I would have found it hard to believe the slaughter and ethnic cleansing that was to come. Nor that it would be reduced to rubble by artillery fire directed by an FOP (Forward Observation Post) positioned a few hundred metres to my right, on the structure that now served as the men's start for the luge. It was bustling with activity as athletes prepared themselves for the sub one-minute run that would see them reach speeds of 140 kph and experience pressures up to 4G as they negotiated the sixteen curves and straights that made up the mile-long track.

The last eleven days, the first seven of which had been spent in Igls, Austria, and the remainder here in Sarajevo, had flown by. The sport had delivered everything I hoped it would and more. Every run on the track, although you were covering the same ground, was a new experience, with every curve and straight presenting a fresh challenge, but tonight the challenges I encountered would be different.

With the day's training runs complete, and the evening meal over, I was back in my room and putting the finishing touches to a sketch map. Twenty minutes later I looked at my watch, *20:07*.

The map wasn't perfect. It was a bit light on detail, but time was tight. The important things, the scale, prominent features and major waypoints, the places where I would change direction, were all spot on, and it would have to do.

The map had gone everywhere with me over the last few days, tucked into the lining of my ski jacket. There was no way I could leave it lying around my hotel room. Apart from running the risk of it being found by a nosey chambermaid or Lurch, the six foot four hotel manager, who bore an uncanny resemblance to the butler from the *Addams Family*, the Yugoslav police and the UDBA (Communist Secret Police) were both well known for their impromptu visits to hotel rooms being used by Westerners; especially when they knew their guests were absent.

Five minutes later I locked the door of my room on the first floor and headed along the tile-covered corridor towards the stairs. But as I reached the bottom step and was about to make my way across the lobby, I spotted a member of the British team leaning against the front desk talking to the female receptionist.

Shit. I just cannot get a break.

There was no way I could afford to be seen as I crossed the lobby. It's true I wasn't part of the team but, having spent the previous week with them at Igls and travelled down to Sarajevo in one of the team vehicles, I had found them more than willing to chat about anything and everything and eager to lend a hand when it came to helping me work on my sledge. Even if this guy didn't follow me down into the hotel basement, he might grow inquisitive about what was taking me so long to do down there; want to know why I hadn't returned and wonder if I needed help with my sledge.

The last thing I needed tonight was anybody else's help.

I retraced my steps, retreated up the stairs to the first-floor landing and waited. It wasn't a case of giving him five or even ten minutes to finish his conversation, what I needed to do had to be done tonight. Which meant he would get as long as it took for him to complete his business and leave. My mind ran over the last few days. If he followed the normal routine, as soon as he'd finished with the receptionist he would head across the lobby and join the other members of the team in the hotel's small TV lounge. However, if he decided to head back up the stairs to his room then, standing where I was on the first-floor landing, I was perfectly placed to say I was also on my way down to the TV lounge.

Two minutes later the faint sounds of chatter disappeared and the lobby went quiet. Not a sound and, as no one appeared on the stairs, I assumed that, true to form, he had headed for the TV lounge. It was time to get going.

Without acknowledging the presence of the receptionist who was still standing behind the desk, I made my way across the lobby and opened the door that led down to the hotel basement. This was where the team stored and worked on their sledges.

The basement was in complete darkness. I had recce'd the route and my exit point from the hotel earlier that day. As a result, I knew that the only light switch was on the ground level at the top of the stairs. If I switched it on, there was no way I could switch it off again from the far side of the basement. So, with my hands planted firmly on the wall, I made my way down the narrow flight of ten concrete steps, counting them as I went. By the time I reached the floor of the basement, my eyes had begun to grow accustomed to the darkness. Fifty feet away, on the far side of the room, with the light from the car park shining beneath it, was the door that would take me outside. Now I could just make out the white metal frame that surrounded it.

I twisted the catch and inched the door towards me. A single floodlight, sitting high on the hotel wall, lit up the outside area and the car park. Both were deserted.

Taking a small, pre-prepared piece of wood from my pocket, I pushed it into the latch hole set into the metal door frame. The block would allow the door to close but prevent the catch from seating itself properly. Although it would appear closed and secure, one good shove should open it. Outside I pulled the door towards me, heard a faint click, and I pushed back against it. It held firm.

The time was 20:22. The sun had set just after 17:00 and the outside air temperature was by now well below zero. Dressed in a thin, dark blue hooded tracksuit, a black woollen hat and trainers, I was glad of the Hale-Hanson thermal underwear I was now wearing beneath them.

The constant coming and going of vehicles had removed all traces of snow from the ground, which meant I would leave no telltale footprints as I made my way across the car park, on to the road, and into the forest on the far side.

As with most mountainous regions in northern Europe, the lower reaches of Mount Trebevic were covered in forest. The trees, mostly firs, were packed tightly together in blocks, separated by narrow tracks, which acted as firebreaks should the need arise. Dotted here and there were the now leafless skeletons of silver birch and the occasional oak. In areas where the snow had not settled, or recently melted, the floor was covered by a dark leafy mulch, creating the faint smell of rotting vegetation, which seemed to permeate throughout the whole forest.

Once beneath the cover of the trees I stopped, dropped to one knee, and pulled the sketch map from my pocket. Even though I had memorised it, I still felt the need to check it one more time before setting off.

My target that night was the Lukavica military base. It lay two miles south-southeast of Sarajevo, between my current position at the Osmice Hotel and the village of Lukavica. Three days earlier, on the Tuesday afternoon, I had decided that before attempting my mission, I would need to check the lay of the land around the base in daylight. So, borrowing one of the team vehicles I drove alone through the village next to it and conducted a discreet recce. It was a small village without a single tarmac road, but it was like a rabbit warren with lots of tiny houses packed closely together, separated by a maze of narrow alleyways. It was also well off the main road and if I had been stopped by the authorities and asked what I was doing there, I would have simply said that I was lost and asked to be directed back to the main road and my hotel.

The base itself was only four miles west-northwest of the hotel as the crow flies, but if I was going to stand any chance of avoiding the communist police and army patrols that regularly cruised the area, I would need to remain inside the forest for as long as possible.

The last time I had played this particular game, being on the run, was during the 'escape and evasion' phase of the combat survival course during Selection. At the time, although my life was never in any real danger, the threat of getting caught and receiving a good kicking from the hunter force was genuine, but nothing compared to what might happen to me if I was caught tonight. This was not some isolated area of Britain; this was Yugoslavia, a communist state, and ally of Soviet Russia. As such, I had little doubt that after being brutally interrogated, like so many others caught operating behind the Iron Curtain, I would either be used in some sort of trade off or disappear for ever. It's not as if anyone back in the UK was going to kick up a fuss. At that time, the Regiment had – and still has – a policy of 'No Comment' and confirmed nor denied anything.

There was widespread mistrust between the various regions of the Yugoslav Federation and it had already led to extreme violence and would ultimately lead to the death of Yugoslavia, the start of the Balkan Wars and the terrible genocides of the 1990s. I remembered reading somewhere that you could tell a lot about a nation by its vocabulary . . . Serbo-Croat had a disturbingly large number of words for 'butchery'.

Tonight was a full moon, partially hidden by cloud and, although I had a small Maglite torch in my pocket as a backup, right now there was more than enough light to read the map.

I took the Silva Compass (a lightweight liquid-filled compass mounted on a small sheet of Perspex) from my pocket and set the bearing to the first waypoint – 270 degrees due west. Ten seconds later I was moving almost silently through the forest, and it didn't take me long to find what I was looking for. A narrow, well-trodden track that wound its way down to the foot of Mount Trebevic.

My thought on entering the forest that night had been that it was unnaturally quiet. Now, as I negotiated my way down a steep bank, I saw the reason why. A hundred and fifty metres to my left I saw the red glow of an open fire as it reflected off the polythene sheeting that covered a group of large, round, makeshift huts constructed from cardboard spread over a wooden frame.

Gypsies.

Following years of persecution, first by the Nazis and later by Yugoslavia's communist government, these nomads trusted no one and it was common knowledge that they could be especially hostile to strangers. Seconds later I heard their dogs begin to bark as they picked up my scent on the night breeze. It was time to make myself scarce before they were let loose and took up the chase.

I am not talking about being chased by a pack of Jack Russells, or Lurchers, the dogs traditionally favoured by Irish Tinkers and the

Essex 'Pikey'. No, I'm talking about 150 pounds of lean muscles and large teeth: Sarplaninacs, otherwise known as Yugoslavian Shepherd Dogs, bred for seeing off wolves and bears. Renowned for their ferocious courage, these monsters would not hesitate to lay down their life in defence of family, flock or master, characteristics that had also made them a valuable asset to the Yugoslav military.

I scrambled back over the bank and, crouching in the dead ground, took out my map. Cupping the Maglite in my hands and reading the map in the red glow that shone through the skin of my fingers, I quickly found an alternate route.

On paper, my mission appeared to be relatively straightforward. I was to gather information regarding troop numbers and equipment levels at the Lukavica military base. It seemed to me that it wasn't a major installation and, given its isolated location, deep inside Yugoslavia, that it was nothing more than a local defence asset, and as such would be of minimal strategic value and hardly a threat to either NATO or the West. But no doubt Thompson had reasons to investigate the place that he had not shared with me.

It's hard to explain the way I was feeling at the time, but the greater the target value, the greater the level of security that surrounds it, which in turn elevates the level of risk involved in a mission like this. It's like comparing the slightly elevated pulse rate you might experience when stealing an apple from a market stall, to the heart-stopping adrenaline rush you would get by breaking into a high security vault in London's Hatton Garden. Tonight, for me, there was no rush.

Thirty minutes of steady jogging along narrow winding tracks that ran between blocks of densely packed trees saw me standing at the edge of the forest. In front of me lay 800 metres of open ground, apart from patches of ferns and the odd tree. On the far side of that I could see the string of orange security lights that marked the perimeter of the military base.

As luck would have it, as I left the cover of the forest and moved out on to the open ground, the moon completely disappeared, hidden behind a thick blanket of cloud. More snow was on the way. I just hoped it would hold off until morning. The last thing I needed to do was leave a trail of tracks that led back up to the Osmice.

Air cools more rapidly than the land or water beneath it and, with the ground having been warmed by that day's winter sun, a light mist had begun to form over the area. The faint smell of damp vegetation carried on the light north wind that was now blowing into my face.

It was a Friday and so most of the camp's personnel, those who were not on duty, would most probably be heading home for the weekend. It was the way most peacetime armies operated. I hoped that the Yugoslavs would be no different.

It took me six minutes to cross the open ground. I zigzagged my way, running in a crouch between the few trees and any ferns that were tall, or where the mist was thick enough to hide me. Where there was nothing but flat, open ground – and as I got closer to the perimeter fence, there was ever more of it – I used my elbows and knees, pushing with my toes, to leopard crawl on my belly through the damp grass and patches of settled snow.

Twenty metres from the perimeter fence, remaining in the dead ground – the areas that were in shadow, not lit up by the security lights that lined the camp perimeter – I searched for my target: the hangars that held the resident unit's vehicles and equipment. You can tell a lot from finding out what vehicles a regiment or battalion uses. If their vehicles are predominantly of the light, wheeled variety, they are probably some form of rapid response infantry, like the airborne; fast moving and lightly armed. The heavier the vehicles, the greater the chance of heavy support weapons – anti-tank and heavy mortar, all of which will slow them down. Then of course there are the big boys: the tracked vehicles, the tanks and self-propelled artillery pieces.

It took me ten minutes to find my entry point. It needed to be somewhere close to the hangars, but as far away from the main gate as possible. That way, if I were discovered while entering or leaving the base – and avoided being shot – the sentry would either have to follow me and climb over the fence or return to the guardhouse at the main gate for backup and, possibly, a vehicle. Either way, it would give me enough time to make my escape.

With my hands and feet a metre apart, spreading my weight across as much of the eight-foot-high chain-link fence as possible, I made my way quickly to the top where I jammed the toe of my left trainer into one of the links. Then locking the leg out at the knee, and using it to support my body weight, I carefully slipped my right leg through the gap below the three strands of barbed wire that ran above it, and hooked it over the top of the chain-link, leaving both hands free to deal with the barbed wire.

I took a length of cord from my tracksuit pocket, looped it around the three strands of barbed wire, and pulled it tight, opening up a gap just large enough for me to roll through – but that was when everything changed. An intense, narrow beam of light from a torch cut through the darkness. Sixty metres away a sentry was checking the door of the hangar closest to the fence.

I froze as he turned away from the hangar and looked in my direction. I held my breath: white vapour rising from the top of a fence would of course be an immediate giveaway, as would be any movement on my part. But, as the beam of light snaked its way across the snow-covered ground towards me, I couldn't hold it in any more and breathed gently out through my nose. Like a cat watching a mouse, I waited in silence as the light swept along the base of the fence a few feet below my position. I was hanging helpless on the wire but my eyes were no longer watching the beam of light from the torch; they were now fixed on the AK-47 the sentry was cradling in his right arm. If I made a sound, moved, drew attention to myself in any way, or the sentry raised the beam of his torch just a few feet higher, he would see me.

Then, inexplicably, he switched off the flashlight and to my surprise and relief he turned away. As I watched him make his way down the side of the hangar into the darkness, I heard the thump, thump of my heart in my ears; as if a corps of drums were beating out a tattoo inside my head.

I rolled my left wrist and looked at my watch.

21:53.

It would appear that I had hit the fence at exactly the right time. Assuming that the Yugoslavs worked a similar system to most other armies, the night-time guard force would have begun their tour of duty at 18:00. As a result, the sentry who had just disappeared would have started his watch at 20:00. With each watch or stag lasting two hours, he now had only seven minutes before he was off duty. There was no way he would spend a moment longer than he had to out here in the cold. It was time for him to head back to the guardroom for a much-needed brew.

God bless squaddies.

Still hanging motionless on the fence, occasionally looking at my watch, I listened to the silence and for anything that would tell me the sentry was on his way back. That something he had seen and previously ignored had now awakened his curiosity and he was returning to check it out, but there was nothing. Nothing but the faint whistling of the wind as it blew across the open ground and through the chain-link fence that supported me.

Two minutes later I was standing in front of the steel picket gate to the right of the main hangar doors. I removed two pieces of wire from my pocket, slid up the brass weather cover on the front of the rudimentary padlock, then slipped the wires one at a time into the keyhole behind it.

This wasn't the first time I had picked a lock, and I doubted it would be the last. Back in Hereford they had joked that sending me, a cockney, on an MOE (Methods of Entry) course – a course where I would be taught how to pick locks, break into secure buildings and blow safes – was just some kind of East End job creation scheme.

I quickly removed the padlock but, as I pushed against the door, I heard its hinges creak. I immediately stopped and listened. Nothing. No sudden appearance of the guard force. It would appear the noise had gone unnoticed.

This was one of those situations that required a little nerve, a bit like removing a plaster. You just have to rip it off and get it over with. I took a deep breath and pushed hard. There was a faint squeak, but it was over before it begun and I held my position as I watched the gate swing away from me.

I stepped quickly over the lip of the gate into a large open area, closed the door behind me, and was greeted by that familiar smell of diesel, engine lubricants and fresh paint. It doesn't matter where you go in the world, all military vehicle hangars smell the same. Taking the Maglite from my pocket I switched it on. The floor had been painted using a dark green gloss, and was divided into sections by yellow lines. I knew what I wanted to see, and wasn't disappointed.

Reversed against the outer wall of the hangar, sitting neatly between the yellow lines, were a dozen, Soviet-made ZSU-23-4 Shilkas, lightly armoured, self-propelled track vehicles, which carried a radar-guided anti-aircraft weapon. Although dated, having first been brought into service back in 1962, it's four, water-cooled, 2A7 Auto-cannons set in a 2x2 box formation, fired 23mm high explosive shells at a combined rate of up to 4,000 rounds a minute, although normally only in bursts of 3-10 projectiles. It had a maximum vertical range of 5,000m. Conversely, its 'effective' vertical range, which translates into the operator being able to hit what he's aiming at as opposed to throwing everything in the general direction and hoping for the best, was estimated at only 1,500m. However, regardless of its short range, when manned by a well-trained, and motivated crew, it was still deadly. The insignia on the front panel of each vehicle belonged to one of Yugoslavia's many Air Defence Regiments.

The next three hangars all contained the same as the first, more Shilkas. However, in the fifth hangar, I found something different. A mixture of light tracked vehicles similar in size and design to the British 'Snow Cat', the vehicle used by Royal Marine Winter Warfare Troops. Parked beside them were a number of light wheeled vehicles. They all carried the same regimental insignia, that of the 'Alpini', Yugoslavia's elite mountain troops and, as I had suspected, there were no major surprises.

I replaced the padlock on the final hangar and, after locking it, looked at my watch.

22:57.

I had been in the base for close to an hour. It wasn't large. You could probably walk around it in a little over forty minutes, which meant that a member of the guard force had already visited the area at least once and left. I checked the immediate area, retraced my steps, and within two minutes I was back on the top of the fence. I slipped the quick release knot on the piece of cord, the barbed wire sprang free and, with a little encouragement from me, quickly regained its former shape. I dropped silently to the ground.

As I made my way back across the open ground and on to the track that ran up to the edge of the forest I was feeling pretty pleased with myself, but a bit confused. After discovering exactly what I had expected to find in the hangars, I felt I was being tested. There seemed no logical reason for tonight's sortie. It wasn't as if Thompson or the SF Brigadier down in London were planning an attack in the area and needed to know what level of opposition they would be facing, but, once again, the reason why was not my concern.

I stepped back on to the track I had followed on my way in. But, as I began to jog, pick up the pace, I heard hushed voices in the darkness up ahead and froze.

I wasn't close enough to make out what was being said. It could've been the gypsies I'd seen earlier, checking or setting their game snares. I held my position, but as I considered what I was going to do next, the area was suddenly flooded with light and night became day. For the briefest moment, I stood there, frozen and alone on the track, exposed for all to see.

The light was angled down. Positioned far too high to be hand-held, which meant it was mounted on a vehicle and that immediately ruled out the gypsy theory. Unlike their Western cousins who pull their lavish mobile homes around the country behind Range Rovers and top-of-the-range Mercedes, Yugoslav gypsies are extremely poor and lucky if they own a horse and cart.

Although the searchlight had initially hit me, the beam had not lingered, and was now sweeping the open ground to my right and rear, but it wouldn't be long before it was on its way back. I dropped on to my stomach, and without pausing began to roll to my right, across the gravel track towards the thick undergrowth that bordered it.

I had covered less than three feet when, without warning, the ground beneath me disappeared and I began to fall. A split second later, I felt the sharp rocks that covered the bottom of a drainage ditch bite into my back. I lay motionless as I watched the searchlight sweep back and forth high above my head. I had no idea what was going on. All I knew was that I needed to get away from here as fast as possible. I rolled on to my stomach and quickly scrambled back up the steep side of the ditch.

With the searchlight now concentrating on the track, I could see that there were two vehicles, which meant that it was probably a six- to eight-man patrol, led by either a senior NCO (Non-Commissioned Officer) or officer. If it had been a smaller unit there would have been no need for a second vehicle. I started to crawl forward, staying beneath the ferns. My head was buzzing. What was a standing patrol doing out here on a Friday night? (A standing patrol is a stationary patrol, one set to secure a specific installation or area, as opposed to a roving patrol which, as the name suggests, is continually on the move.)

Whatever the answer, everything had changed. The level of risk had risen dramatically, and I now had a massive problem. I couldn't risk continuing on my present course, travelling the three and a half miles straight back to the hotel. But moving away from the forest and going back across the open ground, past the base and into the village of Lukavica, was also a nonstarter. There was no way I could risk becoming trapped in its narrow streets while trying to evade a determined hunter force. So, moving in a crouch, I headed off in the opposite direction, northwest towards Sarajevo, and even further away from the safety of the hotel.

I couldn't be sure that the patrol had been waiting for me, but if I was to stand any chance of getting away it was time to let the dogs see the rabbit. Inject some confusion into the game.

I stopped, stood upright and, after making sure that at least one member of the patrol had seen me, as the shout went up I began to run and made my way further out on to the open ground, towards a stretch of forest on the far side. As I had anticipated, after spotting me, and in their eagerness to capture me, the members of the patrol were no longer listening to their commander's orders.

I slowed; I needed to get them closer. It was risky, but if I was going to keep them interested and make good my escape it had to be done. Two minutes later, picturing the map in my head, I heard what I was looking for: the sound of running water, a river, a tributary of the Miljacka that runs through the centre of Sarajevo. I was close to the tributary's widest point, a few hundred yards from where it joined the Miljacka, and I also knew from my earlier map appreciation that it was close to forty metres wide from bank to bank. Running as fast as I could I took a deep breath and, with my lips pressed tightly together in an attempt to hang on to the precious air in my lungs, I launched myself into the darkness.

The water was freezing and I felt my cheeks stretch and the muscles of my chest contract as it tried to force the air from my body.

Twenty metres into my swim, heading as fast and as quietly as I could for the opposite bank, I felt the current take hold and begin to carry me slowly downstream. It was then that I heard the first volley of gunshots and felt a change in pressure as the bullets cut into the water and spun past my body.

These guys aren't pissing around; they're playing for keeps.

There was no way they could see me but, given where I had entered the water, they were now shooting at where they thought I might be. If I was going to avoid being hit by a lucky shot, I would have to dive and swim as far as I could underwater, regardless of the pain. Staying on the surface and being a slow-moving target was no longer an option.

I took another breath, bent at the waist, pushed my head beneath the surface and pulled hard with both arms. The constant flow of the river was the only thing that had prevented it from freezing over, and within seconds my head felt like it was being crushed in a vice, but, if I was going to stand any chance of coming out of this alive, I needed to block out the pain and push on.

I stretched out my arms and, as I started to pull through another stroke, my fingers made contact with something solid. On the next stroke I felt it again, but this time, instead of brushing along it, I grabbed it and wrapped my fingers tightly around it: it was a tree root. My chest was getting tight, I was rapidly running out of oxygen, and as a result I was becoming light-headed, so I decided to abandon the swimming and pull myself through the water using the root instead. As the river became shallower and the oxygen in my lungs finally ran out, like a crocodile hunting its prey, my eyes gently broke the surface. Two metres ahead of me was the river-bank.

Staying low and making myself as small a target as possible, I dragged my near numb body from the freezing water, but as I scrambled through the thin layer of ice that had formed at the water's edge and up the mud bank, there was a second volley of gunshots. There had been a brief break in the cloud, and as the moon shone through the patrol had spotted me again.

Like the sound of a distant band saw, the bullets whizzed as they cut through the ferns on either side of me. The only thing I had in my favour was that they were unable to get their vehicles across the drainage ditch and had been forced to abandon them where they were, sitting on the track. Having taken up the chase on foot, they no longer had the use of the vehicle searchlights.

Now out of sight, hidden in the dead ground behind the bank, I stopped, doubled back, and re-joined the riverbank some fifty metres further upstream from where I had exited. With my hands and feet already numb, I lay shivering in the tall grass as I watched my pursuers hover around on the opposite bank. Unwilling to follow me into the river, they were unsure of what to do next. Eventually, their commander got a grip of his men and ordered them back to their vehicles. It looked like my plan might just work.

If I was right, the only way the patrol could follow me now was to drive back past their base, through the village of Lukavica and cross the river by the only bridge in the area, some four kilometres upstream of where they were now. It would take them at least twenty minutes to get to where I was currently hiding but, even when they reached the area, they would still have to try and pick up my trail, by which time I should be most of the way back to the hotel.

I held my position for what seemed to be a lifetime, my patience eventually being rewarded by the faint sound of two vehicles moving along the track away from me. I looked at my watch.

23:34.

The first time I had crossed the river had been bad, but I knew this time it would be much worse. I steeled my mind and forced myself to re-enter the river and start the long swim back the way I had come.

I was no longer able to use my map – water had got into the plastic bag covering it and the map had disintegrated. So, to avoid the gypsies, I decided to stick to the treeline as it shadowed the tarmac road that ran up the mountain, past the Osmice Hotel, and continued on to the bobsleigh track. It was risky, but here and there, where I had a clear view of the road and was sure there was little chance of being intercepted, I took to the tarmac, which increased my speed.

Crouched among the trees on the far side of the road I searched the surrounding area for signs of life. I was in luck, as apart from a single light on the desk in the hotel's unmanned reception area there was nothing. I looked at my watch.

00:17.

It had been a little over forty minutes since the standing patrol had raced out of the forest and I had started my second swim. What I needed to do now was to remain focused and keep moving. My body, predominantly my arms and legs, had started to shake as I left the river for the second time, and although my jog up the mountain had restarted my peripheral circulation, I was now beginning to shake again as my body temperature dropped and the cold began to attack my core. Having spent two years on the Regiment's training wing, I had witnessed the onset of hypothermia in some of those taking part in winter Selection, and knew that if I didn't get warm soon I would be experiencing the condition first hand.

I reached the door of the basement and pushed against it. It held. My first thought was that the block of wood I had inserted into the latch hole had been too narrow, and the catch had caught, locking the door. The second thought was that maybe someone had opened the door after I had left the building, and it had fallen out. I looked down, there was nothing on the floor. I pushed again, harder this time, and to my relief it gave with a loud crack.

I froze, as I stood motionless on the threshold and listened for any sound as my eyes scanned those areas of the building I could see, looking for lights being switched on, but there was nothing. I removed the block of wood, slipped it into my pocket, and stepped inside. I was just about to close the door when I heard the sound of a vehicle pulling into the hotel car park; unusual to say the least at that time of night in Yugoslavia where all right-minded communists would have been tucked up in bed hours earlier. In my frozen state, the paranoia was starting to set in. Could it be the standing patrol from the forest? There were a number of hotels dotted around the area and, as the Osmice was not the closest to the military base, I reassured myself that it was unlikely.

Hidden behind the door, I peered through the crack but could see nothing. I was about to make my way back up to my room when I heard voices. There was no mistaking it; one of the voices belonged to 'Lurch', the hotel manager.

I closed the outside door, sprinted across the basement, up the cellar stairs and, after checking that the lobby was empty and the desk unmanned, headed for the staircase. A minute later I entered my room, but instead of feeling safe, for some reason I felt trapped. I turned the key in the door, lifted my canvas briefcase from the floor beside the table, and turned it upside down, spreading the contents over the bed. I headed into the bathroom, turned on the shower, and stripped off. Then, in an effort to get some warmth into my body, I stepped under the warm water but, as it began to revive my body, there was a heavy knock at the door. Gathering up my wet clothing and shoes, I quickly stowed them out of sight. With a towel wrapped around my waist, and a second draped around my neck, I re-entered the bedroom and unlocked the door.

To my surprise, the two men standing in the corridor were not members of the Yugoslav military, but civil police. The lead officer pushed me aside as he barged into the room. The second, a few feet behind his partner, pinned me to the wall with the palm of his gloved left hand, and levelled the AK-47, suspended on a sling from his right shoulder, at my waist.

The first officer went straight to the pile of clothes and the trainers lying on the floor beside the bed. He picked them up. They were room temperature – bone dry – and he immediately dropped them again.

I felt my heart quicken as he turned away from the bed and made his way into the bathroom, sending the door crashing against the wall as he went, but apart from the hot water running down the drain in the shower tray, the room was empty.

Leaving the bathroom, he re-entered the bedroom, glared at me and in broken English asked, 'Where have you been all night?'

Trying not to shiver, I adopted my best bemused look. 'Here. After dinner, I came up to my room to do some paperwork.' I nodded towards the bed. 'As you can see, I'm not quite finished.'

The two policemen exchanged words in what sounded like a local Serbo-Croat dialect, and after a quick visual sweep of the room and under the bed they left.

I flopped down on the bed, gave them enough time to get down the stairs and leave the building, before standing up again. I made my way to the door, opened it and checked the corridor outside.

Empty.

Locking the door behind me, I went back into the bathroom, dropped the towels on the floor and stepped into the shower for the second time that night. The water felt much hotter than it actually was as it ran over my still freezing cold body. Then, as I knew it would, the pins and needles and the pain began as my body slowly came back to life.

Stood beneath the cascading water, head in hands, elbows resting against the cold white tiles of the shower wall, I breathed a sigh of relief, but it was short lived. As my body gradually began to warm up so did my brain, and the paranoia experienced by all those who work alone behind enemy lines began to grow. It was a new experience for me, and my initial feeling of relief quickly turned to one of anger. The standing patrol in the forest hadn't been there by accident. They were waiting for somebody, and if it wasn't me, then who was it? Then there was Lurch. What had he been doing up at this time of night? More importantly, why had he gone outside at the precise moment the police arrived? Had he somehow known that I had left the hotel the previous evening and, having been pre-warned, had he been waiting for them to turn up so that he could let them in?

Leaving the shower running, I dried myself off and slipped on a T-shirt and a pair of shorts. After checking once more that the door was securely locked, I returned to the bathroom. I smiled to myself as I lifted the toilet seat, removed the soaking wet clothes and trainers from their hiding place in the bowl and, as I threw them into the shower tray, I began to wonder why the police had checked my room but, it seemed, no other?

However, at breakfast the following morning I discovered that others staying in the hotel had received the same late-night visitors. But having come so close to getting caught in the act, the thing I was now finding really difficult to understand was the reason behind my mission. Why the hell had it been necessary?

Two Weeks Later
Thursday, 23 January 1986
Old Covent Garden, London

T HE WALK FROM Covent Garden tube station to what at one time had been London's principal wholesale fruit and vegetable market had taken a little over two minutes. As we entered the glass-covered courtyard I felt Thompson's hand on my left arm.

'That's him.'

I followed Thompson's gaze. Sitting at a table on the far side of what to all intents and purposes was the outside seating area of a café, albeit under a high glass-covered roof, was a man in his early fifties. The café is still there today, although I reckon it now trades under a different name.

The man's clothes were what I would call practical. He wore a checked shirt with an open, button-down collar, beneath a dark brown corduroy jacket. The cuffs were trimmed with leather, as were the patches on the elbows. Sat high on his nose was a pair of gold-rimmed, John Lennon-style glasses that drew your attention to his small, brown eyes; above them was a mop of dishevelled mousey-coloured hair. He looked like an academic. In fact, he reminded me of Mr Goodyear, my former maths teacher. Not the type of person I normally associated with.

Thompson set off across the café, picking his way through the half-empty tables and chairs. I gave him a short start, and then followed two paces behind. We had just reached the halfway point when, as if he had somehow sensed our presence, the man looked up, got to his feet and extended his right hand.

'Good to see you again, Gavin.'

'You too. This is Staff Sergeant Tom Shore, the man we discussed.' Thompson turned to me. 'This is—'

But before Thompson could introduce him, the man cut him

34

short, mid-sentence, and stuck out his hand. 'Hi. I'm Mark Scott.'

The brief I had received from Thompson the previous day went no further than telling me that we were travelling to London the following day and that, once we were there, there was someone he wanted me to meet. As a result, with the introductions over, and now face to face with Scott, I waited for more, like an explanation as to who the hell he was and what he did for a living. It didn't come. So, without thinking, I took his hand. 'Pleased to meet you.' I was still shaking it when a waitress appeared at Scott's left shoulder.

He looked across the table at Thompson. 'Black coffee?'

Although he was dressed like my old maths teacher and I hadn't been told who he was, or what he did for a living, there was no mistaking Scott's Oxbridge accent. As a result, the alarm bells were already starting to ring. He was obviously well educated and from the officer class, but at the same time he was doing everything he could to be something else and make himself more approachable.

Thompson seemed preoccupied, and for some reason it took him longer than I expected to respond. He shook his mind free and answered, 'Please.'

Scott turned his attention to me. 'And for you, Tom?'

Although I can't function these days without pumping at least two cups of strong black coffee into the system, it was different back then. 'Tea please.'

Scott smiled. 'East End boy eh? Brought up on buckets of dock-er's brew?'

I forced a smile. Scott's over-friendly attitude was not winning me over. 'Something like that.'

The waitress left to get our order and Scott sat down again. 'Is this the first time you've been to Covent Garden?'

I glanced around the large open area filled with tables and chairs, then at the overpriced craft and gift shops that surrounded it. 'No. My granddad used to bring me here some Saturday mornings, but it was a different kind of place. Back then it was full of fruit and veg stalls, and the only place to get a mug of tea and a bacon sandwich was from an open-sided wagon standing outside.'

Our drinks arrived, and as soon as the waitress had left, Scott got down to business. 'I understand that you've recently returned from Yugoslavia.'

I said nothing. There was no point. Scott already knew the answer to his question. Besides, what interested me more was what else he knew.

'Did you enjoy it?'

'It was OK. Although Yugoslavia would not be my first choice as a holiday destination.'

Scott stared at me but said nothing. It was one of those looks you get from a junior officer when they're not sure whether you're taking the piss or not. Eventually he said, 'I'm talking about the special task Gavin set you.'

Given that my 'special task', as Scott referred to it, took place outside the UK, I now had to assume he probably worked for MI6 or one of the lesser known agencies – those that the British public never hears about. I also wondered again if, given its low strategic value – those ZSU-24s I had found were hardly going to have set the intelligence world alight – my mission in Yugoslavia had not been some sort of test. Something Scott had a hand in.

'Enjoy is not the word I would have used. Let's just say it was interesting.'

Scott rested his forearms on the table and leaned forward. 'Right, this is what's going to happen. Firstly, apart from the three of us sitting here this morning, you are not to talk to anyone back at the Regiment about your special task in Yugoslavia, or about this meeting. Is that clear?'

I had heard the speech so many times before, I responded with a somewhat uninterested and automatic, 'Roger that.'

Scott leaned back in his chair. 'Now tell me what you know about BAOR's [the British Army of the Rhine] response to a Warsaw Pact offensive in northern Germany.'

For some unknown reason, the 'need to know' gene immediately kicked in, and I found myself not wanting to tell him. I have no idea why, especially as the information Scott was asking for was hardly a national secret.

Also, Scott's question was a loaded one. Any senior NCO, regardless of his trade or regiment, who did not know the answer should not have been doing the job.

But I turned to Thompson, who nodded his head.

'Well, in brief,' I said, 'it would be nothing more than a holding exercise. BAOR, with the support of the West German Bundeswehr and Luftwaffe, will do everything in its power to slow down the combined Soviet/East German advance, bringing it to a halt on the eastern side of the Rhine. The aim would be to give Western politicians and NATO generals time to talk to the Soviets in the hope that together they could come up with a compromise that would prevent the situation escalating into an exchange of nuclear weapons, and the start of World War Three.'

Scott smiled. 'Short, but very comprehensive, a textbook answer.'

'Thanks. But I don't know what I'm doing here.'

Scott leaned forward again, rested his arms on the table and lowered his voice. 'We've lost contact with one of our agents, a local man who lives and works in the town of Zinnwald, fifty kilometres south of Dresden and twenty-five kilometres north of East Germany's border with Czechoslovakia.'

I could now feel my sarcasm gene coming up for air. 'Well, I doubt that it's the first time one of your agents has come to his senses. Realised that he's playing a very dangerous game and taken the gap – got out while he still could.'

Scott was clearly not amused. 'This agent has always proved reliable in the past. The information he provides is always of the highest quality.'

'That may be, but what precisely do you expect me to do?'

Scott sat back, turned side on, and draped his left arm over the back of his chair. 'Find him, or find out why he's dropped off the grid.'

I felt my jaw drop. 'Not being rude, but I'm a Special Forces soldier, not a spook. Isn't this why you – I assume you're MI6 – exist? Don't you have field agents already on site? People who are far more capable of carrying out this type of work than me?'

Scott's attitude changed again. He became relaxed, maybe slightly arrogant; he reminded me of a politician about to lecture a junior civil servant.

'Who I work for isn't important, but if we were having this conversation forty odd years ago, then I would agree with you. The SOE was the ideal tool for this type of operation, but sadly they were closed down shortly after the end of the Second World War. Since the start of the Cold War the role of our field agents has changed dramatically, and not always for the better. Unlike members of the SOE, who were primarily high calibre military personnel, the best Britain had to offer, the modern breed of agent has no military training whatsoever, and therefore no understanding of what he is looking at when it comes to military hardware.'

Scott had opened the door for me. I smiled.

'But I wouldn't be working on military matters. I would be going in to find a missing agent, which in itself requires no military expertise or training. It only requires someone who is able to blend into the local population. Be invisible and then report back.'

He lifted the cup to his lips, took a sip, and placed it back on the saucer. 'These days our people are primarily involved with the management of foreign agents and the interpretation of the information they provide. It's true that they still operate amongst the civilian population of the target country, but any meetings between them and their contacts are typically pre-arranged by a handler. It will take an experienced soldier, someone with good field craft skills and the ability to think fast, adapt, and look after himself in what is after all a highly hostile environment, to find out what's happened to our man. To find someone who may no longer wish to be found.'

It was a well-known fact that most of those now being recruited by both arms of the intelligence services – MI5, MI6 and others – were being approached while still at university, predominantly at Oxford and Cambridge. Combine that with the fact that much of East Germany was still in the same state that Hitler had left it in – covered by forest – and that being able to move about unseen and unheard was a skill that not only has to be taught but regularly practised. I began to see that Scott might have a point.

But Scott was moving on, trying to add weight to his argument. 'And besides, as you know, second-hand information, the information gathered by third parties, foreign nationals working for us, is never as clear-cut as it first appears. It's always open to misinterpretation and manipulation. For all we know, a large percentage of the Intel we receive from these people could be entirely fictitious, or worse, it could be coming from double agents working for the Stasi or KGB.'

The East German Ministry for State Security or Staatssicherheits-dienst, commonly known as the *Stasi*, were responsible for all matters of state security, but unlike in Britain back then, when the security services concentrated their efforts on threats from outside the country, the Stasi was more concerned with what it perceived as threats from within – dissidents, non-communists, those they considered counter-revolutionaries – and their pursuit of these individuals was both brutal and relentless. Driving them and to some extent directing them was the feared Russian KGB.

I considered asking Scott why he wasn't using the British Commanders'-in-Chief Mission to the Soviet Forces in Germany for the job. BRIXMIS was a small, secretive unit based at 'London Block', deep inside the 1936 Olympic Complex in West Berlin. It was formed in 1946, shortly after the end of the Second World War and pre-Cold War, when there was optimism regarding future harmony with the Russians. A military liaison mission, it operated with Soviet permission behind the Iron Curtain in East Germany. Its objective – and that of SOXMIS, the Soviet equivalent that operated in the British Zone – was 'to maintain liaison between the staff of the two commanders-in-chief and the military governments in each other's zones'. And, even though the mutual antipathy and suspicion of the Cold War had long since soured any goodwill between the two nations, both BRIXMIS and SOXMIS had somehow survived.

I quickly dismissed the idea. BRIXMIS was to all intents and purposes an overt organisation. Its operators, known as 'Tours', were allowed to travel wherever they wanted, apart from a few pre-designated sensitive areas. They wore British Army uniform and travelled in marked cars. It was common knowledge that both BRIXMIS and SOXMIS gathered military intelligence where and when they could, and although incidents of open hostility towards Tours – such as being shot at or having their vehicles deliberately rammed by East German HGVs – were infrequent, they did nevertheless happen. As a result, BRIXMIS were unequipped for the job Scott had in mind for me. Asking the question would have only served to make me look like an idiot.

I turned to Thompson. 'Can I speak freely, Boss?'

Thompson raised his eyebrows and a grin spread across his face. It was the type of look that said, 'It's never stopped you before'.

I turned back to Scott, laid my forearms on the table and, leaning forward, said, 'As I said earlier, I'm a soldier, not a spook. I'm not trained for this sort of thing.'

Scott was obviously expecting the answer and came straight back at me. 'You guys work behind enemy lines all the time. Everybody now knows that the Regiment was operating deep inside Argentina during the Falklands War. Hidden outside Argentinian Air Force bases, providing the Task Force with early warning of air attacks. Then there are the Regiment's operations in Northern Ireland.'

Without realising it, Scott had just dug himself into a hole. I was about to take full advantage of the situation and start shovelling the dirt back in on top of him.

'True. But apart from across the water, where we are armed and always have backup, all of our missions are carried out in uniform. We work on the premise that, if seen by a member of the local population or enemy forces, then the game's up and it's time to get out. Besides, I will never pass as a native East German.'

Scott smiled. It was the smile of someone who could smell victory. 'On this occasion, it will be different. This time you will not have to hide, operate in uniform, or avoid being seen by the local population. You will be able to move about freely, within reason.'

I couldn't see how that was going to work.

He's still digging.

'So why send me at all? Why not just send another one of your East German operatives to find out what happened to your man?'

Scott leaned forward again and lowered his voice. 'Because it's not that easy. If, as I suspect, something has happened to him, then I no longer know which of my local assets I can trust.'

I still wasn't convinced so decided to attack the problem from a different direction. 'That's all very well, but how do you propose I get across the Inner German Border? Even armed with the correct paperwork, it's a nightmare getting through the Soviet checkpoints and along the NATO Military Corridor that runs through East Germany from Helmstedt to West Berlin. And that's "*with*" permission from the Soviet and East German authorities.'

'Your cover story, for the use of a better term, during your trip to Yugoslavia earlier this month was that you were there to take part in a Great Britain Luge Association training week. Correct?'

My response was flat, matter of fact. 'Correct.'

'At the end of February there is a World Cup race at Altenburg, East Germany—'

I cut him off mid-sentence. 'Yes, I know. Members of the team were talking about it in Sarajevo.'

'Well, the track is approximately four miles from the town of Zinnwald.'

I slowly shook my head. Scott obviously had no idea about the complexities surrounding the sport of luge and, to be honest, his somewhat blasé attitude to the proposed project was starting to piss me off.

'Yugoslavia and the previous week in Igls in Austria were, as you've just stated, training weeks. There is no way the GBLA will allow me to take part in a World Cup race on any track, let alone one as technically demanding as Altenburg.'

Scott smiled. 'You won't be there to take part in the event. Your cover story will be that the army now wishes to get involved in the sport of Luge. In much the same way as it did with bobsleigh over a decade ago. You will be there purely as an observer.'

Scott's response had a certain amount of logic to it. It had been the same with bobsleigh and biathlon; the combined sport of cross country skiing and target shooting. With both disciplines the military first provided athletes, then, when they began to get results, they fed in the trainers, managers and badly needed funding, eventually pushing the civilians out and taking over the sport completely. George Orwell, author of *Animal Farm*, once described international sport and the modern Olympics as 'war minus the shooting'. It was now widely accepted that both East and West regularly used foreign sports competitions as a cover for their espionage activities.

'So, how do I get in?'

'You will travel as part of the British team, but in a separate vehicle. That way you will have a little more flexibility once you are in East Germany. I believe you speak a little German?'

'Yes.'

'How much?'

'I picked up a little during my first year in the army while serving with my regiment in BAOR, and I've recently completed a three-week intensive German course in the Regiment's language lab at Hereford.'

'Good. The GBLA have agreed to let you join them. You've already been added to the team list. The paperwork regarding you and your vehicle, a former DET car recently compromised across the water, has already been submitted to the appropriate authorities. The DET was the Regiment's pet name for 14 Field Security and Intelligence Company, a small, highly secretive unit that carried out undercover surveillance operations against groups and individuals suspected of being involved with the IRA, or Loyalist paramilitary organisations across the water.

Scott continued. 'However, the GBLA are not aware of the real reason you will be there and that's how it should remain.'

I said nothing while I considered my response, but thirty seconds later I was ready.

'Well it sounds simple enough. But, if whoever you send is just going to drive across the border as part of the British team and then snoop around, why don't you send one of your own guys? Someone from Century House? It doesn't sound like any of my specialist skills are going to be required.'

Scott leaned back in his chair, took a sip of coffee and, still holding on to his cup, said, 'Firstly, you have experienced the sport first hand, which nobody from Century House has. That gives you credibility and a reason to be there. Secondly, members of the British team already know you. Thirdly, I suspect that, following the time you spent in Igls and Sarajevo, your face will be recognisable to the majority of the other national teams, including the East German and Soviet team. All of which should help you avoid too many awkward questions.

'Finally, all Western teams travelling to Altenburg are billeted in the Dynamo Zinnwald sports centre. It's the East German centre of excellence for winter sports. It employs the very latest training methods and technology in its pursuit of excellence and, as a result, the centre is well guarded, and extremely secure. I need someone who is capable of breaking out of the centre, locating the missing agent's flat, and gaining entry to it and finding out what's happened to him. Then, once you've completed your mission, break back into Dynamo Zinnwald . . . all undetected. The whole mission should take you four hours. Tops.'

What Scott was proposing was nothing new. The Regiment regularly worked on behalf of, or alongside, the intelligence services, especially *across the water* and, although dealing with spooks is rarely a rewarding experience, Thompson's silence throughout told me that the battle was already lost. As such, there was little point in me protesting further. Sadly, Scott's proposal and my suitability for it did have a certain logic about it.

'Does your guy have a name?'

'Littman. Thomas Littman. The last we heard he was working at the Tin and Tungsten mine. Living in the Projects on the south side of Zinnwald. Block Eleven, Flat Three. It's on the ground floor.'

Scott offered me his hand and, although I had taken an instant dislike to the man, etiquette demanded I take it.

'Welcome aboard.'

I turned and looked at Thompson who again, to my surprise, said nothing.

Ten minutes later, with Scott having paid the bill, the three of us left the café through different exits. Scott, presumably making his way back to Westminster Bridge Road on the south side of the river, while Thompson and I headed for Covent Garden tube station and on to Paddington.

As we walked past the Royal Opera House, I turned to Thompson.

'How long have you known Scott, Boss?'

His eyes fixed firmly on the road ahead.

'I've known him since childhood. Why? Something bothering you, Tom?'

I practically grunted. 'What? You mean, apart from the fact that it would appear that I've just been recruited by MI6. I'm about to head off behind the Iron Curtain, alone, and unarmed . . . I know that there is no way I can risk getting caught carrying a weapon as I pass through the Soviet and East German checkpoints, but that doesn't mean I have to be happy about it. And I'm not, Boss.'

I heard Thompson chuckle. 'Anything else?'

Having been given the green light, I immediately followed it up. 'Well, now that you've asked, Boss . . . Yes, there is. Why was this meeting conducted in a public place, a café in central London? Why did it not take place at MI6's headquarters?'

Thompson remained facing forward, his eyes focused thirty feet along the pavement.

'S . . . Scott's . . .' Thompson stuttered. It was like he was having trouble remembering the man's name, but it didn't last long. 'Scott's a little paranoid at the moment. Littman isn't the first of his agents to disappear from the Dresden area and as a result Scott suspects that the organisation has a leak. But he has no proof. Following the discovery of the Cambridge Five and the subsequent defection of Kim Philby back in 1963, the organisation is getting somewhat tired of being told they have a leak. A mole.'

As I turned away from Thompson I looked to the far side of the road and wondered just how much of what had happened over the past six months – me becoming PV'd, my strange non-mission in Yugoslavia and the meeting we had just attended – had all been part of someone's private agenda. Perhaps Sarajevo had been nothing more than a test? If that was the case I was confident it hadn't been for Thompson's benefit. He knew exactly what I was capable off. Besides, there was no way he would have selected me for the task if he wasn't one hundred per cent sure I could pull it off. However, Scott was a completely different kettle of fish: a spook. Maybe he had required proof. But, if that was the case, then I was seriously unimpressed. Apart from the fact that the training run had almost got me killed, it didn't bode well for the future.

On the other hand, for a Special Forces soldier, pitting yourself against the odds and winning through is what it's all about. If it weren't there would be no point in putting ourselves through the selection process.

I was still staring across the road when I said, 'And apart from that, as far as everyone else is concerned, I don't exist, and I assume that's how Scott would rather it stayed?'

It took Thompson a second or two to respond. It was like his mind was somewhere else but eventually he answered, 'Exactly.'

As we travelled down the escalator that led to the platforms that ran below Covent Garden tube station, my mind shot back to that morning in Hereford a few months earlier.

Passing the PV process would most likely open a multitude of doors, not all of them good, but they were doors that when opened could lead me to opportunities most soldiers can only dream of.

Conversely, I knew even then that what I was about to do had the potential to turn into a living nightmare.

East Germany

WHILE THE EAST Germans and Russians were without doubt still my enemy, they were by no means each other's friends. I knew I would soon be entering a country at war with itself.

Just over forty years earlier the Russian and German armies had been slaughtering each other on the streets of Berlin. During the battle for Berlin, which was fought over four days from 16 to 19 April 1945, the Soviets lost a staggering 81,000 men, with another 280,000 falling sick or wounded. The Germans lost over 92,000 men with another 220,000 wounded and 480,000 captured. Although the civilian population of the city suffered a little better by comparison, with only 20,000 dead, it was the German women and children, the survivors of this carnage, that paid the heaviest price. Thousands were either raped, enslaved or brutally murdered by the advancing Soviet troops as they tightened their grip on the city. The largely uneducated, basic Soviet soldier viewed this as nothing more than 'a just revenge'; a payback for the horrors the German troops had inflicted on Russia during the previous four years. But it created wounds within the German populace that even today are still extremely raw.

Although East Germany was a communist country and a committed member of the Warsaw Pact, a country that would have no choice but to side with the Russians against the capitalist West, its people had not forgotten their recent past. Most viewed the Russians as nothing more than a barbaric occupying force – which of course is what they were.

By the same token, the Russians had been attacked by the Germans twice in the twentieth century, losing more than 10.4 million military dead – 8.7 million of those occurring in the Second World War alone. That justified the Russian view that East Germany had to be kept well under control and that the two German states should never be allowed to reunite.

It had been shortly after the end of the Second World War, at the Potsdam Conference in July and August 1945, that the four victorious Allied powers – the United States, Britain, France and Russia – having formally abolished Hitler's government, divided up a defeated Germany into what would soon become known as Allied Occupied Germany.

In the capitalist West, you had the Federal Republic of Germany (FRG), commonly referred to as West Germany. While in the East, you had the communist German Democratic Republic (GDR), East Germany or, as the East Germans and Soviets referred to it, the Deutsche Demokratische Republik (DDR). It seemed to be a given in those dark and dangerous days that if a country was a dictatorship, it contained the word 'democratic' in its title, as if this was somehow going to fool its downtrodden citizens into thinking they lived in a democracy. Separating them was the heavily fortified Inner German border, which stretched for over 1,393km – a structure that on 5 March 1946 Winston Churchill had referred to as the 'Iron Curtain', a name that would stick for over forty-three years.

Berlin, once the capital of the Third Reich, like the rest of Germany, had also been divided up into four zones with the Soviet zone in the Eastern half of the city, and the US, British and French controlled 'zones' in the West. Although they were locked deep inside the Soviet sector, they were still considered to be part of democratic West Germany.

Between 1945 and 1961, some 2.5 million East Germans fled to the West through West Berlin, reducing the GDR's population by around fifteen per cent. Ominously for the communist regime, most of these emigrants were its well-qualified young. The country was haemorrhaging the cream of its educated professionals and skilled workers at a rate that risked the East German state becoming unviable.

During the summer of 1961 this exodus reached critical levels and, on a fateful weekend in August, the communists' vast undertaking to seal off East Berlin from West Berlin and close the 'escape hatch' began.

On Sunday, 13 August 1961, Berliners woke up to find themselves separated from their friends, family, work, and in some cases even their homes. The day became known as *Stacheldrahtsonntag* (barbed wire Sunday).

Within a few weeks, the improvised wooden and wire obstacles spread throughout the centre of the city were starting to morph into a formidable cement structure, 3.6 metres high, backed up by over 40 miles of barbed wire fencing, and more than 300 watch-towers. The structure would soon become known as the 'Berlin Wall' or, as the Germans referred to it, '*Der Mauer*'. It was a heavily fortified, guarded and booby-trapped barrier almost a hundred miles long, which not only divided the city in two but encircled the whole of West Berlin, cutting it off from the rest of the world.

By February 1986 the Wall had stood physically unchallenged for almost twenty-five years. West Germany had become a flourishing democracy of some fifty million people anchored into what was known as the Western NATO alliance, while the DDR was a struggling social experiment, a third of the size of its West German sister, and allied to the communist Warsaw Pact. Compared to easy-going, liberal Western Europe, being behind the Iron Curtain was like being on a different planet; a dangerous, hostile planet, and the further east you moved, the more threatening and oppressive that planet seemed to become.

It was there that I was now heading.

Map of Cold War East Germany

The map below shows the geographical location of Berlin in relation to the Inner German Border and the Federal Republic of Germany (West Germany). It also shows the places that appear in the book: the likes of Dresden, Leipzig, Karl-Marx-Stadt, Zinnwald, and Prague (Czechoslovakia): the areas I was operating in at the time.

Monday, 17 February 1986

Herleshausen – On the Inner German Border

I WAS FIFTY kilometres south of Kassel on Route 7 and heading south towards Frankfurt when I saw the sign for Route 4. I took the slip road and a minute later I was heading east, towards Herleshausen.

Apart from stopping for fuel and the occasional coffee – motorway tea on the Continent is not a pleasant experience for an Englishman – I had driven nonstop since leaving the ferry terminal at Zeebrugge in Belgium.

As I made my way along Route 4, the first signpost I saw read 'Herleshausen 40km'. However, there was no mention of the fact that I was fast approaching the Inner German Border, East Germany, or that I would soon be entering one of the most oppressive states on Earth.

The road surface was good, just as other West German *autobahns* were, but within a few miles of crossing the border, the old, rough concrete slabs that had been laid by the Third Reich to move Hitler's panzers would replace the smooth black tarmac.

East Berlin was the same. Once you were behind the new buildings that lined the 'Wall', those seen by the tourists from the West, you were instantly transported back to 1945, the year the Russians 'liberated' the city. Evidence of the fierce fighting that had taken place at the time was everywhere. There were large empty spaces where there had once been grand buildings, and the facades of those that had managed to survive the carnage still carried the scars of artillery strikes and heavy machine-gun fire. In fact, many were just that: facades of once elegant buildings with nothing behind them but timber supports to stop them falling over. That was East Germany and East Berlin during the 1970s and 1980s.

A second road sign loomed up on my right, 'Karl-Marx-Stadt

220km'. Below it was a sign that read 'Dresden 290km'. A few seconds later, I saw the watchtowers that marked the progress of the Inner German Border, the only features on an otherwise barren landscape.

By the time it eventually fell, 2,000 people would have lost their lives trying to cross this Inner German border, the section of the Iron Curtain that separated the FRG from the GDR and which now stretched out before me. Although estimates vary, it is thought that up to another two hundred would die trying to cross it in Berlin, with many losing their lives along the heavily fortified 'death strip', a sterile area that ran along the East German side of the Wall, containing anti-vehicle trenches, barbed wire, and beds of nails, all under an array of blinding floodlights.

As the road dipped away, I spotted the single-storey, flat-top buildings that marked the official border crossing point. I slowed the car as I approached the first of the barriers. A West German border guard, a member of the Bundesgrenzschutz, stepped out on to the road. I lowered the window and handed him my passport and travel documents.

After a cursory inspection, the guard handed them back, waved his hand in the air, and the heavy metal barrier that marked the end of the FRG, and the beginning of the GDR – the Iron Curtain – was lifted.

I pulled slowly forward, weaved around the concrete tank traps put in place by the Soviets and, as the car reached the second barrier, I applied the handbrake. I looked into the rear-view mirror. The first barrier was being lowered back into place behind me.

There's no going back now.

I was between worlds. Trapped between East and West. Stranded in no man's land.

Now, if I had been German, a border guard would have simply inspected my papers and my car, searched the boot and the car's interior before allowing me through. But I was a foreigner driving a British-registered car, so for me the process was different. I climbed out of the car and walked calmly towards the Russian soldier standing beside an East German border guard, both of whom were sheltering behind a Perspex weather shield on the central reservation.

If I had been travelling through the military corridor from Helmstedt to West Berlin, I would have waited patiently for the Russian to come smartly to attention and salute. It's true, I wasn't an officer, but it was all part of the ritual. Regardless of rank, everybody saluted everybody. But now, I was no longer protected by my military status, and didn't want to be – the last thing I needed was for the Soviets and East Germans to know that I was a member of the NATO forces. I looked at the East German border guard, a member of the Grenztruppen. Not even a smile. I handed him my papers.

The guard practically snatched them from my hand, inspected them, gave them back, and with a ramrod-straight left arm pointed to a building on the far side of the road.

That short walk from the guard post to the admin block was a daunting journey. This wasn't the NATO corridor between Helmstedt and West Berlin – which made for a far more controlled and safe environment for British military personnel, crossing the border. This was a civilian checkpoint on the Inner German Border, at the time one of the most dangerous places on Earth. And although deep inside I doubted it would happen, as I walked across that exposed patch of tarmac the atmosphere was so tense that, with every step, I waited to be recalled, arrested or even for a bullet in the back.

On reaching the admin block I opened the door and stepped into a large empty room. The only clues as to where I was were the two portraits hanging on the wall opposite. Those of Mikhail Gorbachev, the then Soviet President, and Erich Honecker, the head of the SDP, the East German Communist Party, the joint rulers of East Germany.

I turned to my right. Stretching the full width of the room was a chest-high wooden counter. Rising above it, practically all the way to the ceiling, was a frosted glass screen. Between the counter and the glass screen was a foot-wide, four-inch-high gap. No bigger than a domestic letterbox.

I pushed my passport and travel documents through the gap. Then I took a step back behind the white line painted on the floor, and looked up at the camera screwed to the wooden panel that ran above the frosted glass screen. I knew it would be there. The process was the same when entering the Military Corridor at Helmstedt. Hand your papers to the faceless shadow behind the frosted glass screen. Step back behind the painted line, and have your photograph taken while he or she photocopied your military ID card and travel papers.

My journey along Route 4 from Herleshausen towards Karl-Marx-Stadt and on to Dresden was uneventful. The steady rhythm of the car's tyres rumbling over the joins between the concrete slabs became somewhat hypnotic. In places, where new pieces of road had been added, large areas remained unfinished. In fact, a few kilometres west of Karl-Marx-Stadt, two lanes of a large motorway bridge were missing, apparently abandoned mid build.

It was just after 16:00 that I saw the word 'Zinnwald' written on a large yellow sign on the northern outskirts of what turned out to be a tiny town. Three hundred metres later, I turned left and got my first sight of 'Dynamo Zinnwald', the East German centre of excellence for winter sports. It resembled a small red brick village, containing buildings of all shapes and sizes, surrounded by an eight-foot-high, chain-link fence topped with barbed wire. It bore an uncanny resemblance to the compound I had broken into in Yugoslavia. But then, on closer inspection, it became clear that the materials used here – the chain-link and barbed wire – were of a superior quality, and I knew that unlike down in Yugoslavia where the perimeter fence had been designed to keep me out, this one was designed to keep me in.

At equally spaced intervals along the fence, sitting on top of tall concrete posts, were powerful security lights. The main entrance to the centre was a miniature version of the border crossing point at Herleshausen – two barriers with a sterile zone between. The guard on the gate was armed with a pistol and dressed in dark green military-style uniform, and as I waited patiently to be admitted, a two-man roving patrol approached the guardhouse, both armed with AK-47s. As far as I was concerned, it looked more like a prison camp than an elite sports complex.

After completing the formalities at the guardhouse, I parked the car exactly where instructed. As I opened the car door and stepped out on to the tarmac I saw a member of the British team, a tall thickset man, heading across the road in my direction.

'Here, let me help you with your bags. We've just got time to take them up to your room. The evening meal is at five thirty.'

The dining room and kitchen, like the majority of the complex, were housed in a 1960s style red-brick building. It had a flat roof, and large metal-framed windows that reminded me of my secondary school back in Dulwich, south east London.

I stepped inside and took another trip back to the sixties. There were three rows of six-foot, Formica-topped tables arranged in pairs, laid end to end. Ten metal-framed chairs, complete with Formica seats and backrests, surrounded each pair of tables. My time at school hadn't been the happiest part of my life. My days a mixture of trying to learn while at the same time having to deal with the bullies who cruised the playground like sharks. I just hoped my time in Zinnwald would be a little more enjoyable, but I wasn't holding my breath.

Thursday, 20 February 1986

Zinnwald, East Germany

I T WAS AT breakfast three days later and with the dining room close to empty that I was invited to join a mixed table of Austrian, German and Italian sled technicians, all of whom were always eager to practise their English. Although the rivalry among the athletes was as fierce as ever, most of those sat around the table were former athletes and had known each other for many years.

I had just started my second cup of what was jokingly referred to as 'coffee' when I fielded a question at nobody in particular. 'If "Dynamo Zinnwald" is a state-run centre of excellence for winter sports, what is the significance of the "Dynamo" prefix? I've only ever heard the term applied to football clubs in communist countries. The likes of "Dynamo Dresden" or "Dynamo Moscow".'

An elderly but fit-looking Austrian who had been studying the previous day's training times stopped what he was doing and lifted his head. 'Have you ever heard the word "Traktor" applied in the same way?'

I remembered reading about 'Traktor Zagreb', the Yugoslav Ice Hockey Champions when we were down in Sarajevo. 'Yes.'

'Well. Any sports club, in fact, any organisation in Eastern Europe that carries a "Traktor" prefix, is run and administered by the military, specifically the army. Here in East Germany, that means the NVA – the Nationale Volksarmee.'

Given his comprehensive answer, I had a good idea what was coming next, but still felt compelled to ask the question again. 'And Dynamo?'

The Austrian's face changed. His expression became serious, like he was dragging up some unpleasant memory, something from his past. 'In other communist countries, any organisation that carries a "Dynamo" prefix is run and administered by the state police. Here in East Germany that means the Stasi.'

I knew all about the East German Stasi. It was the official state security service of the DDR, and has often been described as one of the most effective and repressive intelligence and secret police agencies in history. Although I didn't know it at the time, the Stasi held files on just about every person in the country, forcing its citizens to betray friends and even family members as the price of survival. What I did know though was that its reputation was fearsome and its reach long. Stasi headquarters were in East Berlin, but it also had regional offices, one of which was on Bautzner Straße in nearby Dresden.

One of the Stasi's main tasks was to spy on the population, mainly through a vast network of citizens turned informants. Although it wasn't known at the time, the situation regarding Stasi informers was much worse than people realised. It has been estimated that by 1989, one in sixty East Germans was working either officially, or unofficially, for the Stasi – close to 300,000. People were informing on their work colleagues, friends and even members of their own families.

They fought any opposition to the regime using both overt and covert measures including the process of *Zersetzung*.

During the Honecker era – from May 1971 to October 1989 – the Stasi used the accusation *Zersetzung* to silence political opponents by repression.

German historian Hubertus Knabe wrote:

The goal was to destroy individuals' self-confidence, for example by damaging their reputation, by organising failures in their work, and by destroying their personal relationships.

The use of *Zersetzung* is well documented due to numerous Stasi files published after the fall of East Germany, where it is estimated that up to 10,000 individuals had fallen victim to this barbaric process, with over 5,000 sustaining irreversible damage.

In addition, its Directorate for Reconnaissance was responsible for both espionage and for conducting covert operations in foreign countries and, under its long-time head Markus Wolf, this directorate

surrounded the local parks and schools in East London. The ones that had never managed to keep me out during my school days. But there was no way I could risk damaging this fence on my way out of the complex in case the damage was spotted by an alert guard and there was a welcome committee awaiting me on my return. Conversely, damaging it on my return – although it would obviously be better if I didn't – was not such a concern with close to a thousand athletes, coaches and officials to process. Moreover, with most of them due to leave for home in a few days' time that should not prove too much of a problem.

On the other side of the fence was a narrow dirt track, just wide enough for a single vehicle to travel along as it patrolled the outer perimeter. Beyond that was the Zinnwald Forest where, even then, small packs of wolves that had migrated south from Poland still roamed free.

The Mining Projects where Littman lived were at the far end of the town, four kilometres away, but there was no way I could just walk there along the main road. The only way I was going to stay out of sight was to travel through the Zinnwald Forest alone, unarmed, and in the middle of the night.

I completed my run, showered, and, just before midday, carrying an account sheet, that was used to record the team's daily expenditure, I made my way back to the canteen. I couldn't face another cup of East German coffee, so waited patiently at the hotplate for someone to appear. I glanced over my left shoulder through the dining-room windows at the guardhouse.

'*Kann ich Ihnen helfen?*'

I turned back to the counter and the owner of the voice who was now standing behind it. A young woman, between five foot six and five foot eight tall, with cornflower blue eyes; her high cheekbones accentuated by her swept-back, platinum-blond hair. She was beautiful.

She spoke again. '*Guten Tag.* Can I help you?' Those last four words spoken in near perfect, unbroken English stopped me in my tracks.

I stood there speechless for a second or two. Then I asked, 'Would it be possible to get a cup of tea, please?'

I watched in silence as she turned to the boiling vessel sitting on the metal table behind her. The pale blue overall she was wearing clung to her body, showing off her trim figure to its full effect.

She turned back, placed a mug of hot water and a teabag on the counter in front of me, and asked, 'Milk?'

I was just about to answer her when something caught my attention. About ten feet away, leaning against a door frame, staring at us from the kitchen, was a weasel of a man in his late forties.

'Er . . . No thank you.' I looked back to the kitchen. The man was still there, and still staring. 'I hope I've not got you into trouble.'

She turned her head and followed my gaze. When she turned back, she was smiling. 'No. It's OK. Our government is trying to change the way the world looks at our country. Now, with permission, we are encouraged to talk to Westerners – forge new friendships.'

I stifled a smile.

You poor deluded creature, you have no idea.

I then remembered my conversation with the Austrian about the meaning of 'Dynamo' earlier that morning.

Or maybe you do?

I thanked her, dropped the teabag into the mug, grabbed a teaspoon from the cutlery tray and headed for a table beside the window. With the mug cradled in both hands I brought it to my lips and stared at the main guardhouse on the far side of the road. I wasn't interested in the building itself. What interested me were its occupants. The comings and goings of the East German guard force. If I was going to have any chance of completing Scott's mission, I would need to know how many patrols there were. How many men made up each patrol. When their stags started and finished and, more importantly, how long it took them to complete a single lap of the perimeter.

It was far too dangerous to record the information in plain language. For all I knew the cute blond who had just made me my tea could, even now, be watching me. Reporting my actions to her superiors.

Before leaving my room, I had put together a simple code. I would enter the guard force's activities on to the cash–flow sheet disguised as items of equipment along with their purchase price. For instance, 'the Start of a two-man Stag at 12:00' became '2 Speed Suits – at DM 120.00 each'.

The timing of my arrival at the canteen had once again not been by accident, or a random act. Realising that sitting here for too long might raise suspicion, I had arrived just a few minutes before the expected stag change at 12:00. Lunch was served at 13:00, so sitting here until then would not look too much out of place. However, the information I would gather over the next hour would be crucial if I was to time my exit from, and return to, the complex precisely. Being seen doing either or, even worse, being captured was not an option.

It was 13:47. Lunch was over, and I was back in my room. I was sitting at the table that doubled up as a desk when there was a knock at the door.

'Come in.'

It was one of the British athletes. 'Do you have a minute?'

I turned over the sheet of paper I was working on. 'Sure. What's up?'

'We've just heard that the track session scheduled for this afternoon has been cancelled.'

That was all we needed. With all of the Western teams as good as locked down inside the centre, most of the two hundred-odd male and female athletes were now on the brink of going stir crazy. There was only so much physical training you could get them to do and, as pre-race tensions grew, tempers were beginning to fray.

'Did they say why?'

I felt my eyebrows rise as, uninvited, he parked himself on the end of my bed.

'It's something to do with the timing mechanism at the men's start. Apparently, when the sledge passes the ladies' start, instead of recording the split time like it's supposed to, it's now stopping the clock, which means there is no time being recorded at the finish.'

'So what happens now?'

His voice lifted slightly. 'They've moved this afternoon's training session back to this evening – from seven till ten. They say that they have identified the problem and will have it fixed by then. I've told the rest of the team to be ready to leave here at five forty-five.'

Although I was only there as an observer, during the past week

I had done my best to be part of the team, helping out where I could, doing anything that needed doing, taking as much pressure as I could off the athletes. In fact, doing what comes naturally to a British Special Forces soldier: playing the hearts and mind game.

'Anything I can do?'

He smiled. 'Would you mind trying to book us a light meal for five o'clock and a hot drink and sandwich for when we return from the track? I would do it myself but I suspect a lot of teams will be trying to do the same, and I still have work to do on my sled before tonight's session.'

'No problem.'

I remained seated and watched as he closed the door behind him. *It looks like it's tonight then.*

I glanced at my watch. *15:07.* It was time to pay another visit to the pretty blonde in the kitchen.

It was just after 23:30 when I peered through the wire-reinforced window that made up the top half of the door that led out of the accommodation block. Plumes of steam were rising from manhole covers through the orange glow of the security lights. To be honest, painted black and surrounded by black tarmac, I hadn't noticed them before, but now, as I exited the door, it was dark and they seemed to be everywhere. It reminded me of the type of scenes used to increase the tension during a New York crime drama. Only on this occasion, the dangers were real. The only good thing was there was no sign of anybody.

I was wearing the same dark blue outfit I had worn for Thompson's mission in Sarajevo. I stayed in the shadows as I moved from building to building and got closer to my target. I could of course just not bother. Tell Scott that I couldn't find Littman or anything about what had happened to him. After all, there was no way he would ever know any different – but that wasn't my way.

As I approached the rear of the building, which housed the indoor luge and bobsleigh start ramps, I heard hushed voices coming from the far side of the building. Someone was approaching my position along the fence line, but I wasn't surprised. In fact, I would have been disappointed if they hadn't been there.

A few seconds later a two-man foot patrol came into view. My eyes locked on to their AK-47s and I stepped back into the shadows and checked my watch.

23:38. Smack on time, talk about predictable.

I had calculated that it took a patrol approximately twenty minutes to get from the guardhouse to my present position at the rear of the indoor start house. It would take them a further twenty minutes to complete their circuit of the perimeter and report back to the guardhouse. Each watch or stag lasted two hours, which meant this patrol had begun its stag at 22:00 and was already halfway through its third and final circuit.

Seven minutes later, having given the patrol sufficient time to clear the area, I was balanced precariously on the horizontal waste pipe that ran out of the first-floor washrooms, with a firm grip on the down pipe. My feet were five feet above the top of the chain-link fence. I pressed my back into the brickwork and steadied myself. The fence looked a lot higher, and the landing area on the other side a hell of a lot smaller from up here.

However, there was no time to think about that right now. In a few minutes I would be outside the wire; my situation would change and not for the better.

I bent my knees slightly. Took a deep breath and released my grip on the down pipe. As I tipped forward, using my arms to give me extra drive and lift, I launched myself upwards and towards the dirt track on the far side of the fence.

There is usually something comforting about the smell of a forest at night, the crisp freshness, the smell of the trees, and wet grass as it's carried on the evening breeze. A cloak of darkness, black enough for a man to hide behind, but comfort wasn't the feeling I was getting tonight. This was an ancient forest and given its location and the violence that had occurred here during the last hundred years, and more recently during the Second World War, it now had a feeling of evil about it, a coldness, the type that comes with immense suffering was now shadowing my every step.

I had covered around three and a half kilometres. Jogging where I could. Walking where the track was not clear or the exposed tree routes made it too dangerous to do so, or when the glow of street lamps broke through the trees.

My journey was slow. Convinced I was being followed, I carefully backtracked, only to discover it was a wild boar. Not wanting to get involved with something that weighed close to three hundred pounds and is renowned for savagery if startled, I slowly backed off and circled around it but, although a necessary precaution, this cost me precious time.

As I reached the treeline, the full extent of the Projects that housed the mineworkers was laid out before me. Long narrow blocks of flats, council apartments, were arranged in neat rows, cresting a hill at the opposite end of town to Dynamo Zinnwald. All I had to do now was find Block Eleven, Flat Three.

A few minutes later, standing in the shadow of Block Ten I stared at my target. Flat Three was one of four on the ground floor. The curtains were open and, apart from a single light coming from what appeared to be a bathroom window on the third floor, the building was in darkness.

There was only one lock on the front door of Flat Three, an East German version of a Yale. I took hold of the handle and gently slid the door from side to side. It was a loose fit. It rattled in its frame; it was the type of fit that hopefully would work in my favour. I put my shoulder to the door just above the lock. Hauled sideways on the handle, against whatever extra compression the hinges had to offer, then, pulling my shoulder back three inches off the door, I hit it. Nothing. It held firm. I pulled my shoulder back slightly further and hit it again. Harder. On the third shove it gave, and the door swung away from me.

The inside of the flat was dark. The air smelled damp. Like it wasn't being lived in − and there was something else. Something unpleasant. I secured the catch, pushed the door closed and switched on the small Maglite torch I had brought with me.

The first room I entered was the kitchen. Again, it was like taking a trip back to the sixties. A single wooden draining board beside a porcelain sink and above it a pair of cupboards. My heart skipped a beat when I saw the dirty dishes lying in the sink. Maybe I had been right when talking to Scott back in Covent Garden. Maybe Littman just had second thoughts about his future survival and, as a result, had quietly dropped off the grid. Maybe he was still living here. It was as I moved closer and shone the Maglite on to the dishes that I noticed the blue mould growing on the food welded to the top plate. Standing on the wooden draining board beside the sink was a carton of milk. I lifted it. It felt half full. I gave it a squeeze. It was solid, and as I raised the opening to my nose I discovered the source of the *something else* I had smelled when I first entered the flat.

An assortment of men's clothing hung in the bedroom wardrobe. There was shaving kit in the bathroom, and what passed as a linen basket was half full. I wiped my hand around the edge of the sink. The dust that covered it was sticky. It hadn't been used for a while. I didn't waste any more time looking for anything else. According to Scott, Littman was an experienced operator, which meant that there would be nothing of any importance hidden in the flat. There was nothing here for me. Not now. It was time to leave but, as I reached the front door, I saw it from the rear. I noticed that the hinges were new. The wood surrounding them had been repaired, which all pointed to the fact that the door had been recently forced and the hinges replaced.

Three Years Later –
Thursday, 3 August 1989
Bethnal Green, East London

A YEAR AFTER my return from Zinnwald, and following sixteen years of military parachuting, trudging over mountains carrying heavy weights while wet and cold which, believe me, is a brutal way to earn a living, my body was beginning to break down. In 1980 I had had major surgery on a serious ankle injury, the result of a close encounter with a piece of Russian-made ordnance. In 1983 my body was doing its best to absorb these new additions and the surgeons had to go in and operate again. While I had managed to adapt to the lack of feeling in my right foot, my right hip was now slowly beginning to disintegrate and would eventually need to be replaced. As a result, I was now eating Brufen 400s (anti-inflammatory painkillers) like Smarties, just to keep pace with my colleagues in the Regiment. In 1987 I was promoted to Warrant Officer (Sergeant Major) and then, rather reluctantly, I returned to the Green Army and a somewhat gentler life in BAOR in West Germany.

I have always been lucky with my commanding officers. I don't know why, maybe it was my plain talking, calling a spade a spade and never backing down when I knew that I was in the right. Or maybe it was the fact that all through my army career I'd always given one hundred per cent, which earned the respect of those both above and below me. Also, joining a unit straight from Hereford, and so bringing with me skills and knowledge that were not readily available to the Green Army, had probably gone a long way to making me more welcome at my latest posting.

However, it looked like it might all go wrong on the third day at my new regiment. I was still in the process of rearranging my office, clearing out the previous tenant's crap, when my new colonel, a tall slim man with brushed-back hair, wearing service dress trousers and an olive green Pringle jumper, walked in unannounced. Caught up with what I was doing and forgetting where I was, I inadvertently called him 'Boss'. Standing directly behind him was his adjutant. He was close to six inches shorter than the colonel, of medium build, and was a dislikeable character, as I would find out later, with an extreme hatred of anything airborne.

He coughed loudly and said, 'Here we respect rank and call our officers "sir".'

But before I could apologise for my error in elevating the CO from a 'Crap Hat' – any non-airborne or special forces soldier – to the lofty status of a Regiment officer, the colonel smiled and said, 'No, that's OK. I can live with "Boss" when it comes from the sergeant major.'

As you can imagine, the CO's comment immediately made the adjutant and me the very best of mates. An adjutant is a jumped-up captain, who has the ability to make a soldier's life – and the life of junior officers – utterly miserable, as he is responsible for discipline in the regiment. But it seemed that my new CO had taken a liking to me. While I never took advantage of this new relationship, it soon became clear that as long as I did my job well, I was virtually bulletproof as far as the adjutant and others like him were concerned. All of which made life a lot easier.

Unlike Hereford where you are always training for something, involved in missions that would take you to different areas of the world, or operations across the water, I found a soldier's life in BAOR in West Germany to be something of a non-event. Our whole existence revolved around the threat posed by the Soviet Union and members of the Warsaw Pact.

We still lived with the threat of an attack by the IRA, who in 1987 and 1988 stepped up their campaign of bombings and shootings against British soldiers and their families based in Germany.

Then there were the home-grown terrorists, like the German Baader-Meinhof Group – otherwise known as the 'Red Army Faction – RAF'. Although it traditionally targeted big business and government institutions in Germany, it had also carried out a number of operations against US military targets in the Frankfurt area, killing several civilians and members of the US armed forces in the progress. The worrying thing was that intelligence sources were now reporting that the two groups, the IRA and RAF, appeared to be sharing both intelligence and recourses. As a result, it was now every soldier's responsibility to keep himself or herself up to date with the growing rogues' gallery of photos hung on the noticeboards of the barrack's guardrooms.

It was just before 09:30 when I crossed Grove Road and passed through the ornate wrought-iron gates that led into Victoria Park. I had spent the previous three days at my aunt and uncle's home, a council flat opposite Gunmakers Lane in Old Ford, enjoying a bit of leave. It was in the heart of London's East End, and a brisk ten-minute walk from the park entrance.

The telephone call from Scott had come totally out of the blue and, if I was honest, as a surprise; not least that he had managed to track me down. I hadn't seen or heard anything from him in over three years. My journey from the mining projects back to Dynamo Zinnwald had gone without incident and getting back over the wire into the complex had been relatively stress free. However, the same could not be said for the meeting, a few days after my return to the UK; the one where I met Scott and delivered my less than positive report regarding the fate of Littman, his missing agent.

Thompson was tied up on Regiment business and I met Scott on my own that day. The meeting took place at the Newington Butts, a pub on the corner of St George's Road, at the point where it joined the Elephant and Castle complex.

The Butts, as it was known locally, was on the site of an old coaching inn, just over a mile from Century House, then the London headquarters of the Special Intelligence Service (the SIS or, as they are more commonly referred to, MI6). Close enough for Scott to casually walk to in about fifteen minutes, but perhaps far enough for him not to bump into anybody else from the office. Although Scott had been polite at that meeting, I could tell he was far from pleased and had probably expected me to have done more; to have been more inquisitive and confirmed my suspicions about the fate of Littman.

Like my two previous meetings with Scott, this one was also happening in a public place, well away from SIS Headquarters. Conversely, given what Thompson had said about Scott believing that a mole existed within the organisation, I put his choice of locations down to professional paranoia and natural spook mentality.

As I made my way past the line of upturned wooden rowboats, their numbered bows pointing towards the park's boating lake, I saw the wooden kiosk set a few metres back from the water's edge. Scattered around it was a collection of weather-beaten metal-topped tables and chairs. It was the type of place where hardy individuals could purchase tea and coffee dispensed in white polystyrene, take-away cups. For anyone brave enough, set out on the counter beneath a clear plastic canopy, were yesterday's cheese rolls. Beside them were rock cakes, which, from childhood memory, would more than live up to their name.

As I drew closer to the kiosk Scott spotted me and stood up. He was dressed in a smart, dark blue suit over a white shirt and a loosened tie, but nothing could hide his sallow complexion, prob-ably the result of a fast-food diet, combined with long nights spent worrying about life and death situations happening thousands of miles away. Events that were no longer within his control.

Scott extended his right hand. 'Tom.'

The short time I had spent in London had been a welcome break from regimental routine in BAOR, which at times can become more than a little tedious. And, as we're telling the truth here, I must admit I was beginning to miss the buzz, the pressure and purpose that comes with being a valued member of an elite organisation: the rush that has always been a part of regimental life in Hereford. But I knew too that as soon as this meeting was over I would be heading for the Joint Movements Centre (JMC) at Luton Airport and the 20:10 flight back to RAF Gütersloh in Germany.

I dropped my bag beside the table and, taking Scott's hand, shook it. 'Mark.'

Scott retook his seat. As I turned towards the kiosk I said, 'Give me two minutes to grab a tea. Do you want anything else?'

He shook his head. 'No thanks, I've only just got this.'

With tea in hand, I took my seat on the opposite side of the table, and taking a sip I looked across at Scott. 'Having heard nothing from you for close to three years, I had assumed we were done.'

Scott took a sip of his coffee, then said, 'We will never be done. Not in this lifetime.'

It appeared that the rumours were true. Like the Italian Mafia, once you're in, or in this case working for the spooks, there was no getting out.

He placed his cup on the table and, still hanging on to it with one hand, said, 'There have been some new developments. I want you to go back into East Germany.'

I wondered if Scott would tell me that Littman, his missing agent, had somehow miraculously resurfaced, but I knew really that this was extremely unlikely to be the case. What I had found at the flat in Zinnwald told me that, at best, he was already dead.

My response to Scott's comment was unenthusiastic. 'To do what exactly?'

'I don't have the complete picture yet but a few weeks ago Littman's replacement left a message in a Dead Letter Drop which was later retrieved by a BRIXMIS Tour. The message was short. It mentioned an Operation Konev, and that whatever this Konev is, it has something to do with Zinnwald and will begin on October the seventh of this year, in less than nine weeks.'

I sat quietly and said nothing as I waited for more but, after close to a minute, I felt compelled to ask the obvious question. 'And?'

Scott's sarcastic look had disappeared and been replaced by one of regret. He reminded me of a small boy who had accidentally broken one of his favourite toys.

'There is no and . . . There was nothing else in the message. No details. And now, like Littman, he appears to have also dropped off the grid.' He leaned back in his chair. 'We have to assume that Operation Konev is some sort of military operation that will be launched on October seventh, from the area around Zinnwald.'

Of course, Scott was right. It had to be something big otherwise there would be no reason to risk reporting it, and things don't come much bigger than a full-scale attack by the Warsaw Pact.

By the 1980s British operations were being given computer generated and, for the most part, random code names, which gave little or no hint as to what they were actually about. Conversely, that was not always the case with the operations conducted by the Soviet Union, which had a much more macho approach to such things. I knew that there had been a Marshal Konev, a hero of the Soviet Army. But I was confused. Given the enormous resources at his disposal, why had Scott not managed to find out who or what Konev was about without needing to involve me.

'So, what has all this got to do with me?'

Scott continued, 'In short, I need someone to go in and try to find out what this Operation Konev is and, once we know, to then monitor troop build-ups and their movements. Give us a heads-up before whatever Konev is kicks off. But it needs to be someone with experience, a soldier. Someone who has the ability to be invisible, move about unnoticed, who knows what he's looking for and is capable of quickly identifying a potential target. Someone who understands the calibre of the forces involved, can predict any pitfalls the enemy might face and the probable outcome, and if necessary suggest a local response. In short, the type of operator that began to disappear back in 1945 when the SOE was disbanded – someone like you.' Then, as a kind of afterthought he asked, 'By the way, how is your German these days?'

I smiled as I recalled a recent event that took place back at my current regiment. I was using a German gym five days a week, which meant I was being forced to speak German on a regular basis, and as a result it had improved dramatically. My wife on the other hand spoke very little German, but thought it would be a good idea to learn the language properly. I had agreed to accompany her to evening classes provided by the Army Education Corp. At the end of the first session the female major in charge called me over and said, 'No point in you coming back. Although your German grammar leaves a lot to be desired you speak street German to a colloquial level. It's better than mine, I can teach you nothing.'

'Not bad. Improving.'

Although I could see the logic behind Scott's proposal, I also felt that such a plan could create more problems than it solved.

'With all due respect, just how do you propose I get back into East Germany? Travelling through the Soviet checkpoints as a legitimate member of the GB luge team was risky enough. But now, with the East German authorities becoming increasingly jittery, as a Westerner travelling alone, without a legitimate purpose, it's going to be all but impossible.'

In the six months leading up to this meeting, the financial and political situation in East Germany and the surrounding Warsaw Pact countries had begun to rapidly destabilise. Living conditions in East Germany were deteriorating and the local population was becoming increasingly frustrated with its leaders. It was believed that the Communal elections held on 7 May 1989 had signalled a major turning point in the East German people's attitude.

It was also said that around 100,000 people had answered the opposition's call and publicly boycotted the elections. Of course, this did not stop the authorities from announcing, as they had done in previous years, that ninety-nine per cent of citizens had cast their vote and overwhelmingly supported the only list. Upon publication of this data there were, of course, formal protests, supported by partial results provided by independent election commissions.

Another wave of protests had followed a month later, on 4 June 1989, after the communist authorities in China massacred students in Tiananmen Square. Within hours of the event in China, leaflets and graffiti drawing parallels to East Germany began to appear in many East German cities, and demonstrations were organised in both Leipzig and Berlin.

But the biggest blow to the communist regimes of Eastern Europe came when, on the same day, in partially free elections, the population of Poland almost unanimously supported 'Solidarity', the Polish Trade Union led by Lech Walesa, and his anti-communist movement. This became a major turning point not only for Poland, but for the entire communist bloc in Eastern Europe. At the end of the same month, following political changes in Hungary, the country removed controls along its border with Austria. These events were a clear signal to the people of East Germany that Poland, Hungary and Czechoslovakia could serve as staging posts on the road to the West. These three countries had quickly become known as the 'Third Country Route'.

However, I knew that as the threat to their absolute authority grew, the KGB and their lackeys the Stasi would be pushed into increasingly extreme measures in order to try to preserve it.

I thought about the camera above the booth at the Herleshausen checkpoint.

'After my last trip to Zinnwald, the East Germans now have my picture, and a name to go with it,' I told Scott.

He slipped his hand into the inside pocket of his jacket and removed an envelope. 'This envelope contains your new passport.'

I took out the passport and flicked through it to the main page. The holder's photograph was of me, but it wasn't new. It was the same age as the one on my current military ID Card, a few years old and in keeping with the issue date on the passport. It also came as no surprise that my name had been changed. I tossed it back on the table.

'Well, that all seems to be in order, but you still haven't told me how I'm going to get in.'

Scott nodded down at the table. 'The envelope also contains two flight tickets. The first is an open return from Dusseldorf to Vienna, via Munich. The second, another open return from Vienna to Prague—'

I stopped him mid-sentence. 'I'm just going to fly into a Czechoslovakia controlled by the Soviet Union?'

Scott stared at me for a few seconds before continuing with his brief. 'Along with the air tickets, there is a Business Visa issued by the Czech Embassy in London. It will enable you to enter Czechoslovakia without too much fuss. Although in the West, Vienna was once known as the "spy capital of the world", on the other side of the Iron Curtain this title was held by Prague. These days Czechoslovakia itself is of minimal interest to anybody, either East or West.'

I knew that Scott was right about that. The feeling within NATO was that Russia only kept hold of Czechoslovakia because it plugged a gap in the Iron Curtain. In reality it now had little strategic value. There was no way either NATO or the Warsaw Pact was going to risk the wrath of the United Nations by launching an invasion through Austria, a neutral country, which bordered Czechoslovakia.

I left the envelope sitting on the table. 'You forget one thing. I'm no longer at Hereford, and Thompson is no longer my CO.'

Scott smiled. 'The powers that be have informed your current CO that you are to be released from the regiment until the end of

February next year, the end of the upcoming luge season. You will be working alongside the Great Britain Luge Association with a view to introducing the sport of luge to the army. In fact, your current CO has already volunteered to take on the role of Army Secretary. And, in September next year, at the start of the new luge season, you will take over as National Team manager in the run-up to the 1992 Winter Olympics in Albertville, France. The British Olympic Association have put their full weight behind the proposal.'

I had considered asking Scott why he wasn't using someone else from Hereford, but his last statement had already covered that – I was the one with the luge background which made me acceptable to the BOA and, besides, I knew the area.

It looked like Scott had all the bases covered. With my new CO keen to get involved in the luge programme, if I refused to take on the job it would not only severely piss him off but be tantamount to refusing a direct order. Anyway, the thought of getting back into the game, feeling the rush once more, was too enticing to resist. But I was far from done with Scott.

'What happens when I get to Czechoslovakia? How do I get from there across the border into the GDR – East Germany?'

'That will be down to my people on the ground in Czechoslovakia, your contact in Prague. But, if everything remains the way it is, you will probably travel by either bus or train from Prague to Dresden. Travel between the two countries is somewhat relaxed at the moment although, given the current state of affairs in Eastern Europe, that could all change at a moment's notice.'

Scott was right, of course. In the summer of 1989 the world was once again witnessing public demonstrations of dissent in East Germany similar in some ways to those that had gone on in previous years. But in the past, such events had been sporadic, random, and rarely affected more than a few hundred people.

This year it was becoming a mass phenomenon. First thousands, then tens of thousands, of East German citizens (predominantly its young people and members of some professional groups), fed up with conditions at home and the hopelessness of life in the German Democratic Republic, decided to try and reach West German territory. Some of them sought a way out by taking refuge at the West German embassies in Berlin and Warsaw, while others took advantage of the chance to travel to Hungary without needing a passport or visa, and then to Czechoslovakia, placing even greater strain on what were already fragile East-West relations.

I needed more reassurance.

'What level of support can I expect when I get to the GDR? I'll need both accommodation and a means of transport, neither of which I can get without producing a valid East German ID card and talking to someone. All of which will increase my chances of getting caught.'

'While you're in East Germany, support will be provided by the Bewegung.'

I raised my eyebrows. 'Who, or what, is this movement?'

'The Bewegung – the Movement – is a small underground organisation trying to bring about government reforms in East Germany by peaceful means.'

I couldn't help myself and shook my head. 'Good luck with that one.'

Scott ignored my remark and continued. 'They will provide you with accommodation and feed you. They will also provide you with everything else you need, but a word of warning to the wise. You will be working alone, among members of a fledgling under-ground movement, in much the same way members of the SOE did with the French Resistance during the Second World War.'

The fact that both Littman and his replacement had recently disappeared without a trace added more than a little weight to Scott's last comment. I pushed him for more information.

'Were Littman and his replacement members of this Bewegung?'

Scott raised his eyebrows and gently shook his head. 'No. The Bewegung is a relatively new addition to the East German freedom movement – in fact, I would go one step further and say that they are still at the embryonic stage, still trying to find their place in the pecking order among the many groups now seeking to bring about reforms.'

Great.

Now some of you may be thinking that Scott was being melodra-matic, given that this was central Europe in the late 1980s and not Nazi-occupied France at the height of the Second World War.

However, what you need to understand and keep in mind is that to most of us in the West at the time, the term 'Cold War' was just a turn of phrase, meaning nothing more than the ongoing war of words and posturing between East and West – communism and capitalism. But to a soldier, someone like me, I knew that once I crossed the Inner German Border and entered the East, if I were caught that 'ongoing war' would be a very real war. What is more, the reality of what was happening on the other side of the 'Wall' was nowhere near as clear-cut as you would have thought, even if you kept a keen eye on the mainstream news.

'So who is my contact within the Bewegung?'

Scott said nothing for a second or two; he just sat and stared. Then he said, 'I have no idea. Up until now I have had no dealings with the Bewegung. In fact, up until a week ago I didn't even know that they existed. The only two contacts I had in the Dresden area are either missing or dead. Everything regarding your travel from Prague to Dresden, and who your contact will be once you arrive, has been arranged through my people in Czechoslovakia.

'But given the large number of Stasi and KGB informers that exist at all levels of East German society, once you're there, there will be no guarantees about who can and who cannot be trusted. Fail to understand that, and where these people are coming from, where their individual loyalties lie, and you will inevitably make some bad decisions, miss possible opportunities which, in the end, could cost you your life.'

I sat staring at Scott for a second or two. He was preaching to the converted.

You're just full of good news.

'Understood. So, what's my cover story? If you're right and this organisation is riddled with informers, I can hardly tell my new friends in the movement that I'm an ex-British Special Forces soldier, sent there to find out about some top secret Soviet operation.'

Scott was not warming to my particular brand of sarcasm and snapped at me.

'Of course not. I suggest you tell them that you're working for the Foreign and Commonwealth Office and that you are in East Germany as an observer. Say that you're there to monitor the situation and at the same time assess the organisation's progress, to see if there is any way in which the British Government might be of assistance.'

Scott's idea of a cover story was weak to say the least and his 'so what' attitude was once again beginning to piss me off. It was also making me increasingly nervous. Telling an East German organisation that I worked for the FCO would immediately flag me up as a member of British Intelligence and at the same time turn me into a high-value target for the Stasi.

But at this point none of it seemed real. The conversation we were having and the operation that it concerned were still very much hypothetical; nothing but a series of questions fielded by me, and answered by Scott. As a result, my responses up until now had bordered on the sarcastic, my flippant attitude only mirroring Scott's own.

'OK. When this is all over, assuming that I'm not captured or killed – ' my sarcasm gene had kicked in once again '– how do you propose to get me out of East Germany?'

Scott screwed up his mouth. 'I haven't worked that out yet, but it would seem logical to simply reverse the procedure. Bring you out via Prague. Hence the open return air tickets.'

Scott's casual attitude was making me nervous again.

Nothing is ever that easy.

'So, when do I leave?'

'You're to arrive in Prague on Wednesday, the ninth. Seven days from now.'

I immediately saw another problem. 'As you've just said yourself, the luge season doesn't kick off until the end of September. How am I going to explain to the colonel that I need to disappear at the beginning of August?'

Scott now had the look of a man who had just won the battle.

'As far as anyone else is concerned you are spending the time attending meetings with the British Olympic Association and International Luge Federation, bringing yourself up to speed with the politics of the sport, and also supervising the team's pre-season testing and training. As I said earlier, your current CO is totally on board, so you shouldn't have any problems.'

It would appear that, once again, Scott had all the bases covered, but there was one thing he hadn't explained.

'Let's suppose I do manage to find out what Operation Konev is, how do I get the information back to you? I can hardly jump on a plane and report back to London. It could take me weeks, possibly months, to get out of East Germany.'

Scott reached into his wallet, took out a slip of paper and handed it to me.

'The last six figures are a grid reference for an RV (rendezvous point) just outside Dresden. The first three are irrelevant; they're a distraction, the dialling code for Zwickau. You need to be at that location at zero four hundred on August the seventeenth, when a BRIXMIS Tour will deliver your communications equipment. Any special requests?'

I didn't hesitate. 'Yes. A Clansman 319.' My flippant attitude had all but disappeared; now, all of a sudden, this was very real indeed.

In those days communications, getting messages between East and West, were not only near-on impossible, they were a nightmare. Of course, back then there were no mobile phones only landlines, and if you wanted to make a call from East to West you had to book it in advance through an official body – the local police – who would then inform the Stasi, who would openly monitor the entire call.

When it came to military communications equipment, most of it was intended for use on the battlefield, which meant it was short range. It was also heavy and transmissions could be easily tracked by enemy listening stations, of which there were many on both sides. But, the Clansman 319 was a totally different kettle of fish.

At that time, the 319 was considered to be state of the art. It was lightweight and able to transmit on both HF and VHF bands, and up to aircraft frequencies for ground-to-air communication; it also had an Electronic Message Unit (EMU). This was a small alphanumeric keyboard that allowed for the transmission of pre-configured written messages when lengthy voice communications were too risky. All of which had earned it its nickname of 'The Spy Radio', and had made it the object of an ongoing love affair with British Special Forces.

'OK. It seems straightforward enough, but I will need to do some serious homework. How do I get in touch if I have questions?'

Scott scribbled a telephone number on the back of the envelope and pushed it across the table.

'My home phone number. Don't use it unless you have to, and never call me at Century House. If you're right about what happened to Littman and possibly his successor, it's now far too risky.'

I shoved the envelope containing my new passport and the flight tickets into my bag, picked it up and, together, Scott and I walked through the park gates on to Grove Road. I stuck out my hand and waited for Scott to take it. 'I'd like to say it's been a pleasure. But I'll save that until after I get back.'

Scott hesitated as if he was expecting more but when it didn't come, he simply said, 'Er, OK. I thought we could talk further as we walked down to the tube at Bethnal Green?'

I was getting the same feeling I'd had in Yugoslavia and after my first meeting with Scott in Covent Garden, that once again I was not being given the whole story. As a result, the last thing I wanted to do was spend any more time than was necessary with him.

'I'm sorry, but I've arranged to have lunch with the family before heading back to Luton.'

And, to my surprise, he just let it go.

Now, before we go any further, some of you reading this book, and especially this current chapter, will probably consider my perception of the real world, and my willingness to take the things Scott was telling me at face value, rather strange. However, in my defence, as soldiers, and especially Special Forces soldiers, we had to believe that what we were doing was for the greater good. More importantly, we also had to believe that those in command, or in Scott's case in control, were also operating in the same way; obeying the same rules. Otherwise there was no way we could do what we do.

But, to quote Jakub Bożydar Wiśniewski, the former Polish Ambassador to the Organisation for Economic Cooperation and Development (OECD), 'the term for the greater good is the phrase that always proceeds the greatest evil'. And it's not until after you leave the Brotherhood, are exposed to the cut and thrust of the outside world, and armed with that beautiful thing called hindsight, that you realise that some of those you trusted with your life, those whose orders you followed without too many questions, were, in the end, only out for themselves.

★

After watching him walk across Grove Road, I turned to my left and headed back to Old Ford. My head a mass of questions.

With regards to Operation Konev, the experience and knowledge I'd gained at Hereford, along with what I had seen during my trip to Zinnwald three years earlier, told me that any East German/ Soviet operation that was launched that far south would initially be of no interest or threat to BAOR, which was based in the north of the country. Zinnwald was too far to the south, practically opposite the American sector, and the only high-value target in that area was the Rhine-Maine air base, which lay close to Frankfurt, the largest American air base in northern Europe. That meant the Americans would immediately assume control, making it their problem, while Britain took a back seat until the shit really hit the fan and the whole of Europe went to war and the world was plunged into chaos again.

On the other hand, logic dictated that if the East Germans and Soviets were gathering a whole armoured division down in Zinnwald, there was no way they could effectively employ it during a strike on somewhere like the Rhine-Maine air base because there was nothing but forest between Zinnwald and Frankfurt. They would first have to move the entire force 70 kilometres north to Dresden. Then west 290 kilometres, around Karl-Marx-Stadt, and through the Herleshausen border crossing, before heading south again, down Route 7, the autobahn that runs from Dortmund to Frankfurt.

Some of you may remember that the Nazis stormed through the Ardennes during the Second World War and think, *That was forested.* However, during the Second World War there was no satellite surveillance so the Allies had no pre-warning regarding the build-up of German armour, so were unable to prepare a suitable response. This was something that could not happen now. Moreover, the forested areas the German panzers encountered, as they moved north and northwest in an effort to surround Antwerp, had a good road and track network that provided easy passage for both their panzers and logistical support, the bowsers (fuel tankers), field workshops and supporting infantry. Once they had cleared the forested areas, they were in perfect tank country, wide-open plains with rolling hills.

But things were different now. In 1989. Large swathes of Eastern

Germany were covered by tightly packed forestry blocks, and the infrastructure that existed – the autobahns and large built-up areas in and around Frankfurt – on the Western side of the Inner German Border presented the East Germans and Soviet Union with a real problem: even in the event that they decided to take the sensible option and head north, the logistics involved would be enormous. The majority of East German roads were in an abysmal state of repair and, as I'd discovered in 1986, the autobahn that ran west from Karl-Marx-Stadt to Herleshausen wasn't even complete. It would take the Soviets days to get just one tank regiment to the border. They'd be spotted long before they reached their start line. Once the threat was identified or their intentions were known, and the tank transporter convoys were out in the open, the American Warthogs – their formidable A10 tank busters – would show up and, backed up by heavy bombers, they would cut the East German and Soviet convoys to pieces.

On the other hand, given that Czechoslovakia and its Eastern Bloc neighbours were rapidly becoming a thorn in Moscow's side with their growing demands for more freedoms, if the Soviets decided to re-invade Czechoslovakia then, in my opinion, Zinnwald, being less than eighty kilometres from Prague, made it the ideal launch point.

When I reached the end of St Stevens Road I turned right and joined the queue of others waiting at the bus stop. It was a little over ten minutes before the number eight bus arrived. Once on board, I went straight upstairs and took a seat on the right-hand side, on the opposite side of the bus to the pavement. I didn't want to get spotted by Scott as we drew alongside Bethnal Green tube station. I didn't want him to find out that I had lied in order to avoid spending any more time with him.

I stayed on the bus until it reached Liverpool Street. Once there I took the tube to Russell Square.

From there, it was a short walk from the square, along Montague Road to the British Museum, which at the time shared its space with the British Library.

The British Library is the national library of the UK. The second largest library in the world by the number of items catalogued, at that time over 150 million. It is also what's known as a legal deposit library, meaning it receives copies of every book produced in the UK and Ireland and has an extensive catalogue of notable articles from around the world. Like the obituaries of the famous, and in some cases the infamous.

As I entered the library, that unique smell of printed paper invaded my nostrils. There is something homely, comforting, about the smell of a book, and even during the dark times, the endless hours spent sitting in hides, down in what we referred to as 'bandit country' in South Armagh, on Northern Ireland's border with the Irish Republic, I would always have a book.

In those days, you needed to have a pass with a photograph to gain access to the British Library, but where there's a will — as I approached the woman sitting behind the desk I took out my Military ID card.

'Good morning. I'm a member of the armed forces and I'm completing a thesis for a promotion exam. I'm looking for an obituary for a former marshal of the Soviet Union, name of Konev.'

She stood up, went to what looked like a small metal filing cabinet sat on a table behind her, and pulled out one of the drawers. Inside each drawer were two rows of index cards separated into groups by a different colour card that carried a letter of the alphabet on its top edge. Within a minute she had found what she was looking for and directed me to the relevant area.

There were no computers in those days. Yes, they already existed, but in places like the British Library, even today, a significant amount of the information it holds that is not in hard copy, printed format or bound books is displayed on Microfiche. I quickly found the film I was looking for, laid it on the viewer and switched on the light below the glass bed. There must have been sixty or more entries on this one film. All of them had been Marshals the Soviet Union, either talented leaders or butchers, but what all of them had in common was they were now dead.

I worked my way across and down the sheet, and there it was . . . 'Marshal of the Soviet Union, Ivan Stepanovich Konev'. Konev was a Soviet military commander who led the Red Army forces on the Eastern Front during the Second World War. He took back much of occupied Eastern Europe from the Nazis before playing a significant role in the capture of Berlin in 1945.

Born on 28 December 1896 in Lodeino, near Veliky Ustyug, Russia, he was drafted into the Tsar's army in 1916. He fought during the First World War, rising to the rank of junior officer, and graduated from the Frunze Military Academy in 1934.

Following the end of the Second World War, Konev held a number of high-ranking military posts, including Supreme Commissar for Austria. In 1953, Khrushchev appointed him First Deputy Minister of Defence and Commander of Soviet Ground Forces, positions he held until 1956 when he was named Commander-in-Chief of the Armed Forces of the Warsaw Pact. Shortly after his appointment, Konev led the Soviet invasion of Hungary to suppress the Revolution. He died on 21 May 1973 in Moscow. He was seventy-seven years old.

I looked at my watch. It was 14:31. The library was just over a mile from St Pancras station and, even at a casual pace, it took me less than fifteen minutes to walk. Once I was there I grabbed a cup of tea and a sandwich. Sitting alone as I waited for my train to Luton and my flight back to Germany, I tried to work out how I was going to break the news to my wife and fourteen-year-old son that, once again, I was about to disappear.

Wednesday, 9 August 1989

Prague, Czechoslovakia

I FELT MY ears pop. The De Havilland Dash 8 aircraft operated by Austrian Airways was losing altitude. I looked out of the port window. At two hundred feet, the white markings and lights that marked the threshold of Ruzyne Airport's runway appeared and just as suddenly were gone. Seconds later my body took the shock as the aircraft's wheels once again found solid ground.

Parked nose out, along the edge of the airfield apron, were a line of single-seat MiG-21 fighters or, as NATO refers to them, 'Fishbeds'.

At that time, and even today, the majority of Soviet/Russian aircraft names were an elaborate array of letters and numbers. Add to that the noise and confusion of the battlefield and mistakes are easy to make. So, NATO came up with a simple reporting process (identification system). If it's a fighter, its designated name will always begin with an 'F', MiG-21 = Fishbed, MiG-25 = Foxbat, and Sukhoi SU-32 = Fullback. Bomber reporting names always start with a 'B', Tupolev TU-95 = Bear, Tupolev TU-160 = Blackjack. And, as you would now expect, helicopter reporting names always begin with an 'H', Mil Mi-26 = Halo, Mil Mi-24 = Hind, and Mil Mi-6 = Hook.

Each of the Fishbeds carried the giant, red, five-pointed star of the Soviet Union on its wings and fuselage. Prague was only fifty-five minutes flying time from Vienna, but the sight of the MiGs left me in no doubt that if anything went wrong, if Scott's plan was flawed in any way and I was caught operating behind the Iron Curtain, then nobody, not even the Special Projects Team – the Regiment – would be coming to get me out.

At the far end of the runway, as the aircraft turned to starboard and taxied towards the airport's one and only terminal building, it trundled past a group of Mi-24s – Hind helicopter gunships, sitting motionless on the tarmac like giant sleeping insects. Fifty metres further on, to the left of the Hinds, a Hip transport helicopter rocked from side to side as its rotors began to slowly turn.

On the night of 20–21 August 1968, Soviet paratroopers had seized this very airport and facilitated the landing of Soviet troop transports. The Russian invasion of Czechoslovakia had begun and, given the significant amount of military hardware currently on display, it was obvious they had no intention of leaving any time soon.

Subconsciously, I ran my hand along my right thigh. Felt the clasp knife in my trouser pocket, and squeezed. It's unthinkable now, but in those days, twelve years before 9/11, you could take almost anything on to an aircraft.

Five minutes later, with the plane on its stand, the pilot cut the power to the two turboprop engines, their blades still turning when the door opened and, armed only with a clasp knife, I stepped out on to enemy territory.

The tall brunette, who moments before had been standing directly in front of me, crossed the yellow line painted on the floor and walked briskly towards the cubicle. She pushed her passport through the narrow gap beneath the pane of frosted glass, took a step back behind a white line, and looked up at the camera secured to the top of the cubicle.

A corporal dressed in a grey Soviet uniform called me forward to the yellow line recently vacated by the brunette. My heart was pounding in my ears as I handed him my passport. I watched in silence as he examined it meticulously. A few seconds later he looked me up and down, checked my appearance.

I was not overly worried about the passport's authenticity. I assumed that it was genuine; obtained using some government back door into the London passport office. I knew the system existed; the Regiment had used the same door on a number of occasions. Conversely, if it was a fake, then it was a given that Scott would have access to a team of highly skilled artisans who turned out such things on a regular basis for MI6, and the quality of their work would deceive any number of Soviet corporals.

Two minutes later, the brunette was on her way to the customs table on the far side of the hall from immigration.

The Soviet guard returned my passport and, after what sounded like a grunt, waved me towards the cubicle.

I pushed my passport and visa through the gap, stepped back behind the white line and lifted my head. Regardless of whether it had been issued, or manufactured, the passport would undoubtedly pass muster. My concern was who would ultimately see it and the photograph that was about to be taken. If it found its way on to the same desk as the one taken three years earlier at Herleshausen, then life could become very complicated.

It was just after two in the afternoon when the taxi pulled away, leaving me standing alone on the pavement. I looked first at the card the driver had given me, and then at the large red brick house on the far side of the road. I had decided back in Vienna that it would be safer, draw less attention to me, if I booked into a small hotel on the western side of the Vltava – the river that runs through the centre of Prague – rather than into one of the larger hotels in the historic Old Town traditionally used by tourists – although the building I was now staring at looked more like a Ramsgate boarding house than a hotel.

I pushed open the polished wood and glass panelled door and walked across the small open area that passed for a lobby. As I reached the reception desk I dropped my suitcase on to the floor beside me. The case contained nothing of any importance, just a few clothes and toiletries, but it was necessary for me to bring it. A visitor arriving in Prague without any luggage might raise suspicion. I lifted my hand, but before I could strike the top of the brass bell sitting on the desk a man appeared through the door on my right.

He was short. No more than five foot eight. His face was drawn and a dark tan covered his bald head and continued down his long, thin neck. The sleeves of his grey suit were shiny and it was baggy at the knees. It had seen far better days.

I put the card on the desk. I had no Russian to speak of, but given Czechoslovakia's geographical position, sitting on the borders of East Germany and Austria, I defaulted to German.

'I was told by the taxi driver that you might have a room available.'

The man stared at me for a moment.

'I speak English if you would prefer it to German.'

I nodded my head and smiled. 'English is fine for me. Thank you.'

The man raised himself to his full height and pulled back his shoulders. He looked like a soldier on parade waiting his turn to be inspected by an officer.

'Perfect. My name is Johan Bartos; I am the owner of this hotel. How many nights will you be with us, sir?'

I had no idea how long I would be stuck in Prague. 'I'm not sure. Maybe only a few days.'

He looked down at the register. 'That will be fine, sir. All I need now is your passport. For the Soviet authorities, you understand.'

With the formalities over, I followed Bartos back across the lobby, through the door, and up four flights of stairs to the second-floor landing. I watched as he unlocked the door and, as he pushed it open, the sweet smell of furniture polish filled my nose. He took a step forward and the floorboards gave a sharp creak.

There'll obviously be no creeping about after lights out.

That thought makes me sound somewhat blasé. But thinking back, considering where I was and where I would be heading in a day or two, it was probably more to do with nerves than bravado.

Bartos glanced around the room. 'I only have two double rooms available at the moment, sir. However, this is the better of the two. I hope it is suitable.'

The room was small. It contained a single wardrobe, a small armchair and, although it was currently bare, a large double bed that looked comfortable enough. To the right-hand side of a tall narrow window, which looked out towards the river, there was a small fireplace.

'This will do just fine.'

Bartos smiled, and with his arms pulled tight into his side he nodded his head smartly.

I smiled to myself.

The only thing that's missing is the click of his heels.

'Excellent. My wife will arrive shortly to make up the bed.' With that he turned and left.

I was standing in the gateway of the Bridge Tower on the Old Town side of the Charles Bridge. Both the Bridge and the Tower, which are said to be one of the most beautiful Gothic gateways in the world, were built in the second half of the fourteenth century. In 1621, the heads of the twenty-one leaders of the Bohemian Nobility Rebellion who had been decapitated earlier in the Old Town Square (Staroměstské náměstí) were put on display in the upper part of the tower, facing towards the bridge, as a warning to the population of Prague. The heads remained in place for over ten years, before secretly being taken down one night and buried in a place that is still unknown today.

Even though it was early evening in late August the air had a chill about it, and the mist rising from the Vltava River that runs beneath it had already begun to envelop the walls of the iconic bridge. I raised the zipper on my Barbour jacket another few inches and looked at my watch.

21:25. It's time to make a move.

The bridge was narrow by modern standards, less than 30 metres wide. It was 621 metres long and appears to sit on the water, rather than rising above it. It had been built for horse-drawn carts and foot traffic. Apart from the forty-odd years, between 1905, when the horse line was replaced by an electric tram, and the end of the Second World War, when a barricade was erected in the Bridge Tower Gateway, it had never been open to motor vehicles.

I slid my hands into my pockets and took a firm hold on the handle of the open clasp knife. It was useless as a stabbing weapon; the blade was too short. But when used in a slashing fashion, if I could make contact with my target's throat, although messy, it was more than capable of killing. I smiled to myself as I recalled the advice of my first platoon sergeant: 'Never bring a knife to a gunfight.'

Years ago, back in the early 1960s, at the start of the Cold War, the Charles Bridge was known as the 'Bridge of Spies'. Yes, I know, according to Steven Spielberg there is also one in Berlin but, believe me, the one I was currently standing on was the real deal.

As I began to walk across it I wondered just how many people's fates had been decided here. How many had lost their lives as a result of the information either passed or sold by the double agents of one side to the other? How, even though Czechoslovakia had long since lost its position as a world centre of espionage, Prague was still a very dangerous place to be.

To some people, meeting a stranger on a bridge in the middle of a busy city is the work of romantic fiction, while others will possibly consider my actions foolhardy, especially when the said bridge has such a shady past. However, from my point of view, although I hadn't picked the location, it was preferable to meeting in a café, restaurant, or hotel lobby. Such places only draw attention to the fact that you are a stranger in town, whereas the Charles Bridge is something that every visitor to Prague should want to see.

Staying close to the north wall of the bridge, I made my way towards the centre and the arranged RV. The light was fading fast and the mist getting thicker, now broken here and there by the twenty-foot-high gothic statues that lined both sides of the bridge. There are thirty figures in all, fifteen along the north wall of the bridge and fifteen along the south. As I drew level with the eighth statue on the south side, that of St Ludmila, the mother of Prince Wenceslas, I slowed my pace and peered into the mist. Thirty metres away was a solitary figure, but the shape and build were all wrong. I assumed that 'Kafka', the person I was here to meet, would be a man but, given the build, the person now standing where he was supposed to be was definitely a woman.

I looked at my watch.

21:29. Well, in for a penny.

I began to walk diagonally across the bridge towards the south wall, and whoever it was waiting there. My plan was simple. Fire a single question at her; if she had no idea what I was talking about, I would just turn and walk away. Disappear back into the mist. Although what I would do after that, I had no idea.

My approach was far from subtle. 'Where's Kafka?'

I saw her flinch. I took another step, and her face came into view. That my contact appeared to be a woman surprised me. But the fact that she was so young, in her mid-twenties, had totally taken me aback, and immediately raised the question as to whether she was experienced enough to see the task through.

I asked again, 'Where's Kafka?'

She looked confused, frightened.

She hasn't understood the question. Bollocks.

Without saying another word, I dropped my head, turned, and began to walk away, back across the bridge, towards the Old Town.

I was twenty feet away when I heard her shout. 'I'm Kafka – Agata Kafka.'

I stopped, stood staring into the mist.

Shit, that's not a good start.

I turned and began walking back towards her. I was less than six feet from her when our eyes met and she forced a smile. She looked like a rabbit caught in the headlights, one that had no idea which way to run.

'Any relation to Franz Kafka, the writer?' I waited for her answer.

Her expression remained fixed, and there was no longer a smile. 'Sadly, no.'

Her short response to my question told me that she was the person I was here to meet. I moved alongside her and rested my back against the bridge wall. 'I believe you have something for me?'

Kafka said nothing for a moment or two, but I suspect it was not because she didn't have an appropriate response. Our entire conversation up to that point, although short, had been entirely in English, so it was more than likely that she was still trying to find the right words.

'I have.'

I held out my hand.

She stared at it for a second or two, then raised her head and looked me in the eyes. Although the word 'idiot' never crossed her lips, the tone of her voice said it loud and clear. 'I don't have it with me. I couldn't risk being stopped by the police carrying a man's identity papers if you didn't show. Besides, it's a bit more complicated than me handing you a few documents. Meet me here again at eleven thirty tonight.'

I thought about the bridge's reputation back in the 1960s and was far from happy. 'Won't it look a bit suspicious, the two of us meeting here, late at night?'

Kafka looked me up and down and smiled. It was the type of smile a teacher might give to a five-year-old, the sort of smile that says 'silly boy'. Her confidence was growing. 'Not really, but see if you can find a different coat. That one shouts "Westerner" at the very top of its voice, and that will draw attention to us. Make people look twice, especially the police.'

Without another word, she turned and began to walk away, leaving me alone on the bridge.

For the second time that night, I stood in the gateway of the Old Bridge Tower.

This is becoming a habit, a bad habit.

I hated repeats. They made me nervous and attending two meetings at the same location, on the same night with the same person, and especially for someone in my current position, was a definite no, no. However, given my predicament – alone behind the Iron Curtain, and with Kafka in possession of what I needed – I had little choice. As I reached the point on the bridge where I had met Kafka earlier that evening, I glanced at my watch.

23:17.

Apart from the odd person scurrying across the bridge, on their way home, or to work, it was empty and, with the antique street lamps not throwing out that much light, the atmosphere seemed even more menacing. I continued to the far side of the bridge and the western side of the river at a leisurely pace. As I reached the end of the north wall, I stopped, leaned casually against it, and looked at my watch again.

23:21. Four minutes. I'll wander around here, look at the statues for another five minutes before heading back across the bridge. If Kafka's not there or, worse, if she's not alone, I'll just keep walking. Plan B will be the river.

Now on my way back, as I drew level with the statue of St Anthony, the seventh on the north wall counting from the western bank, years of training told me that my pace had been perfect and that it was now exactly 23:30. Without shortening my stride, or turning my head, I glanced sideways across the bridge to the south wall.

Someone was there, and they were alone, but in the dark, half hidden by the mist, I had no idea who it was or, this time, whether it was male or female.

I began to drift to my right, across the bridge. I had only taken three or four steps when Kafka's face came out of the mist. She was walking towards me. A split second later her walk turned into a run.

I felt my body stiffen as I prepared to defend myself, and as we came together she threw her arms around my neck. I leaned back. Tried to move away from her, but she held on tight.

As her head came to rest on my right shoulder, her hair blew across my face. The flowery scent of her shampoo, mixed with the smell of cigarette smoke, filled my nostrils, and she whispered, 'Hug me.'

She had taken me by surprise, but there was urgency in her voice, so somewhat reluctantly I did as ordered, and as my arms closed across her back, I heard footsteps coming up behind me. I loosened my grip and, with my hands on either side of her waist, gripping her hips, I tried to push her away. Create some space between us. Give myself room to move if, as I now feared, I was forced to defend myself, but as she pulled me closer she whispered, 'Relax, it will be over soon.'

My pulse was racing. The footsteps were only inches away but then drifted slowly by; I looked to my left away from Kafka and saw the backs of two Czechoslovak police officers as they continued east across the bridge. They were a good thirty metres away when Kafka finally let go.

Taking a step backwards, she straightened her shoulders and smoothed down her coat with her hands.

'I'm sorry about that, but you were right. Two strangers meeting on the bridge at this time of night does look a little suspicious. However, two lovers meeting on the most romantic bridge in Prague, even in these troubled times, would not seem out of place.' She looked me up and down. 'I see you took my advice about the coat. Where did you get it?'

I pulled up the collar of the dark grey overcoat. 'I liberated it from the coat rack at my hotel.'

Kafka now had a disapproving look on her face. 'Well, I hope you're going to return it. We Czechs are poor people. We don't have money to burn, and that coat looks expensive.'

'Of course.' I changed the subject. 'Did you bring it?'

Kafka smiled, but this time it wasn't forced; it was natural. She was apparently feeling more comfortable and why wouldn't she be? She was on home ground and my fate was entirely in her hands.

'Patience, my friend, let us take a walk. Somewhere a little more private.' She slipped her arm through mine, but instead of walking east, or west, she led me straight across the bridge to the north wall. 'Touch the statue.'

I looked it up and down. 'Why?'

'It is the statue of St John of Nepomuk. In 1393 he was thrown from the bridge into the river where he drowned. In modern times, it has become a tradition for visitors to the city to touch the bridge here; it is said to bring good luck, and ensure that they will return to Prague one day'.

I thought about my conversation with Scott in Victoria Park: *it would seem logical to reverse the procedure. Bring you out via Prague.*

Well, I suppose every little helps. I stretched out my hand and stroked the foot of the statue. For the first time since all this had started, it felt like somebody cared, but the feeling didn't last long.

Kafka turned away from the statue and, pulling me after her, we walked west, across the bridge, and in the opposite direction to the two policemen. But as we neared the last statue on the north wall, remembering my reaction to her earlier advance, and with a giggle in her voice, she said, 'Don't worry. You're quite safe. I don't bite.'

Ten minutes later, with Kafka still hanging on to my arm, we crossed the road and headed for the four-storey building on the opposite side. It resembled a large box, and if I had been back in the UK, I would have sworn that it had been built at the height of the inner-city redevelopment period back in the sixties, but here in Prague, behind the Iron Curtain, the building could have been put up as recently as last week.

The glazed brown bricks that lined the stairway leading up to her second-floor flat reminded me of a council estate in South London. Directly behind the front door was what appeared to be a single room. The smell of damp was the first thing I noticed. On the right of the room, standing against the wall, was a Formica-topped work surface. Below it on one side was a single-door cupboard and, on the other, three identical drawers. At one end of the worktop was a stainless-steel sink and draining board, and at the other a small gas stove with an oven below it. Against the wall to my left was an unmade single bed, and beside it a small wooden wardrobe. The only other furniture in the room consisted of a small upright sofa, a wooden coffee table that needed a fresh coat of varnish, and a threadbare armchair. Directly behind the couch was a single window. There was no sign of a door leading to a bath-room, so I assumed she shared it with her neighbours. It's funny how, as we grow older, we can remember such things in minute detail, but if someone were to ask you what you had for breakfast this morning, you probably couldn't tell them.

She took off her coat, threw it on the bed, and waved her hand at the armchair. 'Please.'

I took my seat and watched her walk across the room towards the cooker. She was a pretty girl, tall but not ungainly, with a waspish waist and long legs. Her dark brown hair was cut in a sixties style bob which subtly drew your attention to her high cheekbones and large brown eyes. The style was a little dated by Western stand-ards, but it suited her. She was dressed in a straight, knee-length black skirt and a white short-sleeved blouse with lamb-chop cuffs.

'Where do you work?'

She turned her head and stared at me for a moment or two. 'The Café Slavia.'

I knew the café. I had had coffee there that afternoon after recceing the bridge, but I hadn't noticed her. It occupied the ground floor of an impressive grey stone building. On two of its corners, high above the street, were large, four-sided gothic turrets that culminated in a blunted point. It stood on Národní, opposite the National Theatre, and had first opened its doors in 1884. Shortly afterwards it became known as the regular haunt of writers, poets and other intellectuals who would meet there to discuss their ideas. Later, during the first communist occupation, it had earned a reputation for being a favourite hangout of Prague's dissident community.

She picked up the kettle and swung it from side to side. 'Coffee?'

I looked down at her feet. She was wearing flat shoes, probably to reduce her height and make sure that her feet made it through her long shifts.

'Yes please.'

Kafka placed the cup on the coffee table in front of me. I picked it up and stared at the tar-like liquid as I gently swirled it around. Watched it stick to the sides of the cup, and as I lifted it to my lips the smell of chicory filled my nostrils. I knew the Coffee Crisis was an East German thing, but it was now obvious that it had also been a problem here in Czechoslovakia. Years later I was to discover that the same was true of Latvia and other less prominent Soviet states, who were still serving *Mischkaffee* in the early nineties.

I placed the cup back on its saucer and watched Kafka push her hand down the side of the sofa, into the gap that separated the cushion from the arm, the space where as kids we hunted for the loose change that had dropped out of adults' pockets.

She pulled out an envelope and handed it to me. 'Your Czechoslovakian ID card and travel documents.'

My look apparently said it all, and she immediately answered my unasked question. 'We had no idea how good your German was, so we decided to provide you with a set of Czechoslovakian documents. The only time you're likely to be challenged will be as you cross the border between Czechoslovakia and the DDR. I doubt that any of the Grenztruppen will speak Czech. They feel that it's beneath them. So, as a Czech, your limited German will not raise too many suspicions.'

The word 'we' had caught me by surprise. I hadn't considered that Kafka might be part of a much larger organisation and that a lot more people might know about my existence and where I was heading. I opened the pressed cardboard wallet that contained my ID card. The picture was a copy of the one in my British passport that Scott had given to me in Victoria Park. My new name was, thankfully, easy to remember, although I would need to practise it to get the pronunciation right.

'So what happens now?'

She stood up, made her way over to the sink and, after running our empty cups under the tap, turned around. With her back resting against the worktop, she said, 'Tonight, nothing. Do you think you can find your way back here on your own?'

I re-ran the route from the Charles Bridge to the apartment through my head. It was pretty straightforward. 'Yes.'

'Good. Tomorrow morning, after breakfast, check out of your hotel, then find somewhere to have coffee . . . read a newspaper . . . waste some time. But not in the Café Slavia.'

I looked at her.

She smiled. 'I saw you there this afternoon. I finish my shift at two o'clock tomorrow. Be here at two forty-five. Bring everything you have with you. You will spend tomorrow night here. I will take you to the bus station the following morning.'

She walked to the wardrobe and lifted out a black leather jacket. 'Stand up and turn around.' She held it up to my shoulders. 'It's a bit tight, but it will have to do. We should leave now. I will walk you back to the bridge.'

Thursday, 10 August 1989

KAFKA HANDED ME a bundle of clothes.

'Put these on. I'm sorry, but you will have to change in here. There is nowhere else.' Then, with a cheeky smile, she added, 'I can close my eyes if you're shy.'

I shot her a look. The type of look that says, are you taking the piss?

'I'll cope.'

I was down to my shreddies and socks and ready to re-dress when she said, 'Everything, we can't risk you getting caught wearing anything made in the West. Not even your underwear.'

Five minutes later. Having been bollock naked in front of a woman I had only just met, I was dressed as a Czechoslovakian worker in a pair of brown corduroy trousers held up by a broad leather belt, a hardwearing blue shirt, heavy work boots and the leather jacket I had seen the previous night.

'OK, let's have a look at you.' She smiled as she looked me up and down. 'Turn around. Not bad. In fact, the jacket is a better fit than I thought it would be.' She ran her hands over the front of it like she was trying to smooth out the wrinkles. 'From now on this jacket goes everywhere you go. Stitched into the lining are an East German ID card and some West German currency.'

I knew why I was being given West German currency even though I was going to the East. At the time, although the East German government insisted on parity, one Ost Mark – an East German Mark – to one Deutsche Mark – the West German Mark – the unofficial exchange rate in East German shops and restaurants was closer to 7-1, seven Ost-Marks to one Deutsche Mark.

Her smile faded. 'The Deutsche Marks will help smooth the way if you are forced to go on the run.

'Now put all of your Western clothes in this bag. I will also need your British passport and travel documents.'

I put my neatly folded clothes into the bag, but as Kafka turned back to the sink and filled the kettle, I slipped my British passport down the front of my trousers.

I might need this at some stage.

'What will happen to them?'

She didn't answer, but the look she gave me was along the lines of the one I had given her ten minutes earlier. One of those 'are you taking the piss?' looks. It was then that I realised that everything I had just placed in the bag, along with the contents of my suitcase, was about to go up in smoke, and with them Scott's idea to bring me out through Czechoslovakia once this was all over.

Friday, 11 August 1989

Dresden, East Germany

THE BUS JOURNEY from Prague to Dresden, as Kafka had told me the previous night, took close to three hours. The journey went without incident apart from the fact that the bus itself was not fit to be on the road, and a thirty-minute delay at the border crossing between Czechoslovakia and East Germany, where members of the Grenztruppen had boarded. In fact, in comparison to my experiences at the Helmstedt and Herleshausen checkpoints, it was pretty stress free.

As I stepped off the bus, I kept pace with the rest of the crowd as they headed towards the entrance of Dresden Hauptbahnhof, Dresden's central railway station.

With my head up, observing everything that was going on around me, I did my best to avoid eye contact with anyone, especially the extraordinarily large number of uniformed police that were in the area. *Something's going on.*

As I neared the station entrance, doing as Kafka had instructed, I pulled the corner of a white handkerchief out of the right-hand pocket of my jacket and let it hang over the side. Now all I could do was wait.

Further along the road, two men dressed in civilian clothes were directing the uniformed officers. The body language of the policemen told me everything I needed to know. Their immediate, unquestioning response to the two men's orders had nothing to do with trust or respect, the common bonds that exist between a soldier and his officer, these people were being driven by fear.

Those two have got to be Stasi.

The police officers' fear was understandable. The Stasi were all powerful. They answered to no one and were often likened to the Gestapo in Nazi Germany. They were a law unto themselves, unforgiving and brutal. Question their orders, or disobey them in any way, and there was no telling what might happen to you.

I looked at my watch and felt my breathing pattern change as my pulse rate rose.

09:03. Whoever they are, they're late.

If my contact failed to show, I had no idea what I would do next, or where I might go, but one thing was evident: I couldn't stay where I was for much longer.

I surveyed the surrounding area, and in less than a minute I had come up with what I thought was a workable exit strategy. One that would take me away from the station and its large police presence, but without going too much against the natural flow of human traffic and drawing attention to myself.

I glanced at my watch again.

09:07. They're not going to show. Time to make myself scarce.

I moved to the pavement, but as I waited for a break in the traffic, prepared to cross the road and head into a side street opposite, a powder blue Trabant pulled up to the kerb, blocking my way.

'Get in.'

I leaned forward and peered through the open window. The passenger seat was empty, but sitting behind the steering wheel, although it had been more than three years since our last meeting, there was no mistaking the pretty blond who had made me tea in the canteen at Dynamo Zinnwald, and the years had been kind to her. She was still beautiful.

My mind was racing. Was this a coincidence? Had she merely seen me as she drove past, remembered my face, which I thought unlikely, given the large number of people that passed through the sports centre every year. Or was this something else?

She spoke again, but this time there was urgency in her voice. Her tone was close to pleading. 'Please get in. The longer we stay here, the greater our chances of being arrested.' And her English was still impeccable.

I looked into her eyes, but they were no longer staring at me. I glanced over my left shoulder, followed her gaze to the policeman standing beside the station entrance. He was staring back at us. He took a step forward and, somewhat reluctantly, I opened the door and climbed into the car. As I closed it behind me, there was a loud metallic clunk as she slipped the car into first gear. I swayed back in the flimsy seat as we pulled sharply away from the kerb, and heard her chuckle as I threw my weight forward in an effort to reach the dashboard and steady myself.

'Your first time in a Trabant?'

The young woman's sudden appearance had taken me by surprise. It was Kafka and Prague all over again. I had naturally assumed that all the people involved in this game would be men, but then remembered the female operators of the 'DET', the unit that carried out undercover surveillance operations against terrorist groups across the water. Its female operators were one of its most valuable assets, and when paired up with a male operator (at that time, the British military were still very reluctant to send a woman into a hostile environment alone), it allowed them to move about among the local population virtually unnoticed. Not a job for the faint-hearted and, on reflection, I should have known better.

By the time the car had reached the end of the road, the mental fog and confusion brought about by the young woman's sudden appearance had all but disappeared. We turned right, three hundred metres later we turned left, heading south. It was time to get some answers.

'Pull over. Up there, behind that truck.'

She glanced at me, a look of shock on her face, then back to the road.

'What? We don't have time for this.'

I nodded in the direction of an IFA Tankwagen parked at the side of the road. I was rapidly losing my sense of humour.

'Now would be good.'

Reluctantly, she did as I had ordered.

As the car rolled to a stop, reaching across the gear lever, I removed the ignition key.

'Right. You need to tell me exactly what's going on because I've never been a great believer in coincidence.'

With her elbows resting on the bottom rim of the steering wheel, she dropped her forehead into her hands. Five seconds later she lifted it, and the pleading began again.

'You need to give me back the key. We can't stop here. It's far too dangerous. We need to get out of the city. Now. I'll answer all your questions as we drive.'

I looked into her cornflower blue eyes and, apart from the tears forming in the corners, I could see nothing but fear. I pushed the key back into the ignition.

'OK. But, if you lie to me I'll—'

She cut me short as she pulled the car away from the kerb and back into the traffic. 'I won't lie to you. Just give me enough time to get us out of the city. You have no idea how dangerous it is for us to be here right now.'

As we left the city behind us, we passed a road sign that confirmed we were heading south, back towards Czechoslovakia. Although the young blond woman looked visibly relieved to be out of the city at last, having spent most of the previous night sleeping in the armchair at Kafka's flat, I was way past tired. The paranoia was kicking in and I was rapidly running out of patience.

'OK. Who are you? Why were you at the station? And what's going on in Dresden?'

She kept her eyes on the road ahead.

'My name is Kirstin Huber. I work as kitchen help in the Dynamo Zinnwald sports centre. Although hopefully not for much longer.'

I remembered the conversation I'd had with the Austrian sled technician during breakfast at the sports centre on my first visit: *Any organisation that carries a 'Dynamo' prefix is run and administered by the state police; here in East Germany, that means the Stasi.*

'OK. Suppose I believe you, and just to be clear, I don't. Not yet. Why were you in Dresden this morning?'

Huber continued to concentrate on the road.

'I'm a member of the Bewegung. I was sent to pick up a man from the station. A young woman collecting her father, or boyfriend, draws far less attention than a man. I had no idea it was you until I saw the white handkerchief hanging out of your jacket pocket.'

It all made sense, but I wasn't done. 'And the problem with us being in Dresden this morning? Why did we have to leave in such a hurry?' It was a rhetorical question, I knew what the problem was, I was just pushing – keeping the pressure up – trying to get her to make a mistake.

She glanced at me, then back to the road. 'One of our people was arrested last night. The authorities will have already begun to interrogate him.'

I studied her face. She looked calm enough, but I could still sense her fear. I softened my tone. 'By the authorities, I assume you mean the police – the Stasi?'

Although there was no one else in the car, no one to overhear us, her voice dropped to a whisper. 'Yes.'

'How does that affect me – us?' Again it was rhetorical.

Huber turned towards me, but only for the briefest moment, then her eyes went straight back to the road.

'The man they seized knew that you were arriving today, and were to be collected from the central railway station in Dresden sometime this morning. Thankfully he didn't know who you were, or how you would arrive. In fact none of us did.'

I turned away from her and stared out of the side window. 'So, if the Stasi didn't know who they were looking for, how did they hope to arrest me?'

She sighed. 'It's a tried and tested Stasi technique. They flood the area with police in the hope that they can panic you. Once that happens they have you.'

On reflection, I was relieved that I hadn't known about the arrest the previous night when waiting at the station. If I had, I might well have tried to escape the moment a policeman gave me a second glance and, in doing so, played right into their hands.

'Where are we going now?'

'Zinnwald. There's a safe house in the Projects, a collection of apartment blocks built by the state to house the mineworkers. You'll be safe there.'

She hadn't convinced me. Littman had been living in the Projects when he disappeared or, as I now suspected, had been killed – which meant that someone may have informed on him, and if they were still around I might well suffer the same fate.

'Doesn't the guy who they arrested last night know the location of this so-called safe house?'

My scepticism regarding the term 'safe house' was well founded. In the West 'safe house' normally means just that – houses or flats that have no connection at all to the organisation, agency or individual that are using them. However, here in East Germany, a country where the authorities could turn up at any moment and would not hesitate to break down your door if you were slow to answer; a place where there was no such thing as the rule of law, here the term 'safe house' meant nothing more than somewhere that hadn't been raided up until now. I would feel anything but safe in such a place and, as events were to show, I was right to be worried.

Huber still had her eyes on the road. 'No. The Bewegung, like everything else in East Germany, is riddled with informers. So, no one person knows everyone or everything, we only know what we *need to know*, and that's especially true when it comes to the location of the safe houses. At this moment in time, only two people know the location of the Zinnwald house. You will be the third.'

As we passed a road sign that read 'Zinnwald 30km', I noticed Huber looking in the Trabant's tiny rear-view mirror. She glanced towards me; the fear was back in her eyes. 'Don't turn around, but there's a police car coming up behind us.'

I began to lift my right arm.

'I wouldn't bother; this is a Trabant, not a Mercedes. There's no vanity mirror behind the sun visor.'

I looked up. That was because there was no sun visor. A minute later I heard the two-tone sound of a police siren and caught the reflection of a blue flashing light as it bounced off the Trabant's rear-view mirror.

Huber immediately began to slow the car. Her voice was trembling. 'Unless they ask you something directly, let me do all the talking. If they do ask you a question, use short, clear, precise answers. Remember, you're in East Germany now, and as such you are supposed to be one of us. That means being submissive. If you try to get friendly, or aggressive, with them, they will arrest us both.'

'Understood.' I saw no point in increasing her fear by telling her that my German wasn't perfect, and if push came to shove I would play the stupid Czech, hand over my ID card and hope for the best.

Huber steered the car towards the grass verge, applied the brakes, and brought it to a controlled stop, but instead of pulling in behind us the police car continued towards Zinnwald at high speed. I heard Huber breathe a sigh of relief, but it was short-lived. She was just about to move off again when another police car screamed past. Blue lights flashing, and siren wailing. As it disappeared around a bend in the road, Huber released the handbrake.

'There's a *parkplatz* about a kilometre ahead. We'll stop there for a while. I don't want to get mixed up in whatever's happening further down the road. Even if it's only a simple traffic accident, we may still be stopped, asked for our papers, and questioned. I don't think you're ready for that yet.'

Apart from an antique tractor working its way along a field a few hundred metres to our right, the surrounding area, like the road we were travelling along, was virtually deserted.

I was standing alone at the front of the Trabant, watching Huber trying to compose herself before getting out of the car. She looked drained. It was evident that the arrest the previous night, the events of that morning, and the two police cars turning up when they did had all but finished her off.

I smiled to myself as Huber finally got out of the car and leaned against the Trabant's offside wing. She was slightly built, weighing no more than fifty kilograms, but the panel still bent under her weight. The body shells of these two-stroke pollution generators were constructed from Duroplast. A fibreglass-type material reinforced with recycled fibres like cotton and wood. In reality, they were nothing more than motorised egg boxes. And although powder blue was a fairly common colour for Trabants, as she leaned against it with her near-white blond hair, she somehow made what had always been an ugly car 'girly' – gave it a sense of fun, in a place where fun was very much in short supply. On the downside, I also felt that it might make us stand out – draw some extra, unwanted attention to it and us both.

But I was also beginning to relax slightly. I felt safe out here, surrounded by open fields; I would have no trouble seeing an approaching threat. I was also beginning to accept that if Huber was working for the other side, she could have easily flagged down one of the police cars and turned me in. In fact, if she had wanted to, she could have simply pointed me out to a member of the Stasi in Dresden and nobody, not even me, would ever have known she had betrayed me.

We spent close to ten minutes in total silence before Huber stood up and walked back towards the driver's door.

'Whatever has happened up ahead should be clear by now. It's time for us to go.'

She turned the key in the ignition, the engine burst into life, and a cloud of blue smoke belched from the rear of the little car, but it didn't move. Instead, Huber sat staring straight ahead, through the windscreen.

'By the way, what's your name?'

I paused before answering her. 'Butala . . . Andel Dusek Butala.'

'Is that your real name?'

I turned away from her and looked out of the side window. 'That's what it says on my Czech ID Card.'

I heard Huber blow out heavily through her nose; she was obviously getting frustrated by my evasive answers. 'Is there anything else I should know about you?'

I turned and looked her in the eye. 'I'm an electrical engineer from Plzeň in Czechoslovakia.'

She turned slowly away from me, a half-smile began creeping across her face.

'Do you know anything about electrical engineering?'

I turned back to my right, towards the passenger door window, and felt myself smile.

'I can rewire a plug unsupervised.'

Sunday, 13 August 1989

Zinnwald, East Germany

I HAD SPENT the last two days locked up inside the so-called safe house in Zinnwald with only Huber for company. I was warming to her, and the fact that her English was near perfect made communicating much easier, but until I knew more about her, and who she was associated with, there would be no trust.

It was as I was lying on my bed the previous night, trying to work out a strategy for finding out what I could about Operation Konev, that it suddenly hit me. With close to two months to go before the supposed launch date on 7 October, there would be little or nothing to see right now. Regardless of whether this was a major Soviet push into the West, or into neighbouring Czechoslovakia, the attack force would need to be of a respectable size – nothing short of a full armoured division. That meant six tank regiments – over 300 tanks and 300 armoured personnel carriers, along with artillery and all the necessary support elements. In total, we were talking about close to 17,000 men. There is no way the Soviets could afford to assemble a force of that size and keep it in the field for two months and hope to keep it quiet. The logistics surrounding such an operation would be horrendous. The support structure, feeding, fuel and the discipline issues caused by the boredom surrounding that many men with nothing to do, would be unsustainable. Besides, if that were the case, Scott wouldn't need me down here. A force that size would be spread out over a large area and immediately be picked up by satellite.

This led me to a second line of speculation. Maybe Operation Konev was something much smaller? Or perhaps something entirely different?

It was just after half past five that evening that Huber placed her knife and fork on her plate and lifted her head.

'How would you like to go out this evening and meet some people?'

I didn't answer her right away. Was she talking about a social outing, a visit to a local *Gästehaus* or, given that up until now I had met no one else from the Bewegung, was she talking about something more serious?

Doing my best to hide my enthusiasm I smiled at her. 'Sure. That would be great.'

Huber immediately stood up, and leaving the dirty dishes sitting on the table she picked up her coat and keys and headed out of the kitchen, towards the front door. 'Come on then, let's go.'

I grabbed my leather jacket from the back of the chair. 'Where are we going?'

She glanced back over her right shoulder; she had a mischievous smile on her face. 'Soon.'

Zinnwald, at that time, was a small town; in reality, apart from the mining projects it was not much more than a spreading village. It sat on the main road that runs south from Dresden to the Czechoslovakian border. The road through the town was practically straight, and although wide enough for two cars travelling in opposite directions to pass, it would have been a squeeze for two forty-foot tilts (articulated lorries) to scrape past each other.

Dynamo Zinnwald, the Stasi-run sports centre, was situated at the northern end of the town. At the southern end, between the town and the Tin and Tungsten mine, were the Projects. Between the two there was nothing but a few poorly stocked shops and the occasional house. At the time, it was the epitome of a 'one-horse town'.

Huber parked the car on a patch of waste ground adjacent to the main road and began to head across it towards the town's old Lutheran Church. Ahead of us a stream of people were passing through the entrance.

I felt my heart quicken.

'Listen, Kirstin; I don't do church. If we go in there, I'm going to look as guilty as a fox in a chicken coup.'

'Don't worry. Just follow me. Do as I do, and you'll be OK.'

Once inside the church, I watched her genuflect and cross herself. I did the same, and then followed her as she made her way to the last row of pews.

The church was already half full, but instead of taking her seat with the rest of the congregation, she disappeared through a heavy pair of crimson curtains. Behind the curtains was a short narrow passageway and at the far end a heavy wooden door. I was half a step behind her when she opened the door and entered the room behind it.

I was still hovering on the threshold when I heard footsteps coming along the passage behind me. I was just about to turn and take a look at who it was when a hand was placed in the centre of my back, gave me a gentle shove, and I heard the words. 'Keep moving.'

I took a step forward, regained my balance and, as I turned, like a boxer preparing for combat, I lifted both my hands and stepped to one side. Standing in the doorway was a man in his mid-thirties. I flashed him a warning look. The type of look that left him in no doubt as to what would happen if he ever touched me again.

He quickly took a step backwards.

Smart boy. I doubt that this will be the last time we bump heads. So you'll keep for now.

On the other side of the door was a room with a flagstone floor and grey painted walls. In its centre, sat around a large wooden table, was a group of eight men. A heavy blanket of cigarette smoke filled the room a few feet above their heads, and the air was thick with suspicion, most of it directed at me, the stranger in their midst.

I watched as one of the eight, an elderly looking man, poured boiling water into a mug, and although he was a good six feet away, he was still close enough for me to recognise the strong odour of chicory.

He stretched out his hand and apologised for the fact that there was no milk or sugar.

I took the mug. '*Danke.*'

At the time my command of the German language was more than acceptable, but I was by no means a linguist and, of course, I also had the local dialect to contend with. So what you are about to read is an abridged version of the conversations and discussions that took place that night, with Huber doing the translating where I struggled.

★

Huber was the first to speak. 'This is Andel Butala from Plzeň in Czechoslovakia.'

Sitting on the opposite side of the table was a tall, fair-haired man in his late forties. He stood up and extended his right hand. 'My name is Peter Bonsack. I'm the leader of the Bewegung here in Saxony.'

The dark, thick-rimmed glasses that sat high on Bonsack's nose were reflecting the light from the lamp that hung a few feet above the table, making it difficult for me to see his eyes. Before I had a chance to answer, a powerfully built man with close-cropped fair hair, who was sitting at the far right-hand end of the table, interrupted.

'This is pointless. All we need to know, Herr Butala – if that is your real name – is why you are here?'

I looked to my right, towards the voice at the end of the table. The fact that he had asked his question in English made me pause for a second. Was it because he didn't speak Czech, but assumed that I spoke English, or was there another reason? Even seated behind the table as he was, I could see that he was a big man, and although I couldn't clearly see his face, his aggressive tone and body language told me he was being anything but friendly. Standing behind him, like a butler awaiting instructions from his master, was the man who had followed me along the passage and pushed me into the room.

I made eye contact and answered him in English. 'Well, you obviously know who I am, but I'm sorry, I didn't catch your name?'

The big man's attitude seemed to soften a little as he realised that I wasn't going to be intimidated by the size of his muscles, or his aggressive manner.

'Excuse me. My name is Klaus Metzger.'

I stared at him but said nothing as I waited for more.

'I am one of the managers at the Zinnwald Tin and Tungsten Mine.'

Which might explain the muscles. Metzger would have done his time at the face.

'Like Herr Bonsack, I am also a founding member of the Bewegung here in Saxony. I'm his second-in-command.'

Although I hadn't said anything to Huber, I already knew about the mine, and of course the Projects, having visited them that night in 1986 when looking for Littman.

Given Metzger's opening statement and the fact that both he and his 'butler' had both addressed me in English, I had to assume that most, if not all, of those present had already worked out that I wasn't Andel Butala and neither was I a Czech. Being a Czech was only ever intended to be my cover story while I tried to enter East Germany. I had never liked Scott's original idea of telling the Bewegung that I worked for the FCO – which would have immediately made me a high-value target – so I had decided to come up with my own cover story, that I worked for Amnesty International. However, although working for Amnesty disassociated me from anything to do with the British government, following the Wolfgang Welsch incident back in 1971, it still made me an enemy of the East German state.

In 1964, an East German actor and poet named Wolfgang Welsch, aged twenty at the time, was sentenced to ten years' imprisonment for attempting to emigrate illegally to the West, and for 'incitement hostile to the state'. In 1970, he was in the sixth year of his sentence at the Brandenburg Penitentiary in the German Democratic Republic. He had alerted the outside world to his plight via secret messages written on cigarette papers, which were then smuggled out of prison. In the notes, he described what he called his 'stinking death cell', a 1.2m by 3.5m room, where he lived in solitary confinement, in semi-darkness, without sun or fresh air. A year later, as a direct result of outside pressure brought to bear on the East German government, Wolfgang won his freedom.

I nodded my head. 'Herr Metzger, in answer to your question, I'm here on behalf of Amnesty International.' I gave my audience time to digest this new information before continuing. 'Amnesty feels that organisations such as yours now hold the only key to bringing about a peaceful end to East Germany's autocratic government, and its abuse of human rights. My presence here in East Germany marks a turning point in the organisation's modus operandi. I have been sent to monitor the situation and report back on your group's progress and see if there is any way in which Amnesty can be of assistance.'

I turned my attention back to Bonsack, who had now sat down again. 'Why don't you tell me a little about the Bewegung?' I was of course being polite. I had little interest in their organisation, or their plans for trying to overthrow the East German government. My only interest was finding out what I could about Operation Konev and getting back out of East Germany. But I was also thinking, who better to help me find out what this Operation Konev really is than members of the local population – the Bewegung.

Bonsack smiled, waved his open hand at the empty chair standing in front of me, and cleared his throat. 'Well, the Bewegung is very much still in its infancy, one of a similar number of groups spread throughout the south of the country. But news of our existence is spreading rapidly throughout this corner of East Germany, and similar movements are now springing up all over Eastern Europe, in other communist countries.'

I already knew the answer to my next question, having been told by Scott during our meeting in Victoria Park, but it would have seemed strange had I not asked it. 'What is the organisation's ultimate goal?'

Bonsack's reply was short and to the point. 'To bring an end to the DDR's [the East Germans never referred to East Germany by its popular Western abbreviation, the GDR] one-party state.'

I sat quietly for a second or two, then said, 'And what do you see as your biggest hurdle in achieving this?'

Bonsack replied almost immediately. 'The quislings – spies and informers that work for the Stasi and KGB.'

I had to smile to myself. It seemed ironic that a German should use the name of the Norwegian traitor Vidkun Quisling; a term applied to all Nazi informers in Norway during the Second World War.

'Are they not one and the same problem?'

There was a tone of regret in Bonsack's voice when he answered, 'Sadly no. The two organisations work independently of one another – there's no trust between them – which actually makes life much more difficult for us. It means that if we discover a Stasi informer within our ranks, they will have no idea of who might be working for the KGB.'

Although I listened intently, I was more than a little sceptical about just how achievable the organisation's aims might be. But working on the premise that the East German state couldn't kill everybody if the organisation grew large enough, was well organised, and could hold their nerve when the bullets started flying and the killing began – as it inevitably would – then maybe there was a slim chance that they might just pull it off, although there were some pretty big 'ifs, maybes and mights'.

I glanced around the room, and then back to Bonsack. 'Well, I wish you luck, and I'm sure that Amnesty will do all in its power to assist you in your struggle. To publicise both your efforts and your cause.'

But don't hold your breath.

As the meeting progressed, it became evident that the Bewegung's leadership committee was split down the middle into two factions of four each, headed on one side by Bonsack, and by Metzger on the other. I suspect that in the beginning they had all probably been very good friends, those with a common cause, brought together to fight a common enemy. But as always with these things, it's not long before the individuals within such groups, those vying for leadership, begin to develop their ideas about how to achieve their aim, and the cracks begin to appear. From then on, it's only a short time before they forget about the enemy, their friendship, and begin fighting one another.

Most of those present already argued that without a vast armoury of weapons to distribute, and suitably trained personnel to lead them, there was no way they were ever going to win an all-out war with the vicious Soviet and East German authorities. As a result, their strategy would have to be something different, something a little more subtle. If this had been a Regiment operation and we were attempting to win over the local population in order to defeat a common enemy, we would probably be implementing some kind of hearts and minds strategy. Providing the locals with medical care and education about how to improve their lives and environment, but such a strategy wasn't going to work here. Bonsack was arguing that the Bewegung should organise peaceful demonstrations and that hopefully these would grow organically, forcing the communist regime to make sweeping political reforms.

I turned my attention to the end of the table where Metzger had stopped arguing this would be too slow and ineffective, and that direct action was needed. He was now scribbling furiously on a piece of paper. But before I could find out any more, the door opened, and a priest entered the room.

Although outwardly calm, his eyes and the expression on his face told a different story.

'The lookout you posted at the top of the main street has sent word that the police are gathering in great numbers at the northern end of the town. You must leave now. Before they arrive, and we are all arrested.'

Bonsack quickly cleared the table of papers, while everybody else in the room headed for the door.

I joined the queue and waited my turn to squeeze through the narrow doorway and enter the passageway to escape from what had the potential to quickly become a trap – a Stasi holding cell. But as I reached the door, someone grabbed me by the arm. I turned. It was Metzger.

'Can we meet again? Tomorrow? Alone.'

Caught off guard and eager to leave, I immediately agreed.

Metzger pushed a folded piece of paper into my left hand. 'Be here at 13:30. It's easy to find.'

Huber, who had been two in front of me in the line, suddenly grabbed my hand and led me out of a side door and into a narrow, unlit street that ran behind the church. As we reached the waste ground where she had parked the car, two uniformed East German policemen approached us.

'*Papiere.*'

My heart was pounding in my ears, and for a split second I wondered if the two officers could also hear it. I had managed to compare my Czech ID card with Huber's East German one a few days earlier, and although they were similar I had no way of getting a second opinion. I had also hoped that it wouldn't be put to the test quite so soon.

Remembering what Kafka had told me in Prague, and Huber had said to me in the car as we travelled down from Dresden, I said nothing as I handed over my papers. It was as I stood there, patiently waiting for them to be returned, or me to be arrested, that I noticed the black Volga Sedan parked on the far side of the main street. It was no more than thirty metres away, and sitting in the back reading was a Russian officer.

Illuminated by the street lamp and the car's interior light, I picked out the distinctive blue lapel tabs of the KGB. I knew that I should have been overcome with fear, but the only thing I could think about was how unique it was for a British soldier to be this close to a senior KGB officer. It was then that I remembered the cameras screwed to the top of the booths at Herleshausen, and in Prague Airport, and although in reality there was little chance that my picture would have filtered this far down the chain, I came to my senses. Using small, subtle movements, I slowly tried to reposition myself. I needed to turn myself away from the car and shield my face from the man sitting in its rear seat. But before I could complete the manoeuvre, the Russian lifted his head from whatever it was he was reading, turned and looked out of the side window, directly at me.

'*Sie sind frei zu gehen.*'

Captivated by the face behind the glass, I had failed to hear the policeman. A few seconds later I felt Huber dig me in the ribs. Turning back, I saw that the officer was holding out his hand. In it were my papers. We were free to go.

As we walked across the waste ground towards Huber's car, I glanced back over my shoulder at the Volga. The Russian was still watching us. My heart was racing. I took hold of Huber's arm, picked up the pace, and as we reached the Trabant I turned and looked again.

Both the car and the Russian were gone.

Monday, 14 August 1989

U NLIKE LITTMAN'S FLAT, which had smelt damp and appeared neglected and dingy, the one Huber and I were sharing felt fresh and airy. It had a woman's touch about it but, given the fact that I spent most of my daylight hours locked behind its front door, and doing my best to stay away from its windows, it was beginning to feel like a prison.

Given my mistrust of Huber, it may seem strange that I hadn't been more forceful in my questioning when she appeared without warning at the railway station in Dresden, but you have to put yourself in the mind of someone in my situation. At the time East Germany, in fact anywhere behind the Iron Curtain, was a very dark place. The entire population lived in fear. Even those in power were constantly looking over their shoulder, guarding every comment, fearful of giving something away, being denounced. Everyone knew that your closest friends – even members of your own family – could be informing on you. This meant that I could not afford to alienate Huber. I needed her help to try to find out what I could about Operation Konev. I also knew that without her support, I would not be at liberty for long.

I found out at a very young age that the trick is to never let the opposition know what you're thinking. If I'd bombarded Huber with question after question as we'd made our way south from Dresden, trying to establish whether her being my contact was coincidence or something more sinister, and whether my arrival in East Germany had already been leaked to the authorities, all I would have done was put her on her guard. It would also have encouraged her to fabricate plausible answers to what she thought my next question might be. By keeping it relaxed, appearing to take whatever she told me at face value, just throwing in the odd question here and there, sometimes hours or days apart, I would stand more chance of catching her off guard and telling a lie.

There were some questions that didn't need to be asked; those that would tell her I definitely didn't trust her. Questions like: 'Did you report our conversation in the Dynamo Zinnwald kitchen to your Stasi superiors?' Of course, she had. It's what everybody in East Germany did. It was how they kept themselves out of trouble. But, in reality, it didn't matter either way. At that moment, back in the sports centre, there had been nothing to report – not unless the Stasi wanted to know how I took my tea. The bigger problem for me though, the one I could not avoid however friendly and helpful Huber was being, was that I knew for a fact that all the staff at Dynamo Zinnwald, even if they were not Stasi operatives, had all been Stasi vetted. Right now I had no idea which category Huber fell into.

My feelings at the time are extremely hard to explain now. I was alone in an extremely hostile environment without a friend and not knowing who, if anybody, I could trust. I suppose my mindset can best be likened to that of someone involved in an escape and evasion scenario. But whereas somebody in that situation has a final objective – a safe border for which to aim, something to focus on – I had nothing. I was being forced to stay put in enemy territory and find out what I could about Operation Konev, while all the time waiting to be betrayed. In such a situation, everyone becomes the enemy and nobody, not even Huber, could be trusted.

I was sitting at the kitchen table when I heard the front door open and then close with a click. I got to my feet, lifted the large bread knife sitting on the wooden draining board beside the sink, and stood motionless behind the kitchen door.

A few seconds later, Huber entered the room, and sliding the knife behind my back I let it drop silently on to the draining board.

She glanced at me, turned away, but said nothing. Her performance the previous night, when without any warning she had led me into the lion's den, had done little to improve our relationship. But my lack of trust in Huber was not my main concern right now. By attending the meeting the previous night the secrecy surrounding my presence in East Germany had been seriously compromised and, given the large number of Stasi informers that were known to exist at all levels of East German society, I had to assume that it wouldn't be long before the authorities got wind of it. And if they ever discovered that instead of working for Amnesty International, I was in fact an ex-Special Forces soldier trying to find out what I could about a top secret Soviet operation, my days would be numbered.

'Where have you been?'

Huber placed a white plastic carrier bag on the kitchen table, and without looking at me said, 'Will you relax? I've been to the bakery on the main street. I take it you want breakfast?'

I slid the kettle on to the stove, and as I lit the gas I heard her sigh.

'What's wrong?'

She still wouldn't look at me.

'Two members of the Bewegung were arrested last night after they had left the church. I can't believe we managed to escape.'

I was staring at the blue flame below the kettle.

No. Neither can I.

The kettle boiled, and I poured the hot water into two mugs, carried them to the table, and sat down.

Huber took the chair opposite. A basket of *Semel*, German bread rolls, and a plate of very wet-looking processed ham, sat on the table between us.

'So tell me, Herr Butala. Is that your real name, and do you really work for Amnesty International?'

I ignored both of her questions, picked up a *Semel*, broke it in half, and changed the subject. 'Given the current situation—'

Huber cut me off mid-sentence; the tone of her voice was bordering on hostile. 'And what situation would that be?'

I raised my eyebrows. 'The one that indicates the Stasi already have someone inside the Bewegung feeding them information – if not, how do you explain the massive police presence last night. Zinnwald is hardly a major crime centre and I'm assuming that the man who was arrested on Thursday knew nothing of last night's meeting – which was probably arranged *after* his arrest, wasn't it? Which means they have someone inside. Perhaps it was even one of the eight present at last night's meeting – ten including us – who tipped them off and it's because of that situation that I'm going to need a weapon. In case I'm cornered and can't talk my way out of it.'

Huber didn't argue the point and try to suggest that I was mistaken. Instead, she leaned back and, balancing on the rear two legs of her chair, opened the drawer set into the side of the table. She reached inside and lifted out a Russian-made Makarov 9mm pistol. She smiled as she slid it across the table towards me.

'The magazine is full.'

I considered asking her why she hadn't given me the weapon earlier, but there seemed little point. I knew why. Trust is a two-way thing. Still chewing on the bread roll, I picked up the weapon and examined it. The brown Bakelite panels on either side of the handle carried a relief of the Russian five-pointed star set inside a circle. Even though she had just told me that the magazine was full, like a good soldier I removed it, and after checking that the top round was running free, I slid it back into the base of the pistol grip. Then, holding the weapon by the muzzle, with the pistol grip towards her, I raised my eyebrows.

There was no need for words. She knew what I wanted to know and answered accordingly. 'The original owner has no further use for it. He's dead.'

That was short and to the point.

I pushed the pistol into the belt at the back of my trousers. 'I'll also need a car. Preferably a Trabant, not new but reliable. I have money.' I chuckled to myself.

'What's so funny?'

I leaned back in my chair. 'I can't believe I just used the words "Trabant" and "reliable" in the same sentence.'

I reached into my pocket and took out the folded piece of paper Metzger had pushed into my palm the previous night and slid it across the table to Huber.

'Do you know where this is?'

Huber picked up the paper and unfolded it.

'Yes. It's a small *Gästehaus* on the edge of town.' She screwed up her face. 'It's used by the mineworkers. It's not a very friendly place. Why do you want to know?'

I helped myself to another *Semel* from the basket, and a second slice of ham. I knew that by meeting Metzger I was taking a huge risk, but not meeting him could be equally as dangerous.

'I'm supposed to meet Metzger there at one thirty today.'

Huber held up the piece of paper and waved it from side to side in front of me. 'Where did you get this? Did you leave the house while I was out?'

I shook my head. 'No. Metzger slipped it into my hand last night as we left the church.'

Although we were alone in the flat, Huber leaned forward and lowered her voice; it was as though she was scared of being over-heard. Her eyes told me everything I needed to know.

'Be careful, Andel. Metzger is a very dangerous man. He doesn't believe that Bonsack and the rest of us are capable of bringing about the necessary changes using non-violent means. Some of those who have opposed him in the past have met with mysterious, and in some cases fatal, accidents.'

Given what Huber had just said, I wondered if Metzger had anything to do with the disappearance of Thomas Littman back in 1986.

At 13:25 I was standing beneath the trees on the far side of the road that ran past the bar where I was supposed to meet Metzger. In my right hand I held the Makarov pistol Huber had given me earlier that morning. I pulled back the top slide and released it, let the spring carry it forward again, feeding a 9mm round into the chamber. With the muzzle of the Makarov pointing at the ground beside my right foot, I held back the hammer with my thumb and gently squeezed the trigger. The weapon was now in the half-cocked position. I lifted my jacket, tucked it into the back of my trousers, and as I walked towards the front door of the bar, not knowing what awaited me inside, I prepared myself for confrontation.

The bar was typically East German. A medium-sized, dimly lit room filled with what the antique trade refers to as low-quality 'brown furniture'. The overriding smell was one of stale beer and cigarette smoke, not unpleasant, in fact mildly reassuring; it reminded me of the smell you got when entering a working man's pub back home. On my left, alongside the mesh-covered windows, were a row of three shoddy-looking booths. The walls of the room were bare and, although initially painted an off-white colour, now covered by years of cigarette smoke, the tone was closer to a mustard yellow. I looked up. Half of the lights that hung from the ceiling were missing their glass shades, leaving nothing but the exposed bulbs. Hanging in an ornate wooden frame on the wall behind the bar was a picture of Erich Honecker, the leader of the East German Communist Party and, apart from what looked like three mineworkers sitting in the booth closest to the door, the bar was empty. There was no sign of Metzger.

I made my way to the bar, ordered a small beer and took a seat at a table in the opposite corner to the mineworkers. I lifted the glass to my lips and paused.

Let's hope their beer tastes better than their coffee.

I took a mouthful, and apart from the fact that it was a little warm, it wasn't that bad. From where I was sitting I had a clear view of the three men in the booth, the barman and, more importantly, the front door. I was also aware that the barman and his other three customers had been watching me since I arrived.

I looked at my watch.

13:38. He's late. Does punctuality mean nothing to these people?

I finished my beer and was just about to stand up when the door opened and Metzger walked in. I sat down again and watched in silence as he made his way to the bar and ordered a small beer.

He was dressed in his work clothes: what I would have referred to back in my youth as a donkey jacket over a set of dark brown overalls and work boots. It was only now as he stood in front of the bar that I realised how tall he was, perhaps 6' 3 or 4. Well built, with short cropped hair, he may have been a worker but he also had a presence about him. If I had to label him I suppose he reminded me of Bill Sykes played by Oliver Reed before he went to seed.

As he waited for the barman to pull his beer, he slipped his right hand into his jacket pocket. The barman placed the beer in front of Metzger, and as he reached for it he dropped something on the counter and slid it across to the barman. Whatever it was it was black and shiny. At first, I thought that it might have been a weapon, but it was too slim.

I watched Metzger turn and lean back against the bar. He made eye contact with one of the three men sitting in the booth. It was one of those looks where, although not a word was spoken, it was evident that an understanding had been reached.

Fucking great.

Metzger straightened himself up and made his way to where I was sitting.

I stood up and offered him my hand. It had been obvious from the start that we were never going to be friends, so with the pleasantries over I got straight down to business.

'So, what can I do for you, Herr Metzger? Why are we here?'

Although Metzger had a smile on his face, it was the type of smile you see on a cartoon cat just before he decapitates the mouse. 'Please, call me Klaus.'

I repeated the question. 'So what can I do for you, Klaus?'

Metzger rested his forearms on the table and leaned forward. 'Have we ever met before?'

I felt my pulse rate quicken. Again, I thought there was something familiar about his face but I couldn't place him. 'No.'

Metzger was now staring at me, hard. 'How can you be sure?'

'Because this is my first time in East Germany, and although your English is close to perfect, I doubt that being East German you have spent much time in the West.'

I was bullshitting, of course, trying to find out more about him. I knew enough Germans back in northern Germany who spoke English to know that Metzger's English was not what he would have learned at school. My idea was to encourage him to again raise the subject of who I was and who had sent me, then hopefully I could reinforce my claim of being from Amnesty International and put the subject to bed once and for all. But deep down inside, I knew that Metzger was the type of person who never took anything at face value – didn't trust anybody – and at some time in the near future, we would probably have this conversation, or something close to it, again.

Metzger broke eye contact, picked up his glass, and took a sip of his beer before continuing. 'Aren't you a little young to be doing this kind of work?'

I sat back in my seat and felt the Makarov dig into the small of my back. 'Not really, as I told you last night, Amnesty is now moving in an entirely different direction, taking a more pro-active stance. Where possible we are now attempting to put men on the ground, to collect and report information first hand. In the past, the organisation has relied on the word of others, third parties, who, although they may mean well, provide information open to misinterpretation and manipulation. It is a role that is more suited to the younger, fitter man or woman.'

Metzger took another mouthful of beer and placed his glass back on the table.

'I was hoping that, following what you witnessed last night, you might be able to convince your Amnesty masters back in London that our needs are slightly different.'

That's a strange choice of words. I raised my eyebrows. 'Different how?'

He leaned forward again. 'Instead of playing the long game as Bonsack is insisting on – lobbying Western governments on our behalf, publicising the plight of the East German people through the press, and on television, all of which is very credible – maybe it would be more beneficial to provide us with some military support, weapons, and qualified personnel to train us in their use.'

I resisted the urge to shake my head, but still felt compelled to voice my concerns. 'Firstly, brokering *coups d'état* is something the CIA do; it's not what Amnesty does. Secondly, there is no way you will ever win an all-out war with the East German and Soviet authorities. God forbid it ever comes to war between East and West, but if it did, even an organisation as large and as well equipped as NATO would struggle to hold its own. Given East Germany's geographical importance to the Soviet Union, they will never allow you to win.'

Metzger looked embarrassed, like a child who had just been chastised by a teacher in front of his classmates, and immediately attempted to redeem his position.

'Not immediately I'll grant you, but with outside help we could quickly become a serious thorn in their side, and for a very long time to come.'

I glanced over Metzger's left shoulder. If the three men sitting in the booth were his, and I pissed him off enough, I could very well find myself in the middle of a fight. My eyes ran down the single leg that supported the table they were sitting behind, the large metal plate at its base was bolted securely to the floor.

Metzger wouldn't see it coming and, if I take out the man sitting at the entrance of the booth, with the table bolted down, the other two will be trapped behind his body. Sitting targets. Then, of course, there's the barman. It will be touch and go, but given my training, aggression, and the element of surprise, it's definitely doable.

Confident that if the need arose, I could win, I decided to take the hard line with Metzger.

'Armed rebellion and the Bewegung winning the odd skirmish with the Soviet authorities is not Amnesty's concern. On the other hand, pissing the communist authorities off and getting a lot of innocent people killed in the crossfire will concern them significantly, and if you're not careful, the Bewegung, not the Soviet and East German authorities, could end up being the villain in the process.'

I saw the muscles in Metzger's forearms flex as the anger built in his eyes. It was obvious that the conversation we were having had the potential to become a full-blown argument, or something much worse, and I needed to end it. Quickly.

'Besides, that's nothing to do with me. I'm only here to observe and report back.'

Metzger smiled. 'And how exactly are you going to do that?'

'That's my problem.'

Metzger lost his smile. 'I don't suppose it will do me any good to ask how you managed to get into East Germany undetected?'

I smiled at him. 'Not much.'

To my surprise, Metzger didn't push either point any further. But thinking back now, why would he? He knew that I probably wasn't going anywhere. Time was on his side.

As I walked back across the road to where Huber was waiting in her car, it became clear to me that what I had just taken part in wasn't so much a conversation as a sparring match. One where Metzger had done his own share of digging, tried to find out as much about me as he could. Judging by the questions he had asked, and his reaction to my non-committal answers, whoever he now thought I was and who I worked for, I doubted it was Amnesty International – and, as a result, I also doubted that this would end well. But I didn't have time to worry about that right now, my first priority was to find out as much as I could about Operation Konev.

Thursday, 17 August 1989

Dresdner Heide Forest

It was 03:53 when I switched off the engine of the cream-coloured Trabant that Huber had acquired for me the previous day. The car was close to fifteen years old, and although the bodywork carried more than just a few scars, she assured me that the mechanics were in perfect working order. The seats were the originals, made of heavy-duty grey cloth, worn to the point where they were in danger of becoming a network of holes spread over the foam and springs, not unlike a string vest. However, the engine started the first time and, although a little clunky by BMW and Mercedes standards, the transmission worked, and the brakes did what they were supposed to. On the plus side the cream-coloured paintwork was much gentler on the eye, much less noticeable than the powder blue of Huber's car. I climbed out of the car and looked around me.

I had parked in a small picnic area deep inside the Dresdner Heide Forest, a large nature reserve on the northern outskirts of Dresden, and as I turned the key I heard the car's primitive locking mechanism clunk into place.

Time to find out if Scott managed to keep to his end of the bargain.

It was close to a full moon that night, and as such I had driven the last 300 metres with the lights off, and with the engine revs just above idle. The RV was 400 metres due east from where I eventually parked the car, and I would complete the remainder of the journey on foot, working my way round and approaching it from the south. Three minutes later, having visually checked the surrounding area, I stepped out of the undergrowth on to a moonlit gravel track.

This is the place, but there's nobody here.

Five minutes later, assuming that Scott had failed, or something else had gone wrong, I decided to head back to the car, but as I stepped off the track, and back into the trees, I heard the sound of a vehicle approaching.

Crouched down, and hidden in the undergrowth, I recognised the distinct box-like features of a Mercedes G Wagon, BRIXMIS' current vehicle of choice. Its lights had been switched off and, as it made its way slowly along the track towards me, I looked at my watch.

04:10. They're ten minutes late. They were supposed to be here at 04:00. Before I even arrived. Let's hope I'm not dealing with Muppets.

However, I knew there was little chance of that. Getting yourself selected as a BRIXMIS operator wasn't as physically demanding as Selection, or as mentally draining as becoming a DET operator, but it wasn't a walk in the park either.

I drew the Makarov from behind my back and waited for the vehicle to stop before breaking cover and approaching it from the rear. My eyes scanned the number plate for anything that would tell me it wasn't a BRIXMIS vehicle, but instead a Soviet replica – a trap. It was then that I noticed the car had only two occupants. I froze, raised my weapon to shoulder height and took a step to my right, closer to the edge of the track and the undergrowth.

Where's the third crew member?

BRIXMIS 'Tours' always consisted of three men. An officer, NCO and a driver. With my suspicions aroused, I took another step to my right, back into the cover of the trees. I was just about to abandon the meeting altogether, take a roundabout route back to where I had parked the car, when the front passenger door of the Mercedes opened and a tall, somewhat gangly figure dressed in British DPM stepped on to the track. Some soldiers look smart and impressive in uniform. Others, including me, look like a bag of shit. But there are some who, no matter how hard they try, will always look awkward – like they've stolen it and are wearing it under false pretences. It just so happens that most people who fall into that category are young, very intelligent officers. What we used to refer to as 'light-houses in the desert' – very bright but of no bloody use.

I smiled.

That has got to be a British Rupert.

As I approached him, he turned and nervously offered me his hand. 'Shore?'

I winced as I heard my given name said out loud for the first time in over a week, but then realised that Scott would not have shared my cover name, my false identity with anybody. Not even BRIXMIS.

'Yes.'

'Great. I'm Captain—'

I raised my left hand, cutting him off mid-sentence.

'Best if I don't know. Let's just stick to Tom and Boss for now.'

He nodded at me nervously. 'Understood. Your hardware is in the back.'

'Great. Let's hope it's what I asked for.' Not that I was in any position to kick up a fuss if it wasn't.

I followed the officer to the rear of the vehicle and watched in silence as he opened the single back door and lifted a blanket. Hidden below it was a Clansman PRC-319 radio set.

'Hello, gorgeous.'

I heard the officer chuckle.

As I said earlier, at the time the 319 was state of the art and its capabilities had made it the object of an on-going love affair with British Special Forces.

I slipped one of the carrying straps over my left shoulder, picked up the holdall lying beside it and unzipped it. Inside was a spare battery, a sectional whip antenna, which increased the 319's range from the 20 kilometres that was possible with the standard short antenna, to up to 5,000 kilometres, which meant that I now had a way of communicating with BRIXMIS in Berlin. I would be able to pass on anything I managed to discover about Operation Konev, and the EMU or Electronic Message Unit would allow me to do it without being intercepted. Along with the battery and antenna, there were what the signals fraternity commonly refer to as 'The Harness'; the necessary cables, connections, and a headset. I was just about to re-zip the bag when something caught my eye. Half hidden in the corner of the bag was a small polished black metal plate; it was the bottom end of a pistol magazine. I reached in and lifted it out. It was still inserted in the pistol grip of a Sig Sauer 9mm. I looked at the officer.

'Some guy in glasses turned up at London Block last week. I didn't catch his name. In fact, now I come to think about it, I don't recall him ever telling us who he was. He said that I was to give you that at the same time as the radio. There's also a box of fifty 9mm rounds in the bag.' He reached into his jacket pocket and held out his hand. 'This is my contribution. I acquired it a few years ago. On a childish whim, before I found out that BRIXMIS Tours are never armed. It's never had a round fired through it, but if you're forced to use the Sig, it might come in useful. I've already checked, the Sig's barrel is threaded.'

Nestled in the palm of his hand was a silencer. I smiled as I replayed my recent conversation with Metzger. Strangely, the officer giving me the Sig provided me with a sense of comfort.

Unlike the Makarov Huber had given me earlier, which was designed in 1948 and had been in service with Soviet and Eastern Bloc forces ever since, the Sig Sauer P226 had only been in service since 1983. Compared to the Makarov, the Sig was a far sturdier weapon. And although it was slightly longer and heavier, the extra barrel length along with its increased muzzle velocity improved both the weapon's accuracy and stopping power. That, combined with the silencer the BRIXMIS officer had just given me, would definitely give me the edge if I was ever forced to use it. It had also been my side arm – my backup weapon – when I was at Hereford so I knew its workings and capabilities inside out.

'Cheers, Boss, and if it's not too much trouble, I'd like to request that for the duration of this operation you are the only physical contact I have with BRIXMIS. It will be safer all round. Speed things up if I know who I'm expecting to meet at these little rendezvous.'

'That's already been arranged.'

I was just about to offer him my hand when I heard footsteps crunching along the gravel track behind me. Someone was running towards us. Not knowing if the Sig was loaded, but knowing that the BRIXMIS officer was unarmed, I reached for the Makarov tucked into my belt.

As I drew the weapon and turned, I saw the Tour NCO, the missing third man, jogging along the track towards us. There was no time for introductions.

'There are headlights heading this way, Boss. It looks like the Volga we managed to lose earlier this morning on the outskirts of Karl-Marx-Stadt.' Volgas were large Russian-built saloon vehicles, predominantly black and the preferred choice of the KGB and Stasi whose role it was to track down and hound the BRIXMIS Tours.

Which is why they were late.

The BRIXMIS officer was already moving towards the front of the G-Wagon as the Tour NCO climbed into the rear passenger seat.

'Best you make yourself scarce while we try to lead them away from here.'

As I melted into the undergrowth, I heard the G-Wagon's powerful engine burst into life. A split second later, its tyres kicked up the gravel and it accelerated smoothly away, out of the forest and back towards Dresden. It was followed thirty seconds later by a pair of headlights, which I assumed belonged to the Volga.

With the forest silent again, I walked to the rear of the Trabant and lowered the 319 into its boot. The first thing I had to do was find somewhere safe to hide it. My relationship with Huber had taken another nosedive when shortly after midnight I had left the house refusing to tell her where I was going, or why. As a result, I knew that turning up at the front door with the 319 would do little to smooth the situation.

As I closed the boot lid, my hand drifted on to the pistol grip of the Sig tucked into my belt, and I began to stroke it. I was probably going to need it at some point in the future but, like the 319, for now nobody else needed to know that I had it.

Although the East German state did its best to keep its citizens in the dark about events in the West, news of what was happening in other Eastern Bloc countries, specifically Hungary, Poland and Czechoslovakia, was still filtering through. By mid-August 1989 the West German embassy in Prague had become one of the most important refuges for East Germans trying to get into the Federal Republic of Germany. And by 20 August, so many of them were crammed into the West German embassy in the Lobkowicz Palais, of the Lesser Town Prague, that the West German foreign ministry had no choice but to close the embassy for normal business. At that time, the number of East German refugees taking shelter in the embassy was barely a tenth of the number it would be forced to house and feed just five weeks later.

Tuesday, 22 August 1989

Zinnwald Forest

I DROPPED TO one knee and scanned the darkness that surrounded me. My senses were tingling as I imagined I could see things moving in the shadows. Figures rushing from tree to tree, things that weren't really there.

Get a grip, man. Nobody's going to be out here at one thirty in the morning.

I had been in East Germany for close to two weeks, but as far as Operation Konev was concerned I was no further forward, and in all honesty I had no idea where to start.

Considering Zinnwald was supposed to be the launch point for whatever Konev was, given the short timeframe before it was due to kick off, I would have expected to be seeing a gradual build-up of both East German/Soviet troops and hardware. But in fact, as I had driven around the area either alone, which wasn't very often, or as a passenger in Huber's car, I had seen nothing. There had been no unusual military activity in the area, and it wasn't as if I could simply drop 'What do you know about Operation Konev?' into the conversation with either Huber, Bonsack or anybody else for that matter.

You might imagine there would be local radio broadcasts about such a large movement of troops. But nothing of that nature would have ever been broadcast on East German radio, and doing such a thing without the permission of the state would have been tantamount to treason. Besides, in reality, there would be no need to broadcast it. Even one regiment of tanks on the move makes a hell of a noise, something that can be heard from close to a mile away, and if anything the size of an armoured division was on the move in the Zinnwald area I wouldn't have needed to see it – I would have heard it. Then there would have been the inconvenience – the endless security checks as you drove around the area. The countless roadblocks set up by the military police – you can't move that much heavy armour, scores of tracked vehicles weighing close to fifty tons each, with what can only be described as less than rudimentary steering capabilities, without going some way to protect the local civilian population by stopping or diverting the flow of traffic and closing roads for what could be hours at a time. No, if it happened, it wasn't something I would miss.

Following my meeting with Metzger on 14 August, questions were being asked about my whereabouts. As a result, on 19 August, a few days after my rendezvous with the BRIXMIS Tour in the Dresdner Heide, Huber took the unilateral decision to leave the Projects, and relocate us to an empty cottage some eighteen kilometres due north.

Although its remote location meant that I could now get outside during daylight hours, she was still insisting that I not wander far, and so I still felt like a caged tiger.

The move had been a rash decision; a knee-jerk reaction on Huber's part, and as a result the house was far from ideal. It sat alone on the outskirts of a small farming community. The property was old, in a bad state of repair, and had been empty for some years. Our sudden appearance, along with the fact that there were now two cars parked outside the near derelict cottage, had already begun to draw unwelcome attention from the villagers. I suspected that it wouldn't be long before we were on the move again.

Given the speed of the move from the Projects to our current location, I had had no time to relocate the Clansman radio I had acquired from BRIXMIS. It was still where I had originally hidden it, buried beneath the rootstock of a very large fallen tree fifty metres in front of me. The fact that it wasn't close by and easily accessible had not been a problem so far. Having managed to find out nothing about Operation Konev, it wasn't as if I needed to use it on a daily basis. However, it was far from secure at its current location so I needed to find a new hiding place.

I surveyed the surrounding area one last time. Confident that I was alone, I moved to the rootstock, and using my bare hands began to dig into the soft earth beneath it. Within minutes my fingernails scraped across the thin sheet of plywood I had used to cover the much larger hole I had previously dug beneath it.

I located an edge, then a corner, and hooking a finger beneath it I lifted it clear. Beneath the plywood was a thin covering of plastic, old carrier bags, and below them the Clansman and the holdall.

I slipped the harness over my shoulders. Set my Silva compass to 342 degrees, north-by-northwest, picked up the holdall and, as I moved away from the rootstock, looked at my watch.

02:06.

Unless I got a move on, there was no way I'd get the radio relocated and back to the cottage before Huber woke up and discovered I was missing.

Tuesday, 22 August 1989

Schwarzbachtal

A T 04:42, I was standing beneath the trees of a small copse, two hundred metres short of the entrance to a derelict farm, which stood at the end of a narrow lane, slightly elevated and surrounded by open farmland. I had seen the farm a few days earlier when Huber and I had driven past it on our way back from Dresden.

By East German standards, it was a large sprawling complex consisting of a farmhouse, which stood opposite the main gate, and in front of a large barn. To their right, set slightly to the rear, was the remains of an old pigsty (I know, a mystery, why would you put a pigsty right beside your living quarters? But there you go). At a ninety-degree angle, and to the right of the pigsty, was a stable block with six stalls, and to its rear a small paddock. Directly behind the paddock were two smaller barns that looked to be a more recent addition. A crumbling dry-stone wall encircled the whole complex. It was ideal and, on our return to the cottage, I had found the farm's location on an old road map and plotted its exact bearing from the rootstock in the forest that surrounded Zinnwald.

Twenty minutes later I completed a cursory check of all the buildings. I made sure that none of them were being used as storage sheds, and that the farm was totally abandoned, then I began to search for a new place to hide the radio.

Between the farmhouse and the barn, I found a disused diesel storage tank. I climbed the metal ladder attached to one end of the tank and loosened the wing nuts that held an inspection hatch in place. I slipped my torch through the open hole and, covering as much of the aperture as I could with my upper body, switched it on.

Apart from an inch of diesel oil lying in the bottom of the tank, it was empty. On closer inspection, the tank seemed to be in good condition, weatherproofed, and the internal workings – the intake and breather pipes – were still in place and in good condition. It was perfect for what I needed.

I switched off the torch, and spreading my legs I braced them against the side of the tank, and carefully lowered the radio set through the opening. I used the shoulder straps of the carrying harness to suspend it from a bend in the breather pipe and, after hanging the bag containing the spare battery and harness on to one corner of the 319, I replaced the hatch and screwed it down.

It had been impossible to use the car on this occasion without alerting Huber that I was heading off on my own once again. The last time I had disappeared on my own, the night I'd met the BRIXMIS Tour in the Dresdner Heide Forest, she had gone ballistic on my return. In an attempt to avoid a repeat performance, I had decided to make the entire journey from the cottage to Zinnwald and back to the farm on foot. But now, no longer weighed down by the 10kg radio, and 6kg of battery and harness, I would make good time as I covered the last three kilometres from the farm back to the cottage.

At 05:40, as quietly as I could, I lifted the unsecured window at the rear of the cottage, pulled aside the curtain and climbed in. I looked across the room to the door. The chair I had jammed under the handle was still in place. I quickly discarded my outdoor clothing, dressed in a pair of East German tracksuit bottoms and T-shirt and, quietly removing the chair, I slowly opened the door. Barefoot, and as quietly as I could, I made my way along the short hallway, past Huber's room, and into the kitchen.

I turned on the single brass tap, there was no hot water system in the cottage, so I washed the dirt from my hands, and filled a mug, with cold water. But as I lifted the mug to my lips, the kitchen was flooded with light, and I turned to see Huber standing in the doorway, glaring at me.

'Have you been out of the house?'

I was speechless, not because I didn't have an answer to her question, but because she was standing there in nothing but her underwear. I don't know what I expected to see if such a situation ever arose but, given the fact that we were behind the Iron Curtain, it wasn't the pretty white bra and panties she was now wearing.

Her body was lean and toned, like a gymnast's; she was stunning. I shook my mind free and put on my best innocent face.

'Of course not, why would you think that?'

She was still glaring at me.

'Because I came to your door just after midnight, and when I tried to open it, even though there is not a single key to be found anywhere in the house, apart from the front and back door keys, your bedroom door appeared to be locked.'

There was no point in lying; she knew I'd been out.

'OK. I admit it. I couldn't sleep. I needed some fresh air, so I went out for a long walk.' My answer did nothing to calm her down.

'You shouldn't go out alone at night. It's not safe. There are police patrols everywhere.'

I didn't respond, I was too tired, and besides I knew that trying to come up with some elaborate story on the spur of the moment would be my undoing. So instead, picking up my water, I walked silently past her and returned to my room.

I took the Makarov from where I had hidden it beneath the bedside locker, and replaced it with the silenced Sig that I had been carrying all night. Nobody knew that I had the Sig, and that's the way it was going to stay. I checked the safety on the Makarov, climbed on to the bed, and slipped it under my right thigh.

Two hours later, just before eight, there was a gentle knock at the door. Huber never knocked. Knocking on a door was something visitors did, and we had agreed never to do it. If either of us did knock, then it would be a sign to the other that the house had been compromised. I wrapped my right hand around the pistol grip of the Makarov, pulled back the hammer, and rolled silently off the bed, dragging the mattress with me in an effort to obtain a little extra protection, and knelt on the floor behind it. As I watched the bedroom door slowly open I took up the first pressure on the trigger.

Huber poked her head around the edge of the door. She was now fully dressed and, as her eyes met mine across the muzzle of the Makarov, I saw her swallow.

'I . . . I've made coffee and reheated yesterday's *Semels*. You need to get dressed. We have a lot to do today.'

She left the room and I stood up, lowered the weapon, returned it to the half-cocked position and slid the mattress back on to the bed.

That'll make a pleasant change.

I had good reason to be sceptical. Apart from an occasional trip out, Huber and I spent most of our day cooped up indoors, doing our best to keep out of each other's way, though she had become slightly more approachable, and much more tactile since leaving the Projects. However, every time she changed our routine it caused me nothing but problems. The last major decision she made, moving here from the Projects, had put eighteen kilometres between the Clansman, my lifeline back to the West, and me.

I dressed and headed for the kitchen. Huber was standing beside the sink.

'So why did you knock on my door earlier this morning, and again just now? I thought we agreed we would never do that.'

Huber placed two mugs of black coffee on the table and sat down. Her face and neck were flushed, bright red.

'I'm sorry I forgot.'

I wasn't convinced. 'Well don't do it again, you were lucky this morning, next time I might shoot first and ask questions later.'

I heard her blow out hard through her nose; she had been doing that a lot. Lately it was becoming what psychologists refer to as a 'tell' and what signallers call an 'idiosyncrasy'. Something you do without realising it, something that makes you immediately identifiable to an enemy monitoring station. The only problem was I wasn't sure if it was derisory, or simply a show of frustration, but given the current atmosphere I decided to let it go.

'So what's the big panic?'

She was staring down at the table. 'After breakfast, we need to gather all our belongings together. Make sure we leave nothing behind. Burn everything we no longer need. Once we leave today we won't be coming back.'

I stared at her. 'Where are we going?'

'There's an important meeting tonight; it will be attended by all of the Bewegung's senior members – district commanders from all over Saxony. When it's over, we are to relocate to Leipzig.'

All I could think about was the effort I had just gone to a few hours earlier to recover the radio from Zinnwald. Then – and more importantly – there was Operation Konev, the reason I was here in East Germany. I could hardly discover what was going on from Leipzig – 170km away; even though we had managed the odd trip down to Zinnwald during daylight hours there had been no sign of any additional troop movements or anything else out of the ordinary going on in the area. And if there had been, I would have expected the few members of the Bewegung that we occasionally came into contact with to mention it. But there had been nothing.

'This is all rather sudden, isn't it? We've only been here a few days. What's going on? Do we have a problem? Are you holding out on me?'

Her eyes met mine, their blue was cold, like ice fire, and I heard her blow out through her nose again, but harder, and this time there was no mistaking the meaning – she was fast losing patience with my mistrust of her. She was showing contempt.

Tuesday, 22 August 1989
Zinnwald Forest

I T WAS JUST after 20:30, and about a kilometre and a half into the forest, when we hit a track junction and I saw the lights on Huber's car go out. I immediately did the same. Given what she had told me just before leaving the cottage, we would complete the remaining three kilometres of the journey in total darkness, using the brakes only in an emergency.

I pulled my Trabant up behind Huber's, got out, and made my way quickly forward, where I leaned against her door and held it closed.

With her hand on the door handle, she glared at me through the open window.

'What do you think you're doing?'

I smiled. 'So what did you want this morning?'

Huber stared at me like she had not understood the question. 'What?'

'When you came to my room just after midnight and found the door locked, what did you want?'

She said nothing; it was evident that she did not have a ready excuse, and was unable to come up with one on the spur of the moment, and whatever her reason for knocking on my door, it was clear that she was now unwilling to share it with me.

I stepped back. Opened the door, bowed sarcastically, and held it open while she climbed out.

She pushed me aside, slammed the car door, and I followed her into the woodman's hut, smiling.

The cabin was fairly large, almost square, maybe twenty feet by twenty feet, but as far as I could see there was only one door, the one we had just entered through, and one room, which was crowded with at least thirty people. As you would expect in a woodman's hut in the middle of an East German forest, there was only a small table and two or three chairs, all of which were now occupied. Those without seats were standing around the walls, their faces gradually disappearing behind a rapidly growing blanket of cigarette smoke.

I was already familiar with some of the faces in the room, those that had been at the church the night the police locked down Zinnwald, and I learned from Huber later that the others were long-standing leaders of workforces in the area's factories and mines. When the time came, it would be these men and women who would lead their workmates out on to the streets and call for East Germany's first national strike in over fifty years but, surprisingly, there was no sign of Metzger or any of the other hardliners.

In the absence of Metzger, his deputy, Bonsack had absolute control of the floor and, being an intelligent man who loved to talk, he made good use of it. As a result, all talk of an armed uprising was actively discouraged, and Bonsack and the rest of the committee laid out their plans for a series of rallies they hoped would be the start of a bloodless revolution, one they hoped would spread across the whole of East Germany, and beyond.

I considered what I was doing here tonight. Why had Huber brought me with her? Was it because the Bewegung had swallowed my story about working for Amnesty? Were they about to ramp up their operation and wanted me to observe in full what might become an extremely violent situation unfold, before reporting the full story back to my superiors, who would then bring it to the attention of the world? Or had they worked out that there was more to me than met the eye, if that was the case, that I might be of use in other ways? There was of course a more mundane possibility: that with Huber, my chaperone, about to relocate to Leipzig, they could hardly leave me behind.

It occurred to me that if my suspicions were correct and the Bewegung were about to ramp up their operation, then this would be something I had been trained for. The Regiment regularly sent small teams into friendly countries under the auspices of military advisors, but always with strict instructions not to become involved in hostilities. As a result, I now suspected that my current mission was about to go the same way every one of the Regiment's so-called 'military advisor' operations had gone in the past.

I was a professional soldier. It was not in my nature to walk away from a fight, and I knew that sooner rather than later I would find it impossible to draw the line between observer and full-blown combatant. If the Bewegung were going to succeed, then the time would inevitably come when peaceful opposition failed and things became ugly. It was at that point that I would be forced to disobey Scott and stand alongside the Bewegung as they faced the bullets.

But as I looked around the room, I knew that at least one of those present was a traitor, a Stasi informer, maybe even a deep cover KGB agent, and if the opportunity presented itself, that I might be forced to kill them. And if my suspicions were confirmed, that might even include Huber.

Given the amount of time we were spending living in close proximity to one another, it might seem strange that I was still referring to her as 'Huber' and not Kirstin. Well, it's a self-defence mechanism – a way of making any difficult decisions easier to handle.

Once, during an exercise, a member of another NATO country asked a close friend about me.

'Why doesn't he like us?'

The reply was short and to the point. 'Because one day he may have to kill you.'

The soldier looked shocked and began to stutter. 'B . . . but we're friends, we're all on the same side.'

Again, the answer was short, to the point, and left the man in no doubt. 'Only in your mind, buddy – not in his.'

Of course, he was exaggerating slightly, playing for effect, and although it saddens me to say it now, at the time I viewed my relationship with Huber in exactly the same way.

Sunday, 27 August 1989

Leipzig

I HAD BEEN in East Germany for a little over a month. I'd always taken a keen interest in current affairs, kept abreast of what was happening, but now, as a result of the East German government's ability to control the country's media, I had little idea about what was happening in the outside world – on the other side of the Inner German Border.

I pushed open the door of the *Gästehaus* on the corner of Goethestraße in Leipzig and peered through the half-light and cigarette smoke that filled the bar. As you would expect, from a bar attached to a *Gästehaus* in a major city, its interior was slightly upmarket compared to the one where I had met Metzger a few days after my arrival in Zinnwald. The furnishings were neither plush nor modern in appearance. In fact, the quality of the furnishings, decoration and atmosphere reminded me of a working man's bar in early 1970s Belfast. The only other thing that sticks in my mind was how small the wooden chairs were surrounding every table. The circumference of each seat, and the height, was also strange, so that when seated you were like a half-shut knife – extremely uncomfortable.

It was a good minute before I spotted Huber, Bonsack and two other members of the Bewegung – Gerhard Fischer and Horst Mayer. They had travelled up with Bonsack from Zinnwald and always acted as his minders. It turned out that Metzger had decided to remain in Zinnwald, due to his position at the mine.

The four of them were hunched over a table in the far corner and, as I drew closer, it was evident that their mood was anything but happy.

I remained standing. 'What's wrong?'

Huber lifted her head, looked at me, and then slowly lowered it again. 'The government has announced that all international borders are to close with immediate effect.'

I felt my pulse rate rise. 'What, all of them? Even the ones that lead into neighbouring Warsaw Pact countries like Czechoslovakia?'

Huber continued to stare at the table. It was as though she was now talking to it instead of me. 'No. That's the only border crossing that will remain open. However, their border with Austria is also to close. The orders have come directly from Moscow.'

Taking the empty chair beside Huber, I sat down and looked across the table at Bonsack. 'Peter?'

Bonsack lifted his head and I saw the fight slowly draining from his eyes. The poor guy was dog-tired. I asked my next question, but this time my tone was harsh, almost demanding. 'So, what happens now?'

It took Bonsack a few seconds, but eventually he answered. 'With all but one of our borders closed we are trapped, no longer able to even move further east. Each day the people become more and more frustrated with our leaders. My fear is that as their frustration grows, sooner or later they will take matters into their own hands.'

Bonsack was right, if not properly coordinated; any form of defiance by the East German people would be doomed to failure and inevitably end in bloodshed. It looked like Metzger might get his way after all.

I looked around the table. 'So what? That's it? We're just going to give up?' It was at that moment I realised that I had used the word 'we're' instead of 'you're', and it hadn't gone unnoticed.

Bonsack lifted his head and smiled. 'We're not ready, Andel. The first rally is not planned to take place for at least another month, not until the end of September. I don't think the people will wait that long.'

I knew that unless I could pull them together again, and quickly, the Bewegung – well, Bonsack's side of it at least – were finished. I leaned on the table. 'Well, bring the date forward. It's not as if anybody outside the organisation knows what we have planned.' There it was again. The word 'we', instead of 'you', and it would appear, just as I had anticipated back at the woodman's hut outside Zinnwald, that the Bewegung's fight was rapidly becoming my fight too.

'If you want to mobilise the masses, and avoid the possibility of hundreds being killed on the streets, you need to act now.'

Huber turned towards me. 'It's not that simple. We need to prepare the literature. Then we need to find people we can trust to distribute it. It all takes time, time that we don't have.'

I noticed a hint of frustration in her voice, one that was rapidly turning to anger. I shook my head. 'No, it doesn't.' I hesitated. What I was about to do could jeopardise both my safety and my mission here in East Germany, but given the gravity of the situation, I now felt I had little choice, and if I were going to have any chance of helping save the Bewegung, I would have to risk it. I took a deep breath. 'I have access to a state of the art military radio that's capable of transmitting over three thousand miles into the West, virtually undetected. At the moment, like me, it's doing nothing but trying to stay one step ahead of the Stasi.'

Bonsack lifted his head so fast he nearly cracked his neck. He then sat and stared at me in silence, but it didn't last long, and as was his way he rattled off a raft of questions.

'Where did you get a radio? How long have you had it and, more importantly, where is it now?'

I had the feeling that my rash statement, although full of good intentions at the time, had now opened a huge can of worms, a Pandora's box that I would find impossible to close, but it was done and there was no going back.

I brushed Bonsack's questions aside. 'None of that matters right now.' And to my surprise, he didn't immediately press me for more information about the radio or its current location.

Eventually he spoke. 'So, Andel, what do you have in mind?'

'You need to agree on a date, time and location for the first rally. It should be somewhere prominent, somewhere here in Leipzig so that it's easy to find and doesn't involve too much travelling. And given the current situation it needs to be sooner rather than later.'

I paused, gave them time for everything I had just said to sink in. 'Next, we need a good printer. Someone we can trust. Get him to print a couple of hundred posters telling people to tune into a Western radio station, on a given date and time.'

As I continued, I could see both hope and the fight returning to Bonsack's eyes. His attitude was rapidly changing. I continued.

'A day or two before the rally, I will forward the information regarding its time and location to my contacts in the West. They will pass it on to the West German media, with instructions that the information is not to be broadcast until the agreed time. Hopefully, the protesters will turn out in their hundreds.'

It made perfect sense to me, but I also realised that if I was right and one of those sitting here tonight was working for the Stasi, I was also taking a huge risk. I felt it was a risk I had to take; it was either that, or stand by and do nothing while it all fell apart. I was also aware that those sitting around the table were hearing this for the first time and, as such, they would need a little longer to get their heads around it.

Bonsack leaned back in his chair and a few minutes later he smiled. 'It's brilliant in its simplicity. I know a printer who will be more than willing to help us.'

At the time there was, as far as I could see, very little or no overall command structure in the East German freedom movement. But Bonsack did seem to have a plan and was in contact with a growing number of smaller groups springing up in the south of East Germany.

'Good. All we need to do now is decide on a date, time and location.'

Bonsack sat quietly for a moment or two, then said, 'Two Lutheran priests have been holding a weekly *Friedensgebet*, "Prayer for Peace" service, every Monday evening at the Nikolaikirche − St Nicholas Church − close to Karl Marx Square. The numbers attending are small, sometimes less than twenty, but it would be the ideal place to hold the very first rally.'

Although Bonsack was clearly back on side, it would appear that Huber and the other two still had their reservations.

Huber was the first to speak. 'And who do we get to distribute these leaflets? We are rapidly running out of people we can trust. The police arrested four more of our people in Dresden last night.'

Apart from that one meeting in the woodman's hut in the forest outside Zinnwald, I had only ever met the leadership of the Bewegung down in Zinnwald, and as they kept any physical contact between the cells located in other towns down to a minimum for security reasons, I didn't actually know how big the organisation was. What I did know, though, was that because of the Stasi's relentless campaign to destroy such organisations, it looked like the Bewegung's message was not getting through to the masses. As a result, I thought its aims might never be realised.

I turned and looked at Huber. Even though she was angry and tired, she was still a picture of beauty and, as hard as I tried, I hadn't been able to shake the image of her standing, dressed only in her underwear, that morning at the cottage five days earlier. I shook my mind free.

'That's easy, these are posters, not leaflets, so we don't have to hand them out to anyone directly; that approach is far too dangerous and time-consuming. Instead, we post them on wooden hoardings, lamp posts, street signs, anywhere they will be seen by the general public. The five of us will share the task of putting them where they can do the most damage. News of what we intend to do doesn't need to go any further. In fact, it shouldn't go any further than those of us sitting here tonight. The fewer people who know about what we have planned, the less chance the authorities have of finding out and putting a stop to it. The only other thing we have to do is find out which of the West German radio stations has the strongest signal in the Leipzig area, and confirm the frequency.'

Bonsack rested his forearms on the table and leaned forward. 'What about Klaus Metzger? Surely, as my second-in-command, we should let him know what's going on?'

I thought back to my meeting with Metzger at the bar. Metzger had smiled and said, 'And how exactly are you going to do that?' It struck me now that Metzger already suspected that I had a radio, and that if he found out what we were intending to do he might try to hijack the radio and use it for his own violent purposes, to help create a bloodbath. I looked at the light bouncing off Bonsack's dark, thick-rimmed glasses. 'No. It's safer if nobody else knows.' I glanced around the table. 'Are we all agreed? No one else apart from the five of us here is to know about the plan; nobody.'

Eventually, everybody agreed. I also knew that by keeping the rest of the organisation in the dark, working on the need-to-know basis, that if the authorities did find out, and tried to put a stop to it, then the traitor was one of those sitting here tonight.

Friday, 1 September 1989

Leipzig

I T WAS JUST after 22:00 and, as normal, the streets at this time of night were practically deserted. I was watching Huber staple her last poster over a picture of Erich Honecker, the East German communist leader. It was attached to a wooden hoarding beside Leipzig's central bus station. The poster was old, a remnant of the East German elections held four months earlier on 7 May, but regardless of how old it was, such an act of defiance would be punished severely if she were caught.

I smiled as I turned back to the car, but my amusement was short lived. One hundred and fifty metres away, drawing up to the concrete bollards that divided the street in half, was a black Wartburg 353. As I continued to watch, two men got out and began walking slowly along the pavement towards us. Given that the car was one of the best East Germany had to offer, regularly used by the KGB and Stasi, and the two men that had just climbed out of it were both in civilian clothes, they probably worked for one of the two organisations.

Talk about getting caught with your hand in the till.

I knew that their sudden appearance was not a coincidence. I could understand it if they were local East German police patrolling their beat, but given the car, the plain clothes, and the fact that there was no logical reason for them to be here at this time of night, someone must have tipped off the authorities.

I grabbed Huber by the shoulder, dragged her away from the hoarding and pushed her into my car. 'Get out of here right now; I'll try to draw them away, but whatever happens, do *not* drive back to the house. Once you're clear of the area find some waste ground, and torch the car as I showed you, then find somewhere to lie low for a few hours before heading back to the house on foot. I'll meet you there later.'

As I slammed the car door behind her, and the cream-coloured Trabant pulled away from the kerb, I saw the two men stop. With their car trapped behind the bollards, they were now in two minds. Should they chase me on foot, or return to their vehicle and go after Huber. It was time to force their hand and help them make the right decision. I drew the Makarov Huber had given me a month earlier from my belt at the back of my trousers. Pulled back the hammer and, aiming just a few feet above their heads, I squeezed the trigger – twice in quick succession.

Although I had been carrying the weapon for close to a month, it was the first time I had fired it, and for some reason it didn't feel natural. However, I had thrown down the gauntlet; the big question now was, outnumbering me two to one, would they accept the challenge, or would they return to their car, call for backup, and in the process risk losing us both?

As I climbed through a gap in the hoarding, and on to the waste ground that ran behind it, I glanced over my right shoulder. The two men were running down the street towards me, weapons drawn.

Good decision, boys.

One hundred and fifty metres away, on the far side of the waste ground, was what looked like an industrial estate. If I was right and I could get among the network of buildings, it would be like a maze.

It was true that I had fired the first shots, but the last thing I wanted to do was get involved in a running gun battle with members of the East German or Soviet authorities. Huber had made good her escape. Now it was time for me to do the same.

As I cleared the waste ground and approached the industrial estate, I saw what appeared to be a transport yard surrounded by tall, spiked, angle iron railings, the type of structure that surrounds heavy plant yards back in the UK. There were no vehicles in the yard, but the two diesel pumps, which stood on its right-hand side, were a clear indication of its former use. On the far side of the yard, directly opposite the front gates, standing side by side, were two, two-storey buildings. Through the gap between them, I could see more of the railings as they encircled the entire yard. Half hidden at the far end of the left building, and outside the railings, was what looked like the start of a footbridge.

The two gates leading into the yard were loosely chained,

padlocked together just above the centre, but the gap between them was not wide enough for me to squeeze through. I sat on the floor. Grabbed hold of the bottom of one gate and, using the chain as a fulcrum, pushed against the other gate with my right foot to increase the size of the gap between the chain and the ground, and fifteen seconds later I had managed to squeeze through.

As I headed for the building on my right, I heard the sound of a train approaching. With the Makarov held tightly in my right hand I kicked the door as hard as I could. I saw it flex under the weight of my boot, but the lock held. I kicked it again, and again. On the fourth kick, the lock gave, and the door flew away from me. I glanced over my left shoulder. The two men were now at the gates of the yard, and one of them had begun to climb the railings.

I needed to keep them in sight. Make sure that they saw me enter the building and followed me. If I lost sight of them, and this turned into a game of hide-and-seek, outnumbered, and on unfamiliar ground, I was stuffed. I pointed my weapon into the air and squeezed the trigger. I saw the man straddling the railings duck momentarily, and as the sound of the shot echoed around the yard, he lifted his head and pointed in my direction.

I entered the building, sprinted up a flight of around fifteen stairs, and on reaching the first floor I paused; my eyes flitted over the array of open office doors. The rooms behind them were empty; there was no sign of any furniture, only office rubbish. Both the yard and its office blocks had been abandoned. I turned to my left and saw the second flight of stairs. At the top was what looked like a fire door.

I pushed against the horizontal metal bar that ran across its centre and, as the door opened, I found myself standing on a flat roof thirty feet above the ground.

The gap between the two buildings was a little over ten feet, but the one I was looking at was also a good four feet lower than the one I was currently standing on. All of which created an optical illusion, I told myself, that made the second building look even further away than it was. My mind shot back to Aldershot and my days at P Company. We had a similar test on the Trainasium, the aerial assault course and, like then, this would be a test of confidence.

The size of the gap will slow them down; make them think twice before following me, while the drop on the other side will increase the distance I can travel horizontally.

I suppose the best way of explaining this is, imagine a long jumper. His lift-off point and the landing pit are at the same level. Given the fact that when he touches down, he still has a large amount of forward momentum, if the landing pit were four feet lower than his take-off point, he would be able to cover a slightly greater horizontal distance.

I returned to the fire door, and with my back pressed up against it, looking for that extra couple of inches of run up, I steadied myself. I could hear the sound of footsteps coming up the stairs behind me. It was now or never, but I didn't want to contemplate the consequences of never. So, filling my lungs with air, I started my run.

As I approached the far edge of the roof, I picked up the pace and heard the fire door crash into the wall as it swung open behind me. With perfect timing, like an Olympic long jumper, I hit the flagstone lip of the building, launched myself into the air, and glanced down at the concrete surface thirty feet below me.

A split second later my feet touched down on the neighbouring roof. Still holding the Makarov in my right hand, and in an effort to maintain my forward momentum, I dived forward and rolled. As I came back up on to my feet, I continued the motion, and as I picked up the pace once more, I heard two shots.

I was now back up to full speed and heading towards the far side of the roof, but this time there had been no opportunity to check the size of the gap, I just had to hope that I'd got it right. As I reached the edge of the building, I threw myself up, and forward. Ten feet away and eight feet below me was the footbridge that spanned the railway line. But between the building and the footbridge, twenty feet below me, were the tops of the heavy spiked angle iron railings, a continuation of the yard's perimeter fence.

As I fell towards the footbridge, I heard the horn of a goods train making its way slowly around a sweeping left-hand curve in the track, and looked down.

If you make it, you land on the bridge and catch the train and you're home free. If you don't, you'll be hung up on those railings, and it won't matter any more.

Saturday, 2 September 1989

I T WAS JUST before 02:00 that I turned the corner and stopped. Thirty metres away, standing at the mouth of a narrow alley, was Huber. She hadn't seen me; her eyes were firmly fixed on what was happening at the far end of the street. A few seconds later I stepped up behind her, leaned forward and whispered in her ear, 'What's going on?'

Startled by my silent arrival, she turned to face me, and as though it was the most natural thing in the world her arms encircled my neck.

I slipped my right arm around her waist, pulled her closer, and looked over her right shoulder, down the street towards the house where we'd been living. The house from which we had started that night's operation to distribute the posters. I felt her loosen her grip and turn as she followed my gaze.

'They've found the safe house; they're arresting anyone inside.'

A safe house, as I said earlier, is traditionally a house that has no connection to the individuals or organisation that intend to take shelter there. But here in East Germany it went one step further. Here it meant that the house had not previously been visited by the police or Stasi so wasn't on their watch list. Such houses were also different as it appeared that the Bewegung only used them as meeting places. This was the second so-called safe house that had been raided since our arrival in Leipzig and, as you can imagine, my response to this latest piece of bad news was more than business-like.

'Have they found Bonsack, and the other two, Fischer and Mayer – Bonsack's minders?'

She turned and looked at me. 'I don't think so. There's been no sign of them.'

I was still staring down the street. 'Good. Then we can assume that they are still free and that the details surrounding Monday night's rally are still a secret.' I thought about the two men I had left standing on the roof back at the transport yard. It would appear that our informer, whoever they were, was still at their deadly game.

A movement on the other side of the street caught my attention. Partly shielded behind a lamp post, twenty metres closer to the action than we were, was the same KGB officer that had been sitting in the Volga that night in Zinnwald, but this time there was no sign of his car. It would appear that, as before, he was there purely as an observer and taking no active part in the operation happening less than one hundred metres away. Then, without warning, he turned towards us.

My first instincts were to turn around and, dragging Huber behind me, walk away smartly, but then I realised that might draw even more attention to us. Make him curious. So, with my arm still wrapped around her waist, I pulled her tight against me, then taking a step forward, I pushed her up against the wall and kissed her full on the lips. It was the only physical contact the two of us had ever had, and to my surprise, instead of trying to push me away, she pulled me closer, and slowly opened her mouth.

I looked at her eyes; they were closed. Without breaking the kiss, I rolled her gently to my right and off the wall. Putting her back to the Russian, I glanced over her right shoulder, I felt the weight of the Makarov as it moved in the waistband of my trousers. But using it, actually pulling the trigger, would be a last resort, and it was then that I decided to start carrying the silenced Sig.

To my relief, the Russian turned his attention back to what was happening at the other end of the street. He had apparently dismissed us as nothing more than a courting couple. I tried to break away, head further into the alley, but Huber seemed equally determined to hang on. A few seconds later, and with a firm grip on her right wrist, I headed deeper into the darkness.

'Do you know who that Russian is?'

Huber was scurrying after me, like a young child whose legs were too short to keep up. She turned her head and glanced between us and back over her right shoulder. 'No.'

'Well, we need to find out who he is, and quickly. That's the second time we've bumped into him. Turning up once is chance. Turning up twice is intentional. He's looking for something or someone.' I was now running on auto pilot. 'Did you torch my car?'

Huber was still smiling. 'Yes. Just like you told me to. I dumped it on some waste ground in the north of the city. Stuffed a rag into the filler pipe and set fire to it. By the time I reached the road, it was covered in flames. The body was already beginning to melt.'

'Good girl.'

It was a shame really. I had become quite attached to the old wreck, but as it was the only thing that could tie either of us to the posters, and after what had happened back at the transport yard, it had to go.

'Where's your car parked?'

'Where it always is, on the street behind the *Bahnhof* – the train station.'

'Right. Well we can't go back to the house so we need to find somewhere to get our heads down. Get some rest. Then, when it's light, I need to borrow your car. I have something I need to do, and it's far too dangerous for you to be involved.'

Huber began to protest, but I had stopped listening and was in the process of issuing fresh orders. 'I need you to find Bonsack and the others, but not a word to them about what happened at the bus station last night, or the appearance of the Russian officer here tonight. We need him to be on top of his game on Monday night. There's no need to feed any more crap into his life at this point – that will come later.'

Saturday, 2 September 1989

Schwarzbachtal

I MADE MY way up the lane towards the deserted farm where I'd hidden the Clansman twelve days earlier. Two hundred metres short of my destination, beside a small copse, I pulled Huber's car off the road and parked it beneath the trees.

I scanned the area for any signs of life. There was nothing, no vehicles; no one around. Ten minutes later, I was sitting on top of a stack of old pallets just inside the door of the barn. I picked up the 319's EMU and set to work preparing my message. As soon as I'd finished and had checked the contents, I checked the time.

It was 15:57. I was taking a huge risk visiting the farm and using the radio during daylight hours, but tucked away inside the barn, out of sight behind the farmhouse, I could work unseen, and without having to use a torch.

Using the EMU, once the message was composed, the rest of the process was simple. Sitting at the other end, as arranged during a short broadcast following the meeting in the *Gästehaus* in Leipzig, would be the young BRIXMIS officer I had met in the Dresdner Heide Forest. If he had followed my instructions he would now be sat alone in the communications room (Comcen) at London Block in the 1936 Berlin Olympic complex.

Three minutes later, on the stroke of 16:00, I pressed the send button. The message was gone; sent as a secure two-second-burst transmission. The 319's burst transmission capability made it extremely difficult to locate. Conversely, the longer the Bewegung's campaign went on, the more transmissions I would have to make, and the greater the chance of the GDR's Electronic Surveillance Unit (ESU) locating both the radio and me.

My message contained the date, time and location of the coming Monday night's rally. But, to keep the East German authorities in the dark for as long as possible, I had requested that the information not to be forwarded to the West German media until 16:00 on 4 September, the actual day of the rally, and that it was imperative it was broadcast at precisely 17:00 the same day.

Safe in the knowledge that the Lutheran Church openly supported the need for political reforms in East Germany, the hope was that after reading the posters a large number of Leipzig's citizens would tune into the Western broadcasts, and then gather in the courtyard of the Nikolaikirche (St Nicholas Church). If everything went to plan the rally would begin at 18:30, immediately after the weekly Friedensgebet (Prayer for Peace Service). It was done. The wheels were now in motion, but I was all too well aware that the East German government would not take this open act of defiance lying down – that there were going to be serious repercussions.

Monday, 18 September 1989

Leipzig

S INCE THAT FIRST gathering on 4 September, the numbers participating in each of the Bewegung's weekly rallies had steadily grown. The second meeting on 11 September had attracted over 1,200 people, and tonight more than 1,500 had turned out to show their support. It was clear that the East German people were warming to this new cause, and that even with the genuine threat of being arrested, beaten, and possibly much worse hanging over them, they were still refusing to be intimidated.

However, it was equally clear that the authorities were just as determined to stamp it out. Standing on the fringes of the crowd, I saw uniformed police, backed up by work combat troops, move in to arrest Bonsack and the other speakers, but before they could reach them, they were gone, spirited away by the crowd.

Moments later I spotted Huber heading in my direction, her face flushed with excitement.

'Come with me. I have someone I want you to meet.'

Well, hello, and it's good to see you as well.

With Huber leading the way, we moved quickly and without fuss through the centre of the crowd, eventually coming to a stop beside an elderly woman.

Huber tapped the old lady on the shoulder and she turned towards us.

'This is Klaudia. Until recently she worked as a cleaner at the Stasi headquarters in Dresden. If you can find the Russian officer you're interested in, point him out, and she will do her best to identify him for you.'

I knew the answer to my next question, and what I was looking for was confirmation.

'I didn't know that the Stasi and KGB shared the same building in Dresden?'

Huber spoke to the old woman in German and then turned to me. 'They don't. Apparently the two organisations have never trusted each other and the KGB are always in Stasi headquarters on Bautzner Straße, questioning the civilian workers, looking for information regarding Stasi operations.'

I smiled and began to scan the long line of grey-green, and brown uniforms that now surrounded the square, and eventually I saw one that stood out from all the rest. Taking Klaudia gently by the elbow, and speaking in a whisper, I guided her eyes on to the target.

'There, that's him, the Russian officer with the blue lapel tabs. Do you know who he is?'

The old woman studied the man's face. Her eyes were obviously not what they used to be, and she was struggling. A few seconds later, as if on cue, the Russian lifted his peak cap and smoothed back his hair with his left hand.

Klaudia spat on the floor. There was no hesitation. 'His name is Major Vladimir Putin. He is the head of the KGB here in Saxony.'

At the time the name meant nothing to me. However, the fact that he was the head of the KGB here in Saxony, and seemed to be taking more than a personal interest in what was going on, meant that the operations currently being conducted against members of the Bewegung by the Stasi were not run of the mill.

Wednesday, 27 September 1989
Schwarzbachtal

A S WORD OF events in Leipzig spread, supporters from other East German cities, notably Dresden, Zwickau and Karl-Marx-Stadt, were being drawn to Leipzig to attend the rallies. Two days earlier, on 25 September, with the grounds of the Nikolaikirche no longer large enough to accommodate them, over 8,000 people had filled nearby Karl-Marx-Platz to demonstrate their support. The rallies had also become a regular weekly event, and Bonsack's policy of peaceful protest was gathering pace. As a result, it was no longer necessary for me to broadcast the time and location of each rally to the Comcen in Berlin. In fact, with the support of the Lutheran church, and the Nikolaikirche being the ideal focal point, it had only been necessary for me to make one broadcast, the very first.

I was still no nearer to finding out anything about Operation Konev. However, if the information provided by Scott's man, whoever he was, was accurate, whatever Konev was, it was due to begin in just ten days' time. There was a Soviet Tank Regiment permanently stationed in Dresden, but as yet there had been no reports about additional troop movements, or the arrival of heavy weapons, tanks or artillery pieces in either the Dresden or Zinnwald area, so I was becoming increasingly sceptical. In fact, I was now having serious doubts as to whether Operation Konev had ever been real in the first place. That it wasn't just a clever piece of Soviet misinformation fed to Scott's man, Littman's replacement, the man who had originally fed Scott the information about Operation Konev, before he, like Littman, had also 'disappeared'. Maybe the operation had been nothing more than a deliberate attempt by the Soviets and East Germans to increase tensions between East and West?

★

It was just after 14:00 when I finished tightening the last wing nut on the oil tank's inspection hatch and heard the sound of a car making its way up the lane towards the farm. With the radio safely hidden back inside the tank, I headed for the farm's main entrance. Two minutes later, crouched down behind the dry-stone wall beside the main gate, I saw a car standing beside the copse where I had parked Huber's Trabant. It was a black Wartburg 353. Nobody got in or out. It just sat there, motionless, and I thought back to the night Huber and I came close to being caught outside the bus station in Leipzig.

A few minutes later the car began to move again, but instead of continuing up the lane towards the farm, it reversed back into the copse alongside Huber's car. Shortly afterwards two men dressed in civilian clothes appeared and, after what looked like a heated discussion, they began to walk up the lane towards me.

Given their build, I suspected they were the same two men who had chased me across the rooftops that night in Leipzig, and if that was the case, then – as in Leipzig – their arrival at the farm was not a coincidence.

The farm was situated at the top of the lane, in an elevated position – slightly higher than the copse where I had parked the Trabant – so I had control of the high ground with a good view of anything advancing up the lane and, if it came to a shootout, a clear line of sight. But I had no wish to get involved in a long-range gun battle, especially one that may have included the East German authorities, who would undoubtedly call for backup the minute things turned nasty. So, keeping low, I moved away from the gate and deeper into the farm complex.

Hidden behind the remains of the old pigsty, I watched as, with weapons drawn, their pistols hanging by their side, the two men entered the farmyard and separated. They knew that someone was here – the presence of Huber's car had told them that much – but if they were looking for me in particular, then only one person knew that I wasn't in Leipzig that afternoon, and she only knew because I was driving her car.

As the heavier of the two men disappeared into the farmhouse, I watched the other enter the barn beside the diesel tank. It was time to make a move. If I could find a way of getting between them and their car, disable the tiny short-range car radio carried by all police vehicles, and which I had to assume the Wartburg was carrying, then I might stand a chance of getting away.

It was time to move, but as I moved away from the protection of the wall and on to open ground, the man who had entered the barn reappeared less than fifty metres away. I froze as I watched him scan the surrounding area. Seconds later our eyes met.

Shit, time for Plan B.

The only problem was, there was no Plan B, but I now needed to come up with one very quickly. I turned and headed for the stable block at a run and, as I passed through the open double doors, I heard the shout go up.

'MANFRED – *Er ist hier draußen* [He is out here].'

I ignored the six wooden stalls that lined the right-hand side of a cobbled passageway and passed by without stopping. Pushing the Makarov into my belt, I pulled the Sig from the right-hand pocket of my jacket, the silencer from the left, and screwed it to the Sig's barrel.

The man reappearing from the barn had robbed me of my opportunity to get in between them and their car. My only chance of survival was to either kill or disable one, without alerting the second to my position.

Just beyond the last stall was what at one time had been a small tack area. The metal fixings where they once hung the saddles, reins and bridles were still bolted to the wall. Surrounding them was nothing but bricks: it was the end of the building, a dead end. I could go no further. This was part of my plan: no door or windows meant that the only way my pursuers could reach me was head on. Along the passageway. Whatever the outcome today, this is where it would happen.

I dragged a hay bale on to the floor and, as a large cloud of dust rose into the air, I fought back the urge to cough. I stood it on its end and pushed it tight against the wooden wall that separated the last stall from the tack area. I hoped that the wooden wall was thick enough to stop a round from a 9mm pistol, the weapons I had seen the two men carrying, but just in case it wasn't, the hay bale would catch anything that managed to get through.

Once again, doing what comes naturally to a soldier, I positioned myself behind the wooden wall of the stall and the hay bale, protecting both my head and body from incoming fire, while still giving me a clear view of the passageway and anyone stupid enough to venture along it.

I saw a shadow growing on the wall opposite the stable entrance. Seconds later, silhouetted by the sunlight that was streaming in behind him, I saw a figure turn into the passageway, and move slowly towards my position. I needed him to be as close as possible before making my move.

Judging by the speed with which he was making his way through the empty stalls, kicking open the doors, and clearing each one as he went, he apparently assumed that I had merely passed through the building as I made my escape.

I heard him kick open another door and check inside. There was only one more stall before he reached the tack area, and I adjusted my grip on the Sig. There was no way he could see me. I heard his boot strike the door, felt the vibration, and as it slammed into the wooden side of the stall, I instinctively lowered my head.

Down on one knee, and with my target now safely inside the last stall, I shifted a foot to my right, so that I could see out into the passageway and waited for him to make his move.

Finding the last stall empty, and apparently assuming I had moved on and out of the building, he had relaxed and lowered his weapon. As he re-entered the passageway and turned towards me, our eyes met for the second time and I squeezed the trigger of the silenced Sig – twice.

Members of the Green Army, non-Special Forces, are always taught to shoot at the centre of the largest visible mass, the priority being to hit and stop the target. But in an anti-terrorist situation, those where the lives of civilian hostages are at risk, during an aircraft, train, bus, or building siege, when your target may be sheltering behind an innocent woman or child, using them as a shield, such a strategy is both dangerous and unworkable. On such occasions, you may only have a clear shot at a terrorist's head, and I had spent enough time on the ranges, and in the Regiment's Killing House, to give me the confidence I needed to choose a very precise target.

As two perfectly placed rounds entered the man's left leg just above the knee, I saw his weapon fall to the floor. His mouth was wide open as he grabbed at his wounds with both hands, but there was no sound. It was as though the pain of being shot had frozen his vocal cords, and he collapsed silently on to the cobbled floor.

With the Sig now aimed at his head, I stood up and moved quietly along the passageway towards him. I was five feet away when he began to moan, the sound growing steadily louder with every step I took, and was now interspersed with swear words.

I raised the index finger of my left hand to my lips. '*Sprichst du Englisch?*'

He nodded his head.

'*Gut.* Not a word, if you make a sound before I tell you to, I *will* kill you. Do you understand?'

The man clenched his teeth and nodded his head again as he fought back the pain.

I squatted down beside him, picked up his discarded Makarov, slipped it into my jacket pocket, and pushed the muzzle of the Sig into his left temple. The building was silent once more.

It was over a minute later that I heard a man shouting.

'Dieter. Dieter, *wo bist du?*'

I poked the injured man in the head with the Sig. 'Call to him – Dieter.'

He hesitated. I moved the muzzle of the weapon from his temple to his left leg and began to slowly screw the end of the silencer into one of his two open wounds. It was enough.

'Ahg . . . *Ich bin hier in*, Manfred. *In den stallen.*'

Having served his purpose, I seriously considered killing him, permanently removing the problem, but the cold-blooded murder of a defenceless man is not a soldier's way. In a single movement, I raised the Sig diagonally across my body to my left shoulder and brought the barrel down smartly against his temple. Knocking him out cold.

Holding the Sig in both hands, arms outstretched and raised to shoulder height, I made my way quickly, but calmly, down the passageway to the stall nearest the stable entrance. Crouched just inside, I left the stall door half open and, although I had a clear view of the unconscious body lying at the far end of the passageway, I was hidden from anybody entering the building behind me.

Someone was moving around outside the stable entrance, but I didn't have all day. The longer this went on the more dangerous my position would become. Then there was Dieter, the man I had just shot in the leg and knocked out. He was currently unconscious, but if he came round and found himself alone there was a good chance he would try to warn his friend. It was time to speed things up. Time to let whoever was out there know that someone was in here. Squatting down, with my back resting against the wooden wall, I rested the fully cocked Sig on my right thigh. I removed the Makarov I had taken from Dieter from my jacket pocket, slid back the magazine release button at the base of the pistol grip, and it dropped silently on to the hay-covered floor. I pulled back the top slide and ejected the live round from the chamber. Now empty and perfectly safe, holding the weapon by its barrel, I threw it against the wooden side of the stall creating a loud bang. Seconds later I heard footsteps enter the stable block and move along the passage behind me.

'Dieter?'

Dieter didn't answer but, as his partner turned the corner, he could see his motionless body lying at the far end of the passageway.

The man moved quickly past my position and knelt down beside his unconscious partner.

I smiled sarcastically to myself.

It would appear that Plan B is working.

Still protected behind the wooden sides of the stall, and with the man's back to me, I slowly stood up. I raised the Sig to shoulder height and lined up the foresight on the back of his head, the point where the base of the skull connects to the spine. It would be so easy to kill him, but I needed answers.

To my surprise, although the adrenaline was coursing through my veins, my voice remained calm and controlled as I spoke to him in German.

'Don't move. Put your weapon on the floor. Stand up . . . slowly.'

He hesitated at first. I thought for a brief moment that he was considering putting up a fight, but then he apparently thought better of it. Standing upright, with his weapon at his feet, he raised both hands.

'Turn around. Slowly.'

As he turned I got my first look at his face and immediately recognised him. As far as I knew, the man facing me was not a member of the KGB or the Stasi, but he was one of Metzger's goons. He was the 'Butler', the man who had pushed me in the back as I stood in the passage, before standing obediently behind Metzger that night at the church in Zinnwald.

With my weapon trained on him I moved out of the stall and walked along the passage. Dieter, the man I had shot earlier, was beginning to come round. I glanced down at him, but unarmed, and with two rounds in his left leg, he was hardly a threat. I turned my attention back to the second man. There was no need to continue the conversation in German, I knew that the Butler spoke English.

'Keep your hands up, and kick your weapon over here.'

As his weapon came to a stop a foot in front of me, I issued my next set of instructions. 'Now kneel. Interlock your fingers and put your hands on top of your head, where I can see them.'

He did as he was ordered.

'Now cross your legs at the ankle and sit back on them.'

Again, he did as I said.

I moved closer. 'What's your name?'

There was no hesitation. With his friend lying wounded beside him, and my Sig pointing at his head, he had nothing to lose and everything to gain by being cooperative.

'Manfred. Manfred Adler.'

I had relaxed slightly. As Adler and his partner were not members of the East German authorities, I was fairly certain there would be no radio in their car, which meant there was no way they could have called for backup before making their way along the lane and up to the farm. The lane was also a dead end, and the farm that stood at its head was surrounded by nothing but open countryside. All of which meant there was only one way a vehicle could approach it, head on, up the lane, and I would hear it coming long before it arrived. Although time wasn't limitless, I felt I had enough to get the answers I required.

'Well, Manfred, your answers to my questions will determine whether you and your partner live or die. Do you understand?'

There was no point in playing nice, these people lived in a harsh world, one where human life meant very little, and any show of kindness on my part would be seen as nothing more than a sign of weakness.

Like any good interrogator, I already knew the answer to some of the questions I would ask. What I was looking for was confirmation that Adler would tell me the truth – before I moved on to the questions to which I did not have the answers.

'Metzger sent you here today? Correct?'

Adler nodded his head.

'To do what?'

Adler looked down at his wounded partner who, although in lots of pain, was now wide awake. Adler lifted his head and looked at me once more. 'We were to try and find your radio.'

How does Metzger know I have a radio? I thought back to my conversation with Metzger at the bar on the outskirts of Zinnwald. *I'm only here to observe and report back . . . And how exactly are you going to do that?* Because he had already guessed.

'And if you found it you were to bring it back to him? Correct?'

Adler nodded his head again.

The answer to every question I would ask Adler from now on would have a consequence, and the answer to my next question would determine what I did with the 'Clansman' when this day was over.

'Who told you I was here?'

Adler looked puzzled. 'Nobody told us you were here.'

I extended my right arm. The end of the silencer was now less than half a metre from his forehead.

Fearing he was about to be shot, Adler began to panic. 'It's the truth! After you left the Projects, Metzger told us to check all the buildings in the surrounding area. This farm was just the next on the list. It was pure chance that we recognised Huber's car under the trees in the lane.'

I smiled to myself.

Yeah, that powder blue colour will definitely catch your eye.

I wondered if Metzger had known my whereabouts in Zinnwald all along. There was only one way to find out. 'Did Metzger know the location of the safe house in the Projects?'

Adler stared at me like I was some kind of idiot. 'Of course.'

'How?'

'The same way he knew you had a radio and where to find you that night we chased you over the rooftops in Leipzig. Somebody told him.'

'Who?'

'I don't know – I swear. Metzger never tells us any more than we need to know.'

Besides Huber and me, there were only three other people who knew that I had the radio and where we would be that Friday night – Bonsack and his two minders, Fischer and Mayer. Those who had been present at the bar that night. The list of suspects was getting smaller. Could it possibly be Bonsack? At the time I'd first met them in the church at Zinnwald, Metzger and Bonsack, although outwardly polite to each other, had seemed to be at odds, pursuing totally different agendas – Bonsack being quite happy to try and achieve his goals through peaceful means, while Metzger was, like Bill Sykes in *Oliver Twist,* intent on travelling a more violent path.

It had been clear from the start that Metzger and I were never going to be friends, but in the last few minutes that had all changed. I was beginning to realise that something else – something much more disturbing – was going on and there was only one way to find out what. I turned my attention back to Adler.

'If Metzger knew where I was in Zinnwald, why didn't he come after me straight away?'

Adler stared at me, only this time it would appear that I was not so much of an idiot. 'He knew that sooner or later you would need to report back to your organisation in London. That meant that, somehow, they would have to provide you with the means to do so and, as you can't just telephone, it would have to be a radio. Metzger was never interested in you. He only ever wanted your radio.'

Adler was right; there was no way I could just phone HQ. I had asked one of the American team if it was possible to get a phone call out to the West during my first visit to Zinnwald three years earlier. He had just burst out laughing.

Sure, you go to the main police station in Dresden and book a call. They will tell you to come back the next day, maybe even the day after.

Then, once you arrive, they will sit you down on the opposite side of a table to a Stasi officer, one who speaks perfect English, who will listen to every word you say with his finger hovering over the cut-off switch.

But I wasn't finished, what Adler was telling me made little sense.

'Why does Metzger need a radio? It will be no use to him here in East Germany and now, with the Monday night peace rallies beginning to grow, there's no way any Western government will abandon the process. Not in favour of Metzger's ludicrous plan for some form of violent armed rebellion.'

Adler sneered at me. His confidence was growing.

'The plan for an armed uprising was only ever a front. Metzger thought it might win over those of the movement that were still undecided. He always had another plan.'

I didn't have time to play twenty questions and lifted the Sig again. 'What?'

Adler stuttered. 'Di . . . did you know that the Russian president, Mikhail Gorbachev, is due to visit East Germany on October the seventh, as part of the DDR's fortieth anniversary celebrations?'

I didn't, but it was the first time I had heard 7 October, the date given to Scott, linked to a particular event. But what, if anything, did that have to do with Operation Konev or any large-scale military action.

'No. But what's that got to do with Metzger and his master plan?'

'Metzger is going to kill him.'

I couldn't hide my surprise and laughed out loud. 'Who? Gorbachev?'

However, Adler wasn't laughing. He was deadly serious. 'Yes.'

I stopped laughing, but said nothing. If what he was telling me was true, the ramifications for both East Germany and, possibly, the whole of Western Europe were staggering.

'Why? Doesn't he realise what will happen if Gorbachev is killed on East German soil?'

The panic was once again growing in Adler's eyes, and his voice became shaky. 'I don't know why. All Metzger will say is that the orders have come directly from Moscow.'

My mind was buzzing, but the tone of my voice was bordering on the dismissive. 'And why would Moscow want Gorbachev dead?'

The strain was now beginning to show on Adler's face and he

continued without being prompted. 'Mikhail Gorbachev has become very unpopular in Moscow. Certain elements, especially among the more senior members of the Politburo and KGB, are not happy with his new *glasnost* initiative.'

'And what does Metzger get out of this? I thought you Germans hated the Russians, so why are you going to do their dirty work for them?' Again, for some reason, I was looking for yet more confirmation of this staggering news. Trying to make sense of what he had just told me. Information that turned on their head all my assumptions of East versus West and the way the Cold War worked.

There was a hint of venom in Adler's voice when he replied. 'We do. More than someone like you can ever imagine. But Metzger's priority is to ensure the Bewegung doesn't succeed.'

I shook my head in disbelief. Adler's answer was weak, to say the least.

'That may well be true. But a public assassination? It's never going to happen. Even if Metzger succeeded in killing Gorbachev, there's no way he would personally survive the attack.'

Adler looked at me and I raised the Sig.

'Metzger's not stupid. He's not going to do the job himself! The assassination will be carried out by someone else.'

I was rapidly losing patience. 'OK, listen up. Only giving me half the story is really beginning to piss me off. Who?'

Adler was stuttering again. 'A . . . A three-man cell of the Red Army Faction.'

I knew all about the RAF, or *Rote Armee Fraktion* as they called themselves. In 1970, Andreas Baader, Gudrun Ensslin, Horst Mahler and Ulrike Meinhof formed an association which, at the time, described itself as a communist, anti-Imperialist, 'urban guerrilla' organisation engaged in an armed struggle with the West. They had carried out numerous bombings, shootings and arson attacks on both business and government targets in western Europe over the course of three decades. The Western media, West German government and the military even, soon started calling them the 'Baader-Meinhof Gang' or the 'Baader-Meinhof Group'.

The group's activity peaked in 1977, when on 7 April they had assassinated Siegfried Buback, the attorney-general of West Germany.

Three months later on 30 July they had failed in their attempt to kidnap and murder banker Jürgen Ponto.

On 5 September, the RAF kidnapped Martin Hanns Schleyer, the president of the Federation of German Industries (BDI). The following month, on 13 October, Lufthansa Flight 181, a Boeing 737 named *Landshut*, was hijacked by members of the Popular Front for the Liberation of Palestine (PFLP). The hijackers demanded the release of ten RAF members detained at the Stammheim Prison, two Palestinian compatriots being held in Turkey and a large ransom in exchange for the hostage's release.

The West German government decided that it would not negotiate with terrorists and the 'German Autumn' ended on 18 October when the West German counter-terrorism group 'GSG9' stormed the aircraft in Mogadishu, Somalia. Although all eighty-six passengers were rescued, in revenge for the attack by GSG9, the RAF murdered Hanns Martin Schleyer. On the same day, three leading figures of the first generation of the RAF were found dead in their prison cells at Stammheim.

The group is often talked about in terms of generations.

The 'first generation' consisted of Baader, Ensslin, Meinhof and others. The 'second generation' came about after the majority of the first generation was arrested in 1972. The 'third generation' RAF existed in the 1980s, 1990s and up to 1998.

Although the group had started life as a West German-based terrorist group, Western intelligence and law enforcement agencies had long suspected that the organisation was now receiving financial and logistical support from the Stasi. It was thought the Stasi were also providing its members with shelter, new identities and a haven when they were not carrying out their operations in the West. On 4 October 1990, the *Washington Post* reported that:

> *A former high-ranking East German intelligence official, who recently fled to the West, offered details on how his country became a central base for international terrorism.*
>
> *The defector, who insisted on anonymity, described a GDR that had been a haven for terrorists of all kinds. 'Carlos' (Illich Ramirez Sanchez), an international terror chieftain, was welcomed to East Berlin, as were*

George Habash, head of the Popular Front for the Liberation of Palestine,
Abu Nidal, the ultra-radical Palestinian, and Abu Daoud, who organised
the massacre of the Israeli Olympic team at Munich in 1972. Yasser Arafat,
the PLO leader, was also a frequent visitor. In East German training camps,
terrorists and would-be terrorists were taught sabotage and related arts – some
of the 'students' were Sandinistas, others were Chilean 'dissidents'.

Confirming what Western intelligence agencies had long suspected to be the case. From personal experience, I can confirm that during my time in Rhodesia – now Zimbabwe – members of both Joshua Nkomo's Zipra and Robert Mugabe's Zanla organisations were receiving terrorist training at state-sponsored camps in East Germany, as well as in Russia and China.

I continued to stare at Adler as I recalled Metzger, a few weeks earlier, asking me, 'Have we met before?'

We hadn't, I was sure of that. But it was at that point that I wondered if he had seemed familiar because he had been one of those faces in the rogues gallery of terrorists that hung on the guardroom noticeboards in BAOR.

'Metzger is Baader Meinhof – RAF – isn't he?'

Adler lowered his voice. 'Yes. He was one of the original group. Metzger isn't his real name.'

Without realising it, Adler had just answered the second part of the puzzle. On a personal level, in order to ensure his own survival, Metzger couldn't afford for Bonsack and his peaceful group to succeed. If that happened and relations between East and West improved, every law enforcement service in Europe that had a score to settle with Baader-Meinhof, which was most of them, would be across the border and hunting them down at the first opportunity. Without the Stasi to protect them Metzger and the rest of his organisation would be marked for destruction.

I leaned closer to Adler. 'And how exactly is Metzger going to convince this three-man RAF cell to commit suicide?'

Adler dropped his head and lowered his voice once more. 'He has threatened to kill their families. Their parents, wives, children, everybody, if they refuse to go through with it.'

This guy is a real piece of work, and I thought the IRA was bad.

It was then that I remembered what Adler had told me a few minutes earlier.

'You just told me that Metzger never tells you any more than you need to know. So, what's different now? How do you know what he has planned?'

Adler sounded tired, like giving me each new piece of information was a marathon effort. 'Metzger couldn't set this up on his own. It's far too big for one man. I've been with him since the very beginning. He trusts me more than most.'

'I want details. Where and when this attack will take place.'

Adler was stuttering again. 'I . . . I don't know when and where. Nobody does. Not even the three men who are going to carry out the attack know that. Only Metzger knows the exact time and place.'

Adler's answer had some logic behind it. I had spent years living in an environment where the success of an operation relied on the 'need to know' principle. And, if this really was being orchestrated by elements in Moscow, they would be paranoid about anybody – and certainly not some possibly loose-tongued terrorists – knowing the details until the last possible moment. If word of this plot got back to Gorbachev's people, then they would be dead, not the president.

'So, when will these three men find out the when and where?'

Adler dropped his head and looked at his partner. 'Not until October the seventh. On the morning of the attack.' Then rather excitedly and eager to please, he added, 'But they are already in Berlin, along with their vehicles and weapons. Metzger will phone them with the exact time and location of the assault at eight o'clock that morning.'

I was still puzzled. It was now obvious what Metzger and his group had to gain from all this but, as for the rest of those involved, those back in Moscow who had orchestrated the plan, what was their strategy? What did they have to gain? I extended my arm again, pushed the barrel of the Sig even closer to Adler's forehead.

'What do the Old Guard and the KGB have to gain by killing Gorbachev here in East Germany? Given the security that will surround Gorbachev's visit, its chances of success are minimal. Why not just blow up his car on a Moscow street and blame it on someone like the Georgian separatists?'

Adler stared at me. The stress position I had put him in was now taking its toll. His body would be sore and tired.

'Metzger said that even if Gorbachev doesn't die while he's in East Germany, the mere fact that the attempt was made here would give the Russians just what they want. They will inevitably blame the Bewegung of orchestrating the plot. At the same time, they'll accuse Erich Honecker and his SED party of having lost control of the people. Gorbachev's murder will be the excuse the Russian Old Guard and the KGB need to retake control of the DDR, their only buffer against the NATO forces stationed in West Germany.'

I said nothing, but my mind was racing.

It would be Hungary all over again.

It was then that I remembered what I had read during my visit to the British Library, following my meeting with Scott in Victoria Park: *Shortly after his appointment, Konev led the Soviet Invasion of Hungary to suppress the Revolution.*

Operation Konev wasn't a proposed Soviet invasion of Czechoslovakia, or necessarily the assassination of the Russian president. Gorbachev's murder, or merely the attempt itself, was the catalyst. The trigger for the Soviets to retake full control of East Germany. If I was right, there would be no need for the Soviets to re-invade East Germany – they were already here.

Even as late as 1991 – close to a year after the two German states were officially reunited – and even though the Soviet withdrawal had already begun, around 338,000 Soviet troops still occupied 777 barracks at 276 locations on the territory formally known as the German Democratic Republic. It would simply be a matter of deployment – starting the engines and putting men and tanks out on the streets.

It was all beginning to make sense.

I turned my attention back to Adler.

'OK. So, given his elevated position and the support the RAF receives from both the Stasi and the KGB, why does Metzger still need my radio?'

Adler was staring at his partner lying on the cobbles beside him. His blood loss had been minimal. Leg wounds are like that, unless of course you hit a major artery. However, like all bullet wounds, especially those where bones are involved, the pain can be excruciating – which is why the IRA were so fond of kneecappings.

Desperate for medical attention, he now started pleading.

'Tell him, Manfred! Tell him everything you know. Everything you suspect.'

Adler lifted his head again. 'The Stasi and the KGB are not the only intelligence organisations that Metzger works for. He also has important contacts in the West. Contacts he would rather his masters here in East Germany and Moscow knew nothing about. Your radio will provide him with the means to communicate with these people and organisations directly . . . whenever he wants . . . without the KGB or Stasi knowing what he's up to.'

The logical response to Adler's statement would be, well yes, it's no surprise that the leader of an East German freedom movement would have contacts within the Western intelligence community. It was a well-known fact that Western intelligence agencies were doing what they could to support democracy movements, seizing any chance they could to antagonise the Soviet Bloc by supporting the troublemakers within. But the Bewegung was a relatively new player, with what appeared to be little or no central command structure, which might well make them of little interest to the CIA, for example. And that assassinating the Russian president was the last thing any Western government would want to happen right now. It was quite clear to me there were still nefarious elements to Metzger's plotting I hadn't yet understood.

Adler had fed me just enough information to prompt a string of additional questions.

'If Metzger's networks are as large as you say he will need to keep records: the telephone numbers, radio frequencies, and grid references of Dead Letter Drops. That's far too much information for one man to commit to memory. Where does he keep his files?'

Given how tightly Metzger played his cards to his chest, Adler was rapidly running out of answers and I heard him sigh. 'I don't know, and that's the truth!'

My mind returned to the meeting I'd had with Metzger in the bar just outside Zinnwald and the small object, probably a notebook, he had pushed across the counter to the barman.

'What's the relationship between Metzger and the barman at the bar used by the mineworkers?'

Adler's eyes lit up; at last, he had an answer. 'The landlord? He and Metzger are cousins.'

'Is the landlord RAF?'

'Yes. But not like Metzger. He's just a foot soldier, like Dieter and me.'

My mind drifted back three years to February 1986.

'What do you know about someone called Littman?'

Adler cocked his head. 'Thomas Littman?'

'The very man. Do you know where he is now?'

It is generally accepted by interrogators that when a prisoner or suspect glances to the right, the observer's left, it usually reveals a creative process – he or she is 'making up' the facts – lying. However, a glance up and to the left, to the observer's right, reveals that the subject is remembering facts – telling the truth. Adler's eyes were firmly fixed on the ceiling beam to my right. He was in the process of remembering.

'He's dead. Lying at the bottom of a ventilation shaft in Zinnwald.'

'What happened?'

'Metzger found out he was working for British intelligence and, after interrogating him, slit his throat.'

'How did Metzger find out Littman was working for the British?'

Adler took a deep breath. 'I don't know exactly. All I know is that when Metzger returned from a trip to West Germany, he knew. Someone in the West had told him about Littman.'

Maybe Scott's right. Maybe there is a mole within MI6.

'OK. I have one last question. Once you found the radio, what did Metzger tell you to do with me?'

I already knew the answer. In fact I had a good idea what Metzger had planned for me from that first meeting, but I needed to hear Adler say the words out loud. It was as though they would somehow give me the justification for what I had to do next. I raised the Sig and pointed it at his forehead.

He blurted out the answer. 'We were told to kill you and dispose of your body.'

It was over. I had no more questions and, realising that, Dieter, the wounded man, began to beg for his life. I closed my ears. I had no other choice. I was alone in East Germany and rapidly running out of friends and places to hide. Both Adler and his partner were self-confessed members of a major terrorist organisation who had been told to murder me. If I let them live, especially knowing what I did now, they would report straight back to Metzger. Even if I handed them over to the police, given that they worked for the Stasi, they would probably be released and I would be counting my life in hours. What's more, I was probably the only Westerner in the world who knew about the RAF plot to kill Gorbachev, and the consequences if it were allowed to happen.

Given my personal circumstances, totally alone and under threat, the conversation with Adler may appear to be unnecessarily – even dangerously – long. But I needed answers. I needed to know what I was up against if I was going to stand any chance of surviving the coming days and weeks.

It's convention in SAS thrillers that the soldier is briefed on the over-arching plan – which of course makes the story more interesting for the reader. In reality, soldiers are rarely provided with the big picture. They are given a very specific, very practical task and told to go in, get it done, and get out again, no questions asked. But because Operation Konev wasn't turning out to be the straightforward military recce I'd been led to believe, I started to question the bigger picture. And as things became clearer, I realised that discovering the identity of the traitor in our midst would be crucial to my getting out of here alive.

When Adler and his partner had pulled their guns, and followed me into the farm complex that afternoon, there was only one way the day could end. Only one side would be coming out alive and, because of that, I now had 'no other choice'. And that's what I've been telling myself every day for close to thirty years.

I lowered the Sig and shot Adler twice in the chest. His body swayed back against his thighs and, as I saw the blood begin to flow on his shirt, he fell face first on to the floor, his hands still on his head. Moments later, as the blood began to work its way along the cracks between the cobbles, his partner Dieter began to crawl towards me. But, having already killed Adler, again I was left with no other choice. There was nothing else I could do. I looked him in the eyes.

'*Es tut mir wirklich leid.*' (I am truly sorry.)

Staring down at their dead bodies, I shot each man once more in the head.

★

I quickly went through their pockets, removing all forms of identification, anything that would link them to the Bewegung, anything that might somehow implicate me. I found the keys to the Wartburg in Adler's trouser pocket. Then, one at a time, I dragged their lifeless corpses out of the stable block and into the open area beside the pigsty. I lifted the heavy metal grid that covered what looked like an old slurry pit, rolled them in, one on top of the other, and watched as their bodies slowly disappeared below the surface. It was time to leave the farm and head back to Leipzig, but before I left I had one last thing to do.

Back at the copse, I went through the interior of the Wartburg and, as I had done with Adler and his partner, removed anything that would tie it to the Bewegung.

The boot was empty, not even an oily rag, which immediately raised my suspicions. The East Germans didn't have the type of relationship we in the West have with our cars, and finding one with an empty spotless boot prompted me to ask whether something else was going on? It's the type of thing a child would do – tidy up in order to hide something it didn't want found. I was pretty confident that Adler and his partner wouldn't have risked moving me once they'd killed me, and it could well have been me who was now lying in the slurry pit instead of them. I went back into the car and removed the bottom section of the rear seat. Wrapped in a rag wedged into a recess in the car's bodywork, I found two Russian-made RGD-5 hand grenades. They were flimsy compared to those currently in use by British and American forces, but that didn't mean they were any less deadly.

Where there's one, there will be more.

I shifted my attention to the other side of the car, and there it was, stuffed into an identical recess. I unwrapped the rag. Inside was a Czechoslovakian Škorpion vz. 61. Also known as a Model of 61, a 9mm submachine gun. Besides the Claymore anti-personnel mine, those originally manufactured by the Americans, and now copied by every country on the planet, the British Army's biggest fear was that the Czech Škorpion would find its way on to the streets of Northern Ireland in large numbers. However, it wasn't its impressive rate of fire – 850 rounds a minute – that worried them. It was the fact that with the stock folded away you could conceal it in a woman's handbag.

Being a regular soldier and working on the simple theory of 'finder's keepers', I immediately wanted to take it with me, but then I reconsidered. It's not as if I had anywhere to hide it. So, dropping one of the Russian grenades into my pocket, I stuffed the Škorpion and the second grenade back into the car and replaced the seat.

For a split-second I thought about going back up to the farm and using the 319 radio but just as quickly dismissed the idea. The only people I could have spoken to were BRIXMIS, but I was in no frame of mind to share what I had just learned from Adler – or that I had just killed two men.

As I drove down the lane in Huber's Trabant and began my journey back to Leipzig, I considered what I had done and its consequences. I wouldn't have to worry about Metzger going to the authorities; there was no way he would admit to any involvement in what had happened this afternoon. But our differences would still have to be settled. And then there was the guilt. This wasn't the first time I had killed, but before this afternoon it had only ever been in combat, in a 'kill or be killed' situation. But now, working for Scott, I had been forced to cross the line; the line that separates a professional soldier from a state-run assassin.

Wednesday, 27 September 1989

Leipzig

B Y 19:20 IT was dark and I was back in Leipzig, sitting alone in the *Gästehaus* on the corner of Goethstraße. I had been there for the best part of an hour, was on my third cup of coffee – which wasn't getting any better – and my legs and arse were once again rapidly becoming casualties of the tiny chairs. I was still trying to get my head around what Adler had told me. If I had been anywhere else in Europe I would have said he was mad, but this was East Germany and, given that Metzger was Baader-Meinhof, logic counted for nothing.

If Adler had been telling the truth, then what Metzger had planned for me was nothing personal. He couldn't have cared less who it was that had turned up in East Germany as long as they brought a radio with them. You have to put yourself in Metzger's position. He was about to try and assassinate the president of the Soviet Union, one of the most powerful men in the world and, as such, he would know exactly what the fallout would be.

He would know that, whether the team in Berlin were successful or not, if the Soviets retook control of East Germany, there would be no guarantee that his life would remain the same. Some might think that he would be treated as a hero of the Soviet Union, while in reality those back in Moscow, those who were ultimately responsible for planning Gorbachev's assassination, might well be looking for a scapegoat. Someone to pin the blame on, in an effort to placate the Soviet people, those to whom Gorbachev had promised so much. There was no guarantee that they wouldn't simply arrest every member of the Red Army Faction they could find. However, if Adler was right and Metzger did have contacts in the West, the only value he had to them was if he could keep providing vital information. Make himself invaluable to the outcome of what would soon become a ramped-up Cold War. But in order to do that he would need a way of keeping his channels of communication open, while at the same time ensuring that the KGB and Stasi never found out what he was up to. And for that to happen he needed my radio.

For my part I had to assume that as soon as the assassination attempt was made, all access to the Eastern Bloc would be put on hold; all air and land borders would be closed. Even the road and rail links which ran along the NATO 'corridor' from Helmstedt to Berlin – those through which NATO military personnel were permitted to travel – would be suspended. Further increasing the tension between East and West, while at the same time making my return to the West near impossible.

I had no idea how I was going to let Scott know what I'd found out, not before it happened. There was no way I could risk doing it by radio and involving the BRIXMIS officer. Not without being a hundred per cent sure that he would be sitting there alone at the other end. Openly broadcasting news like this would send shock waves around the world. Besides, even if I could get the information to Scott, what could he do about it? It's not as if he could send in the Regiment to stop Metzger and his team. Or get Maggie Thatcher to phone Moscow and tell Gorbachev that he was about to be assassinated.

Part of me said, sod it. Preventing the Russian president from being murdered by his own side was not my problem. After all, the Soviet Union is the sworn enemy of NATO, so maybe I should just let Metzger's men get on with it. But just sitting back and letting it happen would involve taking a huge gamble. I knew that regardless of where Gorbachev was murdered, whether it was here in East Germany, or even deep inside the Kremlin, the Old Guard and hardliners in the Politburo would insist that the West had somehow orchestrated it.

The same had happened on 22 November 1963, but of course, on that occasion, the boot had been on the other foot. Then it had been the 'Hawks' in the US Senate who insisted the KGB had somehow been complicit in the assassination of President John F. Kennedy and, thankfully, although there had been some very serious sabre rattling on both sides, eventually it came to nothing. But now, with Eastern Europe in turmoil, and the Soviet Union struggling to keep control of its Warsaw Pact allies, such accusations could be even more dangerous.

In fact, what worried me most was that if Metzger's men succeeded, and Gorbachev was murdered here, on East German soil, it would give the Soviets exactly what they wanted: an excuse to retake control of the country, plunging Europe into crisis, and bringing the world closer to war than it had been since the Americans and Russians faced each other across what remained of Berlin in 1945. Back then, as allies, and having just defeated the Nazis, for a few crucial hours it was touch and go as to whether they would turn on each other, and the Second World War would continue. Even if on this occasion it didn't come to all-out war, with the Soviets once again in complete control of East Germany – and with the heightened security – there was no way I was getting out.

I watched Huber walk across the bar and take her seat on the opposite side of the table, but there was no friendly greeting from me, what I needed was information.

'Did you find Bonsack and the others?'

'Yes, they're on their way. But we have to move again. The police raided the safe house on Bahnhofstraße early this afternoon. Luckily no one was there when they arrived.'

That was another thing that was puzzling me: the way that Huber and Bonsack and I had managed to stay one step ahead of the East German police and Stasi. It had been clear to me since the night I was chased across the rooftops in Leipzig that either Bonsack, Fischer, Mayer or Huber, one of those who had been present at the meeting back in August, was a traitor. So, the big question was: *Why are we all still free?*

Sunday, 1 October 1989

Dresdner Heide Forest

I T'S AN UNWRITTEN rule that no two RVs are ever held at the same location, but sticking rigidly to such rules can at times create their own problems. With every new grid, and with both sides normally operating at night, and on unfamiliar ground, the chances that one side – in this case, either me or the BRIXMIS Tour – might fuck up and get it wrong are greatly increased.

I took one last look at the map, folded it, and slid it beneath the passenger seat of the Trabant. The days were getting shorter and, as a result, the nights were longer and much colder, and there was dampness in the air, but I was happiest out here – alone. There is something safe and very comforting about the smell of a forest at night, and that feeling of closeness that comes with the dark.

Using my Silva compass, I headed north-northeast through the Dresdner Heide Forest. I held that bearing for six minutes, about 500 metres, before swinging due west and coming at the RV from the opposite side. There, parked nose out beneath the trees, on the edge of a small clearing, was the familiar sight of the BRIXMIS Mercedes G Wagon.

I had spent the last three days trying to figure out what I was going to do about Metzger and his master plan to bring Europe to the brink of yet another world war. Then, that morning, sitting alone in the kitchen, I remembered something that had been said to me many years before: *The only thing necessary for the triumph of evil is for good men to do nothing.* It was a quote by Edward Burke, and it was then that I made my decision, but before I did anything I would first need to establish my fallback position.

Seconds later I was standing beside the driver's door of the Mercedes. The driver flinched as he turned and saw me, but as he began to lower the window I heard someone step up behind me.

I reached into my jacket, wrapped my hand around the handle of the Sig tucked into the front of my belt and, as I spun around, I pulled back the hammer with my thumb and raised the weapon to head height.

With the Sig's muzzle digging into his forehead, the Tour officer inhaled sharply and held his breath. A split second later, his eyes widened and filled with horror as, holding back the hammer with my thumb, he watched me squeeze the trigger and return the weapon to the half-cocked.

'Creeping up on people like that will get you killed one day, Boss.'

As I lowered the weapon, I heard him breathe out and saw him smile nervously.

'Sorry. I was just making sure you weren't being followed. Believe me, it will never happen again.'

I tucked the Sig back into my belt. 'No problem, it's not as if anybody died – this time.'

I could still feel his body trembling as I laid my hand on his shoulder. 'I want one final meet. At this location on October the tenth.' By then it would all be over.

The officer stared at me. 'A repeat?'

'Yes. I can't afford for anything to go wrong – for us to somehow miss each other.'

'Time?'

'O–three–fifteen?'

The officer's eyes were questioning, but in the end he said nothing and seemed prepared to let it go.

But it wasn't that easy. If my plan was going to stand any chance of success, his involvement was crucial. There were things I needed him to do. I had messages for him to relay, and in order for him to achieve that there were things he needed to know.

'My work here will be done by then. Tell London I have what they want, and I'm ready to come in. Tell them I can get myself to Prague, but I need a new British passport, complete with tourist visa and flight tickets back to the UK. And that I'm expecting you to bring them with you to the meeting on the tenth.'

The officer grinned as he shook my hand. 'Wilco.'

Monday, 2 October 1989

Leipzig

IT WAS ONLY five days before Metzger's team were due to make their bid to assassinate Mikhail Gorbachev and, as a result, I was in a constant mental struggle, worrying what I should do about it. My daily routine was now becoming tedious and, as a result, the paranoia was increasing. I spent most days lying low, staying away from crowds and familiar places. Even when sitting alone in a quiet coffee shop or bar, I was always looking over my shoulder, searching for someone who didn't fit in, planning my escape route as soon as I sat down. Although the regular Monday night rallies with their attendant police, troops and added security measures brought the chances of arrest even closer, it was all out in the open. I could see the enemy, the threat, which also meant I had something genuine to focus on.

I made my way through the crowds crammed into Karl-Marx-Platz and found Huber exactly where we had agreed. Standing beside the wall that surrounded the Nikolaikirche. She looked nervous and, as I drew alongside her, she grabbed my hand and squeezed it. For a second or two it gave me a warm sort of comfort.

'Where have you been?'

I turned my back to the wall, and with my eyes wandering over the crowd I said, 'There are roadblocks everywhere; the whole city is crawling with police and troops. I had to park your car on the industrial estate behind the bus station.' I turned towards her, and for the briefest of moments I saw the excitement in her eyes.

'They are expecting over ten thousand people to attend tonight's rally.'

I looked around me; I had never seen so many people crammed into the square, and the noise was deafening.

'That's great news.' But as the words left my mouth, her expression changed. She had bad news as well. 'What's wrong?'

'In response, the authorities have drafted in a huge number of police, militia and work-combat troops.' She paused; there was more. 'And this afternoon Erich Honecker issued a *Schießbefehl*, a shoot-to-kill order to the military.'

I wasn't surprised at her last piece of news. We had been incredibly lucky up to now, but with the rallies being held at the same location, at the same time, and on the same day every week, it meant the authorities had plenty of time to prepare.

Although, as always, the atmosphere at the rally was charged with a mixture of hope for a better future and a fear for what the authorities might do to those attending it, tonight there was something else: there was a new, more confident kind of optimism that I had not experienced at previous rallies. As the rally drew to a close, watching from the corner of the square it would appear that the turnout had been enormous, but a few minutes later I spotted Bonsack, and he looked far from happy. I turned to Huber.

'What's wrong with Peter?'

She followed my gaze, and I heard her sigh. 'I don't know. Yesterday evening, when we were having a beer, I asked him the very same question, but all he would say was that he wasn't happy with the way it was going.'

I cast my eyes over the large number of uniformed personnel that now surrounded the square. It would appear that, like Bonsack, the East German authorities were also far from happy with the way that it was going, and although on this occasion Honecker's military commanders had ignored his shoot-to-kill order, I knew that it would only be a matter of time before they were forced to carry it out.

Earlier in the day, in an attempt to limit the number of people able to attend the rally from outside Leipzig, the East German government had given notice of a state-wide curfew. It would come into effect at nine o'clock that night, and stay in force until five o'clock the following morning. Anybody caught breaking the curfew would be shot on sight.

I turned to Huber. 'Well, there's little we can do here now. Stay close to me just in case things turn ugly and we have to make a run for it.'

Huber tightened her grip on my hand and smiled. 'I didn't know you cared.'

I glanced across at her. Her face was beaming.

Friday, 5 October 1989

Leipzig

B ETWEEN 18:24 ON 4 October and 01:35 on 5 October more
than 8,000 people who had occupied the grounds of the West
German Embassy in Prague, living in what might be described as
medieval conditions, were put aboard eight special trains in what
was to become known as the 'Exodus'. Their passage through the
German Democratic Republic was neither quick nor uneventful due
to violent conflict between police and demonstrators at Dresden's
main railway station.

It was estimated that close to 10,000 demonstrators had gathered
at the station on Thursday night hoping to get aboard the sealed
trains. But police quickly moved in with rubber truncheons and
water cannon in an effort to disperse the crowd. In the first riots,
and the worst outbreak of civil disobedience seen in East Germany
since the 1950s, the demonstrators fought back, hurling paving
stones at the police.

It was later reported that around 2,000 people had lined the
platforms and approaches to the station in order to watch the trains
progress as they passed through on their way to freedom in West
Germany, among them Huber and me. The event was, and still is,
one of the most haunting memories of my life. Hundreds of people
just standing staring, quietly waving at those who were staring back
at them through the locked carriage windows, stateless, stripped of
their national identity and homeland by the East German state. Men,
women and children who had been expelled as antisocial elements.
Some, Huber among them, stood crying as the trains pulled slowly
through the station, while others were beaten back by police and
troops as they tried unsuccessfully to board the sealed trains. And
for the first time since I had arrived in East Germany, knowing what
I was about to do, I wondered if I would ever get back to the West.

Saturday, 7 October 1989

Zinnwald

I T WAS JUST after one in the morning when, with my back to the driver's door of the drab red-coloured Trabant, I removed the East German equivalent of a Phillips screwdriver from my jacket pocket, and placed its point in the centre of the vehicle's primitive lock. The palm of my right hand struck the top of the handle. Nothing. I hit it a second time, felt the barrel of the lock shoot into the recess of the door, and heard it clatter to the bottom. I was in.

I had left the house thirty minutes earlier, telling Huber that I needed to go out. As I had now come to expect, she protested vehemently, telling me that it was far too dangerous for any of us to venture out on to the streets alone and after dark. But she knew I wasn't asking for her permission, and reluctantly she agreed not to ask questions and promised not to follow me.

She had offered me the use of her car, but there was no way I could use it for what I had planned tonight. If the police stopped me, or I was seen leaving the scene, the car would lead the authorities straight back to her, Bonsack and the others. No. Tonight the risk had to be mine, and mine alone.

Inside the car, I depressed the clutch pedal, ripped the wires from the back of the flimsy ignition, twisted them together and as I earthed them on the metal steering column the car's small engine turned over and then, somewhat hesitantly, burst into life. I slipped it into gear and headed east, out of Leipzig towards Dresden and, from there, the fifty kilometres south to Zinnwald.

At 03:45, as I reached the southern end of town, I turned left and, as I drove on to the service road that led to the Projects, I contemplated what I was about to do and the inevitable consequences. If

Adler was right and Metzger was the only person who knew where and when the attack on Gorbachev would take place, then, I calculated, if I waited until the very last minute to stop him the RAF leadership would not have enough time to come up with an alternative plan. But given what Adler had told me back at the farm, I had to assume that there was a possibility he might even be working alone.

However, there was also no way I could just walk into Metzger's flat and gun him down. Not without having to kill his girlfriend as well. Then there was their three-year-old son.

No women, no kids.

Nor could I risk anyone in the Bewegung pointing the finger at me afterwards, otherwise I would have the KGB and Stasi hunting me down as their top target. That I would not survive.

I somehow had to make it look like the RAF had lost faith in Metzger and were, once again, cleaning house; typical paranoid terrorist behaviour.

I parked the car at the edge of the Projects and, staying off the roads, made my way up a slight rise and then between the tall, dark blocks to the one where Metzger lived. Although I didn't know which number flat was actually his, I had seen him come and go while living at the Projects with Huber.

His car, a matte grey Moskvitch, was parked tight against the kerb on the road outside.

I checked the number plate to make sure it was Metzger's car. I couldn't afford to make a mistake. Not now. I looked around me. All the buildings were in darkness. Not a light on anywhere and, at that moment, standing there alone, I could have been the last man on earth.

I removed the Russian RGD-5 hand grenade I had found under the rear seat of Adler's car from my right-hand pocket and, from the left, I took a length of thin, non-stretch electrical flex and a roll of black insulating tape.

I scanned the area one more time, dropped to the ground and, making sure that the grenade's safety lever had enough room to fall free of the vehicle, I wedged it firmly into the vehicle's poor excuse for a chassis. It was then, as I began to apply the adhesive tape that would hold the grenade in place, that I stopped and thought about the consequences of what I was about to do. I shook my mind free and continued with my task. There was no time for that. Not now.

With the grenade secured beneath and slightly to the rear of the driver's seat, I tied one end of the flex to the nine o'clock position on the inside rim of the car's offside rear wheel. I fed the other end through the ring attached to the grenade's safety pin, pulled it taut and, after testing the tension in much the same way a guitarist would check the tension of his instrument's string, I tied it off.

Satisfied that everything was as it should be, I carefully squeezed the splayed ends of the grenade's safety pin together. The pin needed to be loose enough to pull out easily and not snag and rip the grenade from the chassis as the vehicle pulled away, but tight enough to ensure it did not fall out, causing the grenade to explode prematurely.

I ran my fingers over each of the components one more time. I had left nothing to chance. As soon as the car pulled away, whether forward, or in reverse, the rear wheel would turn, pull the pin from the grenade and, five seconds later, Metzger would be dead.

As I made my way back through the blocks of flats to the car I did my best to convince myself that what I had done back at the farm, and what was about to happen now, was for the greater good. Metzger was a terrorist and, to my reasoning, he deserved neither quarter nor sympathy. He was also a terrorist who had ordered my murder. But, deep inside, I knew that by booby-trapping his car, I was in reality no better than him or any other terrorist. Although I hated myself for it, he wouldn't stand a chance. I just hoped he would be alone when he got into his car.

As I reached the stolen Trabant I looked at my watch.

04:21.

I didn't have time to hang around and confirm the kill. Right now, I needed to be somewhere else.

It was 04:43 when, standing alone in the bar, I scanned the room. But nothing jumped out at me and, if I was honest, why would it? It was a working man's bar, and I knew there would be nothing of interest on the public side of the bar. I walked behind the large wooden-topped counter and began my search. The most obvious place to look was under the till, but there was nothing. I quietly shifted the crates stacked neatly under the bar. It was doubtful I would find anything there; I just needed to keep my mind working.

It was as I straightened up, turned, and began to run my eyes over the counter behind me that I had a terrible thought.

Of course, it could be hidden upstairs, in the living quarters.

I quickly dismissed the thought; that wouldn't work. Metzger would need immediate access to whatever it was he had passed across the counter to the landlord, his cousin. He wouldn't have time to wait for him to run upstairs and fetch it every time he needed access to it. No, it had to be hidden down here somewhere, and somewhere behind the bar.

It was as I ran my eyes along the shelves that held the glasses and schnapps bottles that they fell upon the only piece of decoration in the room, the picture of Erich Honecker hanging on the wall behind the bar. The thick-varnished wooden frame that surrounded it was far too elaborate for a mass-produced black and white print. I reached up, lifted it down from the wall, turned it over and laid it flat on the bar. The thickness of the frame meant that the backing which supported the picture inside sat proud of the wall by nearly an inch. In the recess, secured beneath a criss-cross web of some cheap white elastic, was a small, hard-backed notebook. It was the shiny black object Metzger had slid across the bar at our first meeting. I quickly rehung the picture and slipped the little black book into the inside pocket of my jacket. I was just about to head for the door when I heard footsteps coming down the stairs behind me.

Bollocks, I just cannot get a break.

I quickly returned to the public side of the bar and squatted down behind the counter. I was not overly worried about being seen. But I did hope that armed with both the element of surprise and approaching from the rear, it would not be an issue.

As I waited alone in the dark, I could hear the footsteps steadily growing louder, but then they stopped. Whoever it was, was now standing directly behind me, on the other side of the counter. I drew the silenced Sig from my belt and pulled back the hammer, the faint click as it found its stop sounded as loud as a church bell to me, but obviously went unheard by whoever it was that was now making their way around the end of the counter and heading for the front door. As they came into view I froze. It was a woman, probably position the landlord's wife. I returned the Sig back to the half-cocked position and slid it into my belt.

No women, no kids.

Given what I had already done since arriving in East Germany, such a statement probably makes me sound like a hypocrite, but in the quiet times, with nobody to unload on, no way of venting my frustration, the guilt was eating away at me and, as such, I needed something good to hang on to. Some way of convincing myself that I wasn't all bad. There was no way I wanted to kill her, but I might have no other choice.

She was at the door, reaching for the handle when I stepped up behind her. I saw her body tense. She had heard me at the last moment but it was too late. Before she could turn, I threw my arms around her neck and, using the collar of her dressing gown as a weapon, applied a Rear Strangle Hold, a Close Quarter Battle (CQB) technique, designed to render your opponent unconscious, but without killing them. Two seconds later she lay in an unconscious heap at my feet, but she wouldn't be out for long, and it was time I was gone.

Saturday, 7 October 1989

Leipzig

I HAD SPENT the morning alone, watching a live feed of Soviet President Mikhail Gorbachev's visit to East Germany to commemorate the communist state's 40th birthday. It had crossed my mind that Metzger might have given the assassination team stationed in Berlin their instructions earlier, maybe even the night before. As a result, what I was looking at seemed surreal in some respects, knowing what Metzger had planned for him. And even though it was now just after 13:00, I was still half expecting it to happen.

In the end, Gorbachev had a surprise of his own for Erich Honecker, the leader of the DDR. During his speech that day in Berlin, Gorbachev remarked, 'Life punishes those who come too late.' In reality, he was telling Honecker, and his government, that they could no longer rely on the support of the Soviet Union, or the large number of Soviet troops stationed in the country to control the East German population. It would later emerge that Gorbachev had also given express orders that all Soviet troops were to remain in their barracks for the duration of the celebrations.

It was 13:15. I was still staring at the TV, but with Gorbachev still alive all I could think about now was Metzger's black book and what it contained. But that would have to wait until I was totally alone in the house.

A minute later the door opened and Huber entered the room. She was carrying an empty mug and paused as she passed the far end of the table on her way to the sink and our eyes met. She was obviously distressed, and even before she opened her mouth I knew what was coming.

'Klaus Metzger is dead.'

I maintained eye contact. 'How?'

'A bomb.'

I felt my eyes narrow. 'There's been nothing on the news.'

'They're saying that his death was part of an internal power struggle.'

I needed to know more. 'Who?'

Huber turned towards the sink. 'I don't know, it's only what Peter told me.'

'Was anybody else involved?'

'No. He was alone. It was just before six o'clock this morning; he was leaving for work when the device went off beneath his car.'

I was relieved that no one else had been involved, and although it looked like I had quite literally got away with murder, I was far from happy. I had crossed the line at the farm outside Schwarzbachtal, the afternoon I killed Adler and his partner. On that occasion, I had convinced myself that it was either them or me, but last night I had crossed it again and, given what I knew, and what I now had in my possession, Metzger's death would not be the last, not by any stretch of the imagination.

I had probably saved Mikhail Gorbachev's life, and in the process possibly removed Russia's Old Guard's excuse to take full control of East Germany once again. No one would ever know and, at the time, I wanted it to stay that way. God only knows what the repercussions would be for me if Scott and his superiors at MI6 ever found out what I had done. Maybe it would have suited their purpose if Gorbachev had been assassinated. After all, as I said earlier, although the liberal Western democracies vainly decried yet another communist atrocity, did the leaders in the West genuinely loathe the Wall, or was it in some ways rather convenient? Was it a way of maintaining the status quo and ensuring some kind of ongoing fragile peace? Also, both Britain and France had long mooted their resistance to a reunited Germany and, of course, if Gorbachev was assassinated, that would never happen.

However, I had no time to worry about that right now. Right now, I had a more pressing problem. I had to assume that following my break-in earlier that morning, Metzger's cousin, the landlord of the mineworkers' bar, would have already discovered that the note-book was missing. Once the RAF had managed to work out who had taken it, they would do everything in their power to get it back and, in an effort to tie up the loose ends, kill me.

On the day I had arrived in East Germany, as Huber and I had made our way down from Dresden, she had suggested that only two people knew about the location of the Zinnwald safe house: 'You will be the third,' she had said. But before he died, Adler told me that Metzger had known where it was all along.

I looked across the room at Huber. She was standing at the sink with her back to me.

'You once told me that, including me, only three people knew the location of the Zinnwald safe house. Who was the third person?'

Huber turned and looked at me. A second later she turned back to the sink and her dishes.

'Peter Bonsack.'

As I watched her stacking the dishes neatly on the draining board, I wondered whether, if push came to shove, I could do it. It had been obvious from the night the police locked down Zinnwald, the night of the meeting at the church, that the Stasi had at least one informer inside the Bewegung, but the list of who it might be was rapidly shrinking. Knowing what I did now, the obvious choice would have been Metzger or one of his cohorts, but with Metzger dead and his subordinates still down in Zinnwald, the only people who could be informing on us had now been whittled down to just four: Bonsack, Huber, Fischer and Mayer. If push came to shove, could I kill any one of them as clinically as I had killed Metzger and his henchmen back at the farm? I shook my mind free.

'Where's Peter now?'

'I don't know. He said he had to go out.'

I paused for a second. 'What about Gerhard Fischer and Horst Mayer – where are they right now?'

Huber turned and looked at me. 'I have no idea. I haven't seen either of them since this morning when Peter left the house.'

It was just after four thirty in the afternoon, and I was lying on my bed. The light was fading outside, and with the curtains drawn the room was practically in darkness. I heard the front door quietly close; it sounded like somebody was trying to enter or leave the house without being noticed. I slid the Sig from under my right thigh, got up, and went to the bedroom window. The street was quiet, there was no one about and, to my relief, there was no sign of any police cars or unfamiliar vehicles.

Maybe Bonsack's back?

However, as I went to turn away from the window something caught my eye at the far end of the street. Disappearing around the corner eighty metres away was what looked like the back of Huber's coat. I opened the bedroom door and made my way quietly downstairs. The house was empty.

I had no idea where she was going. She had not mentioned that she was going out and, with no word from Bonsack, the paranoia was beginning to creep back into my head once again.

Back in the bedroom, I turned on the light, wrapped my arms around the wooden wardrobe, and taking small steps shuffled it across the bedroom floor towards me. Tipping it backwards, I rested its top rear edge against the wall. Taped to its underside was a clear plastic bag, and inside was the little black notebook.

I sat down on the edge of the bed and began to flick through the pages. I was amazed at just how much information it contained. There were pages and pages of names, some of them in full, some only initials. There were very few addresses, but many telephone numbers, both inside and outside East Germany. There was far too much information for me to examine right now. I had no idea where Huber had gone, which meant I had no idea when she might return.

Two days later, on 9 October, Leipzig hosted the largest demonstration in East German history. Between 70,000 and 100,000 peaceful demonstrators defied warnings from the Stasi, the menacing presence of thousands of armed riot police and work combat troops, and marched around the city centre. In the end, although the warnings and the risk of being imprisoned or worse were very real, the police did nothing, and the stage was now set for a peaceful revolution that would eventually sweep across East Germany.

Tuesday, 10 October 1989

Dresdner Heide Forest

IT WAS AROUND 03:05 when I lifted the Clansman from the boot of Huber's Trabant, threw the carrying strap over my left shoulder and, picking up the holdall, headed north-northeast into the Dresdner Heide Forest. Six minutes later, as I had done on my previous visit, I swung due west.

As I approached the RV, I saw the BRIXMIS officer standing in the clearing. I had to smile. Even though he had done an exceptional job up to now, his tall somewhat gangly, boyish appearance made me question whether I would follow him in a bus queue let alone a battle. To his left, twenty feet away, was the Tour NCO, but something was wrong. His right hand was in the pocket of his combat jacket, the material stretched over what appeared to be something a little larger than his hand.

I lowered the Clansman to the floor, slipped my hand inside my jacket, and pulled the hammer of the Sig back the last half click.

'Boss.'

The officer took a deep breath, pulled his shoulders back, and raised himself to full height. 'Tom.'

I glanced across at the NCO, then back to the officer.

'Do we have a problem?'

The officer stuttered. 'Why . . . why would you think that we have a problem?'

I turned my head slightly to the right and glanced at the Tour NCO again.

'Because your NCO is armed, and BRIXMIS operators are never armed.' I slowly lifted my left hand and opened my jacket, revealing the fully cocked Sig to the young corporal. 'Don't get creative, son. Any sudden movements on your part and both you and your boss will be dead before that weapon clears your pocket.'

The Tour NCO swallowed, then, slowly lifting his empty hand from his jacket pocket, let it drop to his side.

I turned my attention back to the officer.

'Now that we've got that sorted out, what's the problem?'

The young officer looked visibly relieved that I had resolved the situation for him.

'Your handler believes that for your own safety, you should stay where you are for a while longer, just until it's safe to bring you in.'

The adrenaline had started flowing the minute I left the car and, headed into the forest, the fact that the Tour NCO was armed had increased the flow marginally, but the young officer's last statement had all but opened the floodgates. There was now no time for rank or niceties.

'Right, listen up. I've just murdered—' I stopped dead. Although I had thought about little else over the last few days, hearing the word said out loud for the first time had taken me aback. I continued, 'Liquidated three senior members of the RAF, one of them a leading member of Baader-Meinhof, whose accomplices are now hell bent on getting revenge. London needs to bring me in, and quickly – before it's too late.'

I looked down at the radio. 'I can't worry about this any more, I need to remain flexible, keep moving.'

The officer glanced at the radio and then at me. 'But how will you contact us?'

My response bordered on a snarl. 'I'm no longer interested in talking to or receiving instructions from London, or Berlin. The only thing I'm interested in right now is getting out of East Germany alive. I'll make sure I'm sat beside a radio and tuned into Rundfunk, the joint German/American RIAS radio station in Berlin, at eighteen thirty hours every evening. Once London has got its act together, and sorted out how they're going to extract me . . .' I paused, I needed time to think, and a few seconds later I had it. 'Get the station to play *Going Home* by Dire Straits immediately following the six-thirty news. I'll be at this exact location, two days later, at zero one thirty.'

At the time, and even now, thirty years on, Dire Straits had a large and committed following and, although their music is a bit of an acquired taste, *Going Home* is a classic. But, being an instrumental meant that it was rarely played and also playing it straight after the six-thirty news bulletin would be hard for me to miss.

The officer nodded his head and smiled. 'OK. I'll pass on your message but—'

I wasn't finished and cut him off mid-sentence. 'There are no buts, and something else that might encourage them to speed things up. Tell London that I've acquired some critical information, a list of all Baader-Meinhof and RAF contacts in the West.'

In reality, very rarely being left in the house on my own, I had not yet had the opportunity to go through Metzger's notebook in detail. I wasn't exactly sure what it contained but, from what I had already seen, at worst it was a sort of terrorist NOC list. In intelligence circles, agents under Non-Official Cover (NOC) are operatives who assume covert roles in organisations without any official ties to the government for which they work. At best, it was something much more damaging, which also made it both more valuable to the original owner, and more dangerous to whoever had managed to get hold of it, which in this case was me.

I took the officer's hand and shook it.

'You might also like to point out that if I'm captured or killed, then that list dies with me.'

Without another word, I turned and made my way back into the forest.

Saturday, 4 November 1989

Leipzig

I WAS LYING on my bed, the light was out, and I was fully clothed. It was just after 19:00 and tonight, as I had done every night for the last three weeks, at 18:25 I had religiously drawn the curtains in the front room, taken my seat beside the radio, and tuned into Rundfunk. After listening to the 18:30 news bulletin, I had waited for the first record to be played directly following it, but not once had I heard the strains of *Going Home*, and with my personal paranoia now at an all-time high I was convinced I had been abandoned. What I didn't know was why?

Although Huber was naturally still living on her nerves, she seemed to be a lot easier around me, intent on us spending time together, but given what had happened at the farm and in Zinnwald, I was now rapidly withdrawing, spending more and more time on my own.

On 7 October, the same day I killed Metzger, Bonsack had disappeared. Huber was convinced he had been arrested, so two days later, on the ninth, as a precaution, I had taken control, insisting that we dissolve what remained of the small Leipzig cell for the time being and relocate, but not to another one of the Bewegung's so-called safe houses in Leipzig. If Huber was right, and Bonsack had indeed been arrested, then the safe houses were rapidly becoming nothing more than traps.

I was brought back to the present by the sound of Huber's screams coming from the room below. I picked up the Sig from the bedside table and made my way silently down the stairs. Arms outstretched, holding the weapon in both hands, as I reached the bottom step I flicked off the safety and pulled back the hammer. Placing the toe of my right foot gently against the bottom of the front-room door, I pushed. However, instead of discovering a room full of East

German police and Stasi, I found Huber jumping up and down on the spot, her arms waving wildly above her head.

I breathed a sigh of relief and lowered my weapon.

'What's going on?'

Huber was smiling, but I could also see tears rolling down her cheeks.

'We've done it, Andel!'

She ran towards me, threw her arms around my neck, jumped up, and wrapped her legs around my waist. Subconsciously, my hands found her backside and, with me taking her weight, she leaned back and stared at me.

She had that look in her eyes again, that ice-cold fire.

'Following the numbers that attended the Leipzig rallies and in an effort to appease us, the East German people, Erich Honecker has decided to authorise a rally at Alexanderplatz in Berlin. They are expecting over half a million people to attend. It will be the biggest protest our country has ever seen. It's the beginning of the end for the communist regime. Soon we will all be free!'

She then kissed me full on the lips, but it wasn't a celebratory kiss; this was something else, her mouth was open, and her tongue probing.

Eventually I managed to break away from her, and with my hands under her backside, still taking her weight, I stared into her corn-flower blue eyes. Although I had already guessed the answer to my question, I needed time to defuse the situation, so I asked it anyway: 'What was that all about?'

She leaned back on straightened arms, her fingers interlocked behind my neck, and her legs wrapped tightly around my waist, giving the occasional squeeze.

'You once asked me why I had knocked on your bedroom door in the early hours of the morning. Well, that kiss, and the pretty new underwear I was wearing that night at the cottage, was why.' Her eyes widened and her pupils dilated. 'I fell for you the morning I picked you up in Dresden, and although you're not the easiest person in the world to live with, I feel safe around you, and I've loved you more with every day.'

Huber was totally unaware of my personal circumstances. She had no idea that I was married with a young son, and although I was extremely flattered and, as we're telling the truth here, sorely tempted to take advantage of the situation, I removed my hands and, letting her slip gently to the ground, changed the subject.

'Is there any news of Peter?'

Huber's smile faded. 'No. Not even Klaudia, the cleaner who once worked at Stasi headquarters in Dresden, can find out anything.'

'What about Fischer and Mayer?'

'Nothing. It's like they've all just vanished.'

If Huber was right, then we were totally alone. We could expect no help from anyone.

I stood and stared at her. I could see she was dog-tired, and what I was about to tell her was not going to help the situation.

'We need to move again.'

I heard her sigh. 'Why, and where to this time?'

'Dresden.'

Her eyes widened, she looked surprised. 'Further East? Even further away from the border?'

'Yes. We have a saying where I come from: "When you're being hunted, the safest place to hide is among your enemies."'

But I was not sharing everything I knew with her. I knew that with things rapidly falling apart in East Germany, the RAF would be intent on getting Metzger's black book back, would not rest until they had it, and once they realised who had it would tear Leipzig apart to find it and kill me in the process.

Friday, 10 November 1989

Dresden

I REFLECTED THAT moving from Leipzig to Dresden was a massive decision for me. As well as trying to avoid being found by members of the RAF, I had, by now, given up all hope of ever hearing *Going Home* played on the Rundfunk radio station, and moving to Dresden meant that now it would never happen. Dresden was in what was known as the 'dark zone', jokingly referred to by the East German population as '*Tal Der Ahnungslosen*' (Valley of the Clueless). It was one of two corners of East Germany, so far away from West Berlin, and the West German border, that it was impossible to receive the radio programmes being broadcast by ARD, West Germany's public service broadcasters.

At just after 07:30 that morning, I poured boiling water into a mug and watched the liquid slowly change colour. It wasn't coffee, but it was hot and brown, and it would have to do.

The day before, at 19:00, East Berlin's Communist Party spokesman, Günter Schabowski, announced that East Germans would, with immediate effect, be allowed to travel directly to West Germany. Later that evening the government of the GDR attempted to backtrack, calling for its citizens to queue at the migration office the next day, but it was too late. Thousands of East Germans were already on their way to the Wall. However, instead of being met by open barriers, the crowds were met by heavily armed, and somewhat confused border guards who were unaware of the change in policy and, up until that point, had been carrying out their orders to shoot on sight anyone attempting to cross the Wall.

As the *Grenztruppen* officers made a series of frantic phone calls to their headquarters, the East German crowd, which was growing larger by the minute, continued to demand that the gates be opened. Their request was finally granted at 22:45. In an attempt to avoid

a stampede, officials began to let people through gradually, but within the hour they had lost control and the barriers were opened, allowing East Germans unrestricted access to the West.

The Wall – or, as the Germans called it, *Die Mauer* – had been constructed overnight on 12–13 August 1961, and on the night of 9 November 1989, just over twenty-eight years later, it fell.

Huber and I spent the night glued to the TV in a tiny bar on the south side of Dresden, watching as thousands of East Germans poured through pre-existing, official access points, and the newly made gaps in the Wall. They were met on the Western side by huge crowds of West Germans carrying flowers and champagne, starting a round of celebrations that would go on for days.

As the excitement grew, Huber slipped her arm through mine and nestled up against me. Her body was trembling and tears rolled uncontrollably down her cheeks. I had been in East Germany for the best part of three months, but it was only on that evening that I truly realised just how much the events currently being played out on the TV screen in front of us meant to the people of East Germany.

The good news was that I no longer had to rely on Scott to get me out. In theory, with the Berlin Wall down, I was no longer a prisoner, a foreign agent trapped behind the Iron Curtain. I could simply leave with the thousands of East Germans who would be making their way to the West over the coming days – but I also knew it was not going to be that simple.

It was true that the Berlin Wall had disappeared virtually overnight, but the defences that marked the route of the Inner German Border, the endless miles of barbed wire, minefields and man traps, were still very much in place, and as a result my exit points from East Germany were somewhat limited. I would have been a fool to think that the RAF would not have surmised the same, which meant any one or all of these crossing points could quickly become a death trap. Combine that with the fact that with the disappearance of the Wall, and fearing reprisals from members of the East German population, a large number of the country's police force had already left their posts. And in doing so, they had removed any meaningful form of law and order, a situation the RAF would undoubtedly exploit to the full as they attempted to get back what rightfully belonged to them – Metzger's black book.

As I lifted the mug to my lips, Huber entered the kitchen. She was wearing jeans, boots and a thick winter coat. I looked down at the sports bag she held in her right hand. The expression on her face was one of nothing but bad news. I blew out heavily through my nose.

'What's wrong now?'

Her voice was not much more than a whisper. 'We have to go – right now. A Russian patrol is in the process of blocking off both ends of the street.'

The Wall might have fallen but it would appear that the Russians were still here and capable of being as vicious as ever.

I raced to the front-room window and inched the curtain to one side. She was right. At the far end of the street was a roadblock and beyond it a line of cars waiting to pass. My heart skipped a beat. The officer in charge, although to the rear, directing oper-ations, was none other than Major Vladimir Putin.

This guy's like a bad dream.

I had no idea what was going on, what the Russians were up to, but having lived in East Germany for close to three months, whether the Wall was down or not, I knew for sure that their sudden appearance was never a good thing. My fear levels were rising and the adrenaline was once again rushing through my veins.

I turned to Huber who was hovering at the door that led into the kitchen. Behind her I could see the window that led out on to the street that ran behind it. If we were quick, we could get through the window and out on to the street before the Russians got totally organised and sealed off the whole area. We might still be able to get away.

I nodded at the bag. 'Is that everything we need?'

I suspect that without even knowing why, Huber glanced down at the bag in her right hand, then back to me. 'It will have to be.'

'Wait here. Keep an eye on that patrol. If they start to move in our direction, yell.'

'Where are you going?'

'The bedroom, I need to get something, then we're out of here.'

Huber raised her voice as I disappeared along the short corridor to the farther of the two bedrooms. 'Where to?'

I didn't answer. In truth, I had no idea where we would go now.

Taking an apartment on the ground floor is always risky as it's easy for the authorities to gain access, but it's nowhere near as dangerous as being trapped on the upper floors of a building, where your only way out is down a stairwell crammed with the enemy.

Climbing through the kitchen window, we disappeared into the maze of surrounding streets and headed for Dresden city centre. Once there, we stuck to the areas where there was lots of foot traffic. Those areas where we could mingle unnoticed among the crowds. When the shops began to close, but before the crowds completely disappeared, we made our way to Bautzner Straße, on the north side of the Elbe River.

Saturday, 11 November 1989

Dresden

I T WAS JUST after midnight when, with nowhere else to go, and with Huber keeping watch, I broke into an abandoned building.

Between 13 and 15 February 1945, 1,300 heavy bombers of the Allied Air Force (Britain and America) had launched four massive air raids on Dresden, dropping close to 4,000 tonnes of high explosives and incendiary devices, creating a firestorm that destroyed over 1,600 acres of the city centre. As a result, the building we were now sheltering in was less than fifty years old, built after the Second World War. It was in good condition, weatherproof and secure.

While I kept watch, and tried to work out how I was going to get us both safely out of Dresden and back across the Inner German border, Huber slept restlessly on one of the few remaining pieces of furniture.

I knew that it was only a matter of time before life caught up with us, and the narrow escape we had had the previous morning merely confirmed that. What puzzled me was why the Russians were there; why not the East German police or troops? It's not as if the apartment was on a major road junction, which meant they had a definite objective, a specific target. Then there was Putin. What was the local head of the KGB doing leading a run-of-the-mill foot patrol?

At the time, moving to Dresden had looked like the smart thing to do. It was further away from the Inner German Border, so not a place the RAF would think of looking for us.

Now, whatever the reasons for the Russian presence, it would appear that the net was rapidly closing, and that regardless of the risks it was time to get out of Dresden and head back across the Inner German Border.

But, if we were to stand any chance of reaching the West in one piece, I first needed to acquire some form of reliable transport. With the roads already jammed with refugee traffic heading west, we needed an edge – and I knew exactly where to acquire one.

I took hold of Huber's left foot and gently shook it. It was a full minute before she struggled free from an uneasy sleep and opened her eyes.

'I need to go out.'

I handed her the Makarov she had given me back in Zinnwald.

'The magazine is full and there's one in the chamber. Don't go back to sleep. Wait here for thirty minutes, then make your way to the petrol station on Bautzner Straße. I'll pick you up there as soon as I can.'

Closing the side door behind me, I made my way along the alley towards the main road.

Following Bonsack's arrest, I was reluctantly beginning to consider quite seriously that Huber might be working for the Stasi. It's true that she was not the only person I suspected, but to my knowledge she was the only one who knew that we were in Dresden, and I began to wonder if this was the most likely explanation for why, or how, we had avoided capture for so long. However, her passionate kiss and declaration of love a few days earlier had thrown confusion into the mix.

Earlier that evening, as I watched her sleep, I had considered abandoning her. Disappearing into the night and making the trip alone, but if she was the mole, then I needed to keep her close, at least until I was safely back in the West.

I lifted my head, looked towards the end of the alley, and saw the yellow glow of the street lights that lined Bautzner Straße.

As I made my way across the forecourt of the petrol station where I would meet Huber later, I removed the silenced Sig from the back of my trousers, tucked it into my belt, and covered it with my jacket. There was no longer any point in being discreet or subtle. I knew that if challenged now, the situation would rapidly escalate and inevitably end in violence. I crossed the road and made my way towards Stasi headquarters.

It was a formidable-looking structure. Four storeys high, constructed of what appeared to be solid concrete and painted matt grey. It sat on the northern side of Bautzner Straße, the main road that separated the River Elbe from north Dresden and the Dresdner Heide Forest. Up until a few days ago, before the Wall came down, the complex had been heavily guarded, but now, in fear of reprisals, most of the guard force had deserted their post, leaving it virtually unprotected, with only the odd light showing here and there.

I looked around me. The car park was half full. The vehicles were a mixture of East German Wartburgs, Russian Moskvitchs and Volgas. I began trying the doors of those cars sitting closest to the exit. The third car I tried, a Volga, was unlocked, but as I slipped into the driver's seat and looked down, as you would expect, the ignition was bare. I smiled to myself. The absence of an ignition key was a minor problem for a cockney.

Ten minutes later I stopped the car at the western end of the petrol station forecourt, and Huber slid into the passenger seat.

'Where did you get this?'

I felt my squaddie black humour coming up for air. 'It's nice, isn't it? The Stasi car park is full of them, and some of them, like this one, were even unlocked.'

Huber could not hide her horror at what I had done. 'You stole a car from the Stasi?'

'Relax, it's not as if they're going to be using it anytime soon. Anyway, it seemed rude not to, and the blue lights hidden behind the front grille are just the edge we need.'

As we made our way west along Bautzner Straße, I looked in the rear-view mirror.

I wonder?

Fifty metres further on, at the very last moment, and without indicating, I turned sharp right into a side street.

Huber straightened herself up and turned towards me. 'Now where are we going?'

I didn't answer. I was busy putting the car through a 'box' manoeuvre: a series of four right turns, which meant that I never had to stop the vehicle to turn across oncoming traffic and you could keep moving, so the chances of being forced to stop and subsequently ambushed by the following vehicle were near impossible.

As I completed the final right turn, back on to Bautzner Straße, and headed west once more, I looked in the rear-view mirror again.

'We're being followed.'

Huber turned around in her seat and looked through the rear window; she was finding it hard to hide her anger.

'I knew this would happen. It was a stupid idea stealing a car from the Stasi.'

Although it was evident we were being followed, whoever it was seemed to be making no effort to stop or overtake us. At the edge of the city, I pulled the car on to Route 4, a poor excuse for an *autobahn* that ran due west from Dresden, through Karl-Marx-Stadt, and on to the border crossing point at Herleshausen.

I glanced at the police radio hanging beneath the dashboard of the Volga.

'Do you know how to work that?'

Huber followed my gaze. 'Not really.'

'Well, give it a go. It's not rocket science. The frequencies are all pre-set. It's just a matter of clicking through the channels until you hear something you recognise. If we can pick up the radio traffic between that car and its control centre it might give us an idea of what they're planning to do next.'

Keeping my eyes on the road, I listened to the clicks as Huber flicked quickly through the channels.

'Stop. Go back one.'

It was not what I was hoping for, but a traffic report from police HQ in Karl-Marx-Stadt. '*Die Straße im Osten von Nossen wird mit dem Flüchtlingsverkehr blockiert.*'

I looked at Huber. 'If that broadcast is accurate, and the road east of Nossen is blocked with refugee traffic, then we need to find an alternate route. See if you can find a road map.'

After digging around in the rear of the car, Huber sat back down in her seat. 'I've found a map. It looks pretty old, but nothing will have changed that much.'

I smiled. She was right, nothing much had changed in East Germany since the end of the Second World War.

'Good. Now try and find us a way around that traffic jam and back into the West.'

Huber said nothing for a second or two; she seemed to be lost in thought, then she blurted out, 'Where are we going?'

I smiled. I hadn't discussed my plan with her, mainly because of what had happened over the last few months. I was finding it increasingly hard to trust her and, as a result, all such information was now on a strictly need-to-know basis, and up until that point she hadn't needed to know.

'Kassel Ost. A *Raststätte*. Northbound on Route Seven.'

If we were anywhere else in Europe, our choices of where to cross the border would have been endless. But here in East Germany, with the Wall only having been down for a matter of days, I knew that the minefields, vehicle traps and barbed wire fences that made up the Inner German border were all still very much in place.

Keeping one eye on the road, I watched Huber's finger snake quickly back and forth across the map.

Suddenly she stopped, traced the route one more time, and said, 'OK. At the next junction take the road north, back towards Leipzig. There we can pick up the A14, and use the back roads to an old military crossing point between the towns of Muhlhausen and Nordhausen.'

Although they had always been well hidden and heavily guarded, the East German military had left some officially unrecognised crossing points free from mines and other immovable obstacles just in case their long-expected push into the West ever became a reality. But how did Huber know about the military crossing? Given our current situation, my only option was to follow her directions and hope that it didn't end in a trap.

I checked the rear-view mirror again. The last time I'd looked, the radiator grille and headlights of the Wartburg following us had all but filled the mirror, but now there was space all around it, and I could see two men sitting in the vehicle. For some reason, whoever they were, they were slowly dropping back.

Thirty seconds later I looked again, and there was now fifty metres of open tarmac between us. They had fallen even further behind.

What the fuck's going on?

We were sixty kilometres south-east of Leipzig when I looked again, and they had fallen even further behind. Now the gap between us was close to one hundred metres. Fearing a trap up ahead, without warning I turned off all of the car's lights and hit the accelerator. A hundred metres further on, with my eyes more accustomed to the dark, I swung the Volga right, off the main road. At the end of a short slip road, we left the tarmac surface and entered a single lane tunnel which led beneath the A14. Forty seconds later we were bouncing our way through the forest on a rough track.

Huber put her hand on the dashboard to steady herself.

'Where are we going?' She sounded tired, frustrated. 'We don't have time for detours.'

I wasn't listening, and as the track swung back briefly towards the A14, I saw the tail lights of the Wartburg as it continued west. Whoever it was had visibly reduced their speed and, although the gap between us was still growing, it wouldn't be long before they realised their mistake and turned around.

Surrounded by trees and in complete darkness, I did my best to keep the speeding car on the narrow forest track. However, as I exited a tight S bend combination, I saw a large number of dark objects spread across the centre of the track less than twenty metres ahead. They were logs. A log pile stacked on the side of the track had collapsed, and was now blocking our path.

I instantly applied the brakes. Hard enough to slow the vehicle, but not so hard that they locked up the wheels and caused us to skid. A split second later, the bright red glow of my break lights filled the rear-view mirror.

Shit.

Up until a few seconds ago, I had managed to control the car's speed by using a combination of its weight and the gearbox, but confronted by hundreds of tonnes of logs, I had automatically hit the brakes and the bright red glow from my brake lights had lit up the forest, telling the whole world where I was in the process. I flicked my eyes back to the track. If we hit the obstruction without seat belts, the impact could kill us both. My only option was to try and avoid it. I swung the car to the right and, using my left hand to brace myself against the steering wheel, I threw my right arm across Huber's chest, pinning her back in her seat.

Moments later the car came to a bone-crushing halt as it nose-dived into a drainage ditch that bordered the right side of the track.

Turning in my seat, I kicked open the driver's door, climbed out, and surveyed the damage. Apart from the radiator, which was now gushing copious amounts of steam, and a broken headlight, most of the damage seemed to be superficial. However, with the car sitting nose down at an angle of forty-five degrees, and with its rear-drive wheels off the ground, there was no way the two of us were going to get it out of the ditch and back on to the track.

I grabbed Huber's bag from between her legs, picked the map up off the floor of the car, and helped her out of the wreckage.

As we climbed the sides of the ditch, back on to the track, I noticed that she was limping, favouring her left leg, but I gave her no time to think about her injury. I knew from experience that when it comes to the wounded it's best to keep them moving, anything rather than give them time to lick their wounds.

'We have to keep moving, Kirstin. Put some serious distance between us and whoever is in that car. They will have been able to see the red glow of our brake lights in Berlin, let alone from the A14.'

06:07.

It was still dark when the track we were travelling along suddenly opened out into a small clearing and a dozen or so houses.

As we moved along the mud-covered track, which to all intents and purposes served as the main street to this isolated community, I felt Huber's fingers dig into my arm.

'Andel.'

I turned and followed her gaze. Someone was standing in the shadows between two of the houses and, as they stepped out into the moonlight, I saw the sharp edges of a police uniform. There was no way the chase car and its occupants could have reached here before us, which meant this had to be a local bobby.

I took a step forward, and he raised the pistol he was holding in his right hand. I continued to edge slowly forward and, using my left hand, I pulled Huber behind me, shielding her body with my own.

'*Guten Morgen, Offizier. Konnten Sie helfen? Wir verloren unseren Weg, und unser auto ist beschädigt worden.*'

The policeman was having none of it and replied in German, his voice harsh and aggressive. 'No. I cannot help you. Raise your hands above your head, or I will shoot.'

I needed to get us out of there and fast. If I allowed him to arrest us it was all over, but there was also no way I could risk drawing my Sig. I was fast, but not that fast. The moment my right hand started to move towards my belt he would shoot me where I stood and, I suspected, Huber as well. I turned slowly towards her and, with my back to the officer, I reached into her open jacket. As I eased the Makarov from her belt I flicked off the safety and began to turn back towards him. I hoped that, on seeing the weapon, I might be able to force some sort of stand-off. I was guessing that, like most East German policemen, he was used to being obeyed without question and, if challenged, I might be able to shock him into a moment's inaction. Then, while he considered his next move, Huber and I could melt away into the darkness.

'But my friend is injured . . .' I said, and gave Huber a hard shove, pushing her away from me and, I hoped, out of harm's way. But, as she began to fall and I completed my turn, I saw that the policeman had gone. Obviously expecting some sort of trick, he had stepped back into the darkness in an effort to deny me a target and protect himself. A second later the near silence that filled the clearing was shattered by a loud crack and a bright orange flash lit up the darkness between us. The officer had fired.

Instinct took over and, as I went into a crouch to minimise myself as a target, I zeroed in on the last thing I had seen, the bright orange muzzle flash of the policeman's weapon, and squeezed the trigger of my Makarov. Twice.

Still in a crouch, with my weapon held in both hands, arms outstretched, level with my shoulders and expecting a return of fire, I moved quickly forward, but when I reached the point where I had seen the muzzle flash of the policeman's weapon there was nothing. No wounded officer and no body. He had vanished.

My heart quickened as I strained my ears and listened for anything that would tell me where he was, or where he might be going, but there was nothing. Not a sound.

As my eyes continued to scan the darkness, Huber's voice broke the silence.

'Andel . . .'

Keeping my weapon raised and my eyes fixed on the point where I had last seen the policeman, I slowly began to back up towards her.

She was sitting in the mud. I hadn't realised I had pushed her so hard. Then I saw her right hand was clutching her left shoulder. It was shining in the moonlight.

It's wet. She's bleeding.

Despite my best efforts to protect her, the policeman's one and only round had found its target and buried itself deep in Huber's left shoulder and, if that wasn't bad enough, we now had another problem. As I knelt beside her I saw the faint yellow glow of lights as they flickered on in the surrounding houses. The noise of the gunshots had woken everyone in the tiny village.

'Can you stand, Kirstin? We need to get out of here . . . right now.'

Grabbing her under her right arm I hauled her to her feet but, as I turned her around, back in the direction of the forest, I saw that a small crowd was beginning to gather. They were blocking our way.

I levelled the Makarov at the person closest to me, an old man, but he ignored it and continued coming forward, closely followed by what I assumed was his wife.

With little regard for her own safety, or knowing what I might do next, the old woman gently pushed me to one side and wrapped her arm around Huber's waist.

'You should go now. We will take good care of her. Make sure she is OK.'

I knew that, given the importance of what I had in my pocket, the policeman disappearing like he had, doubtless going for rein-forcements, and the occupants of the chase car still out there somewhere, looking for us, I had little choice but to follow the old woman's instructions. I handed Huber's bag to the old man and then looked at her.

'I'll be back as soon as I can, Kirstin.'

Whether she believed me or not, she knew there was little else either of us could do. Despite the pain she must have been suffering, she managed a smile, but said nothing.

I waited until Huber was safely inside what I assumed was the old couple's house, made a mental note of its location in the village and then, making sure that everyone had seen me heading north, I made my way back into the darkness. Once I was out of sight of the village I went to ground and waited to see if anyone was following me. Satisfied that nobody was, using the map I had taken from the car and my Sylva compass I made a mental note of where I thought I was, and turned south-west towards Route 4 where I would turn due west and head towards the Herleshausen crossing point on the Inner German Border.

I started walking.

Two hours later, as the sun climbed higher in the winter sky, in the distance, perched high above the trees on a rocky outcrop, I saw a crumbling structure that brought back memories of my child-hood – Colditz Castle.

It had originally been built as a medieval fortress. Then in April 1945, US troops entered Colditz town and, after a two-day fight, captured the castle on 16 April.

In May 1945 the Soviet occupation of Colditz began. According to the agreement at the Yalta Conference, what was left of the town and its infamous castle became a part of East Germany. I remember reading that shortly after taking control, the Soviets turned Colditz Castle into a prison camp for local burglars and non-communists before becoming a psychiatric hospital where inmates were incarcerated as enemies of the state, strapped to beds, and brainwashed.

Back in 1972 I, like many others, had watched the BBC television series about the infamous POW camp for persistent escapees (designated Oflag IV–C by the Nazis), which is what the castle had been used for during the Second World War. Although it wasn't the same castle I'd seen on TV (most of the series was filmed at Stirling Castle in Scotland), I just happened to have chosen Colditz as the subject of my 'O' Level history project and, having seen and used many of the photographs that were taken at the time, there was no mistaking it. But, given the suffering that had occurred there over the years, my feelings at now seeing it for real were a mixture of excitement and dread.

Saturday, 11 November 1989

Colditz

HIDDEN AMONG THE trees, with my pulse rate steady, but pounding in my ears, I patiently watched and waited. The area seemed quiet enough, but I had thought the same earlier that morning as Huber and I had stood on the outskirts of the village. I had been wrong on that occasion, a mistake Huber had paid dearly for. I looked at my watch.

10:08. I'll give it a few minutes more.

As the minutes ticked slowly by, it became apparent that apart from a few elderly locals, those who had not fled to the West at the first opportunity, the area was pretty much deserted.

My plan at this point, as it was now daylight, was to do what comes naturally to a Special Forces soldier on the run – what I had been taught to do in an escape and evasion situation – go to ground and lie low until nightfall. But as I began to climb the hill, I looked up. The castle was in poor condition and I could hear voices. If I had had any sense at all, I would have turned around and looked for somewhere else to lie low until dark, but something was drawing me towards the castle. For some inexplicable reason, maybe because it was a pleasant memory from a troubled childhood, it somehow felt safe and, even if I only stayed for a short time, I needed to see inside, regardless of what was waiting behind its high walls.

I smiled as I passed through the gates. If the lads back in Hereford could see me now, they'd be wetting themselves with laughter. It was the perfect place to lie low. Who was going to notice one more lunatic in a place like this?

However, unlike the surrounding area, the castle turned out to be far from deserted. It became clear to me that the East German authorities had continued using it as a psychiatric hospital but now, with the country in chaos, the medical staff had abandoned their charges, leaving them free to wander the castle and its grounds unsupervised. As a result, it was now a very dangerous place to be.

I avoided all eye contact with the inmates as I moved quickly across the courtyard. Inside, I passed across a small tiled entrance hall and began to climb a narrow spiral staircase. Whether it was simply the location, or the danger now associated with it, my mind shot back to my history teacher at my secondary school in Dulwich. *The spiral staircases in ancient castles always turn clockwise, which made them very hard to fight your way up.*

Apparently, it was because most people are right handed, and when climbing stairs clockwise your right hand is closest to the inside wall of the continual bend, and the steps are narrow – making it difficult to cut and stab upwards to your right. However, a defender holding position on the stairs had much more room in which to swing his weapon down and to the left – the natural sword swing. But regardless of whether the statement was true or not, it wouldn't be the same now. You don't need a lot of space to fire a gun.

There was only one room on the first floor of what was basically a tower and, although the stairs continued up, I resisted the temptation to move any higher. The higher I went, the more difficult it would be to escape if the need arose.

Even before I had reached the threshold of the room, the stink of stale urine filled my nostrils and ammonia began to burn my nose and throat. I looked around me. The room was fairly large, maybe fifteen feet wide by twenty feet long. It was in a bad state of repair; the plaster was powdery and peeling off the walls.

I moved across the room and sat down on the wooden floorboards with my back against the wall. To my right were the only two pieces of furniture in the room, two military-style tubular steel bedsteads complete with heavily soiled mattresses, which I assumed were the source of the stink. I stared at the three sets of leather straps that stretched across each bed.

There are no prizes for guessing what they're for.

Opposite where I was sitting was what looked like a cupboard. It was built into the wall and had probably been a much later addition. Its door, which was flush with the brickwork, lay partly open.

Sitting in the top left-hand corner, on the same wall as the cupboard, was the main doorway, the same one I had just entered through – minus the door. The only other exit was a tall rectangular window set into the wall to my left, but behind it was nothing but a drop of around twenty feet on to the rock-hard dirt floor of the courtyard. Using it as an escape route would hardly be a viable option if I found myself cornered.

My eyes went up to the ceiling, which hung ten feet above the floor. Off centre, to the left and closer to the door than I was, hung a single light fitting, minus the bulb.

My eyes were drawn to a section of exposed brickwork between the cupboard and the main doorway; an area the size of a large dinner plate, surrounded by the now off-white plaster. Letters had been carved into one of the original stones and my mind began to wander. Were they recent, carved by one of the inmates, or had they been left by an allied prisoner during the Second World War, and had once been plastered over for convenience?

From my current position, with a clear view of both the door and the room's only window, all I could do now was wait for nightfall before moving on.

As my eyes returned to the restraining straps on the beds, I saw something move behind the half-open door of the cupboard on the wall opposite. Someone was inside, watching me. I slowly reached inside my jacket and, leaving the safety on, I pulled back the hammer on the Makarov I had taken off Huber earlier that morning.

With my fingers wrapped around the pistol grip, still hidden inside my jacket, I stood up and slowly approached the cupboard. Taking hold of the turned wooden doorknob, I flicked off the Makarov's safety and inched towards the half-open door.

Crouched on the floor at the back of the cupboard, shaking either with fear or, given the temperature outside, maybe the cold, was what can only be described as a pathetic creature. It was impossible to be certain of his age, but I thought that he was probably younger than me, maybe in his late twenties. His head had been shaved, and sitting proud on what would have been his natural hairline was an angry-looking scar that ran the full width of his forehead. Filthy, and dressed only in an old nightshirt-style gown, his feet were bare and covered with scabs. The sight reminded me of the pictures I had seen when the Allies liberated Bergen-Belsen and Auschwitz.

I crouched down, stretched out my hand and waited. After what seemed like a lifetime, he took it and, with a firm grip, but keeping me at arm's length, and his back pressed tight against the wall, slid past me to my left and disappeared down the stairs.

Alone again, I returned to the wall and looked at my watch.

11:18. It won't be dark for another six hours.

So, with nothing else to do but wait, I removed Metzger's black book from my pocket. I knew that making sense of it would be a time-consuming process, but time was something I had plenty of right now.

As I opened the notebook, I caught sight of the dried blood on my hands, Huber's blood, and wondered what had become of her. Then I was brought back to the present by a figure standing in the doorway. The young man from the cupboard was back.

I slipped the notebook back into my jacket pocket, smiled, and beckoned him over. As I watched his bare feet tread gingerly across the wooden floorboards, I spotted the large glass jar he was cradling in his right arm.

He crouched down in front of me. Even with the heat of the winter sun, the outside temperature was close to zero, but he appeared to be naked beneath the filthy nightshirt. Then, as though it was some precious trophy, he placed the jar on the floor between us.

The contents and I were old friends. It was pickled vegetables. A mixture of tomatoes, cabbage and onions, and if I were forced to eat them it was a fair bet that I would be shitting through the eye of a needle for close to a week.

The young man extended his arm and offered me a lump of mouldy bread.

I took it, and saw the tattoo on his right forearm: a lump hammer and compass surrounded by a wreath of rye. Beneath it were the letters NVA – Nationale Volksarmee – the East German People's Army. At one time, the pathetic creature squatting opposite me had been a soldier. My eyes flashed to the scar running across his forehead and I remembered the *Zersetzung*, the Stasi's notorious programme of psychological destruction, the systematic decomposition of dissidents, those opposed to the communist regime.

Although he was East German, and to all intents and purposes my enemy, knowing that he was also a wounded soldier somehow stripped away the animosity, making us friends.

I watched him rip off a piece of stale bread, dip it into the jar and scoop out some of the vegetables. He then gingerly pushed the pot across the floor towards me, raised the bread to his lips, and urged me to do the same.

Hoping to demonstrate that I was a friend and not a threat, I somewhat reluctantly did as he asked and, although not a single word had passed between us, the action seemed to reassure him, and a few minutes later, uninvited, he took a seat against the wall beside me.

With the foul smell of his body odour, and God knows what else filling my nostrils, and my new best friend looking over my shoulder, I opened Metzger's notebook and began to work my way slowly through the pages.

The book was indexed alphabetically with individual letters of the alphabet cut into the right-hand margin, the type of notebook you could buy in any newsagents back in the UK. Each of its pages had been laid out in three columns. The first column contained names, but I suspected that for the most part they were not real, only code names made up by Metzger to protect the individual's true identity.

In the centre column, opposite some of the names, was what appeared to be a radio frequency. In the third column there were telephone numbers, and although Metzger could disguise a name, it would be near impossible for him to change the phone numbers without coming up with a very complicated algorithm.

As I continued to make my way through the book, it soon became apparent that Adler, the man I had been forced to kill back in the stables at the farm, had been telling me the truth. Metzger had contacts all over Europe and beyond. I ran my finger quickly down the right-hand column looking for any numbers I might recognise.

There were a total of six numbers with the 0044 prefix, but apart from one that began 0044-(0) 128, a Northern Ireland number, the other five were all central London.

I found numbers that I would later discover were for Paris, Bonn,

Rome, Geneva and Moscow. I searched for numbers outside Europe. There were only two, one was a number in the United States, but as for the other I had no idea.

It was just after 16:00 that I decided it was now dark enough for me to leave the castle and begin the two hundred kilometre cross-country trek towards the now redundant, but still highly dangerous, Inner German Border. I knew the vicious *Grenztruppen* were long gone, they had left the night the Wall fell, but the barbed wire, minefields and mantraps were still very much in place and represented a credible threat to anyone trying to find a way through them.

As I passed through the castle gates, I knew that the journey that lay ahead of me was not going to be easy, and neither would it be the last time I would make it. After completing my business with Scott, I would return to what was left of East Germany and try to find Huber. That was if she was still alive.

But right now I couldn't afford to worry about her, or anyone else apart from myself. If I wanted to make it safely back to the West, I needed to concentrate on the job in hand. There were people out there who desperately wanted back what I had taken from the bar just outside Zinnwald – and wanted me dead.

The first thing I needed to do was acquire some transport.

Just over an hour later I was skirting my way around a small village ten kilometres south-west of Colditz. The village struck me as rather quiet, given what was going on in the rest of Germany and across Europe, where people were still out celebrating the fall of the Berlin Wall.

I approached the main street along a narrow alleyway, stopping just short of the road, and stood in the darkness, staring at a small bar on the far side of the street. The road through the village was quiet. In the five minutes I had been standing there I think that only one vehicle had passed by.

On the far side of the road, parked to the right of the bar, was an old Moskvitch. A Soviet-made car that resembled a cross between a Mark 1 Ford Cortina and a Fiat 128, although the workmanship was nowhere near as good – but beggars can't be choosers.

I stood and watched a while longer. I was torn. I knew that I

needed to be quiet, couldn't afford to alert those inside the bar –
but I also needed a ride and I couldn't wait for ever. I took off my
jacket. My intention was to spread it over the driver's door window,
smash it with the butt of my pistol, and hope for the best. With
my left hand pinning the top of the jacket to the roof just above
the door I swung back the pistol, but then paused. *I wonder.* I took
hold of the door handle and gently pulled – the car was open.

Three minutes later, having hot-wired the car, and without seeing
a soul, I was heading away from the village and towards the A4,
the autobahn that would carry me west to what I now hoped would
be a busy but unmanned East German checkpoint.

Sunday, 12 November 1989

Kassel Ost *Raststätte*, West Germany

I T WAS 08:15 when I parked the Moskvitch I had stolen from a village a few miles south-west of Colditz, on the far side of the service station car park, thirty kilometres south of Kassel on Route 7, the main autobahn that ran south from Dortmund to Frankfurt. I spent the next twenty minutes in the *Raststätte* washrooms trying to repair the effects of having lived rough for the last three days.

I wiped the excess water from my hands, threw the paper towel into the wire basket sitting beside the washbasins, and stared into the large rectangular mirror fixed above them. It had been a long night, first walking and then driving across what was still a very effective border. Although I had not seen anybody, I had been unable to shake the feeling that I was being hunted.

With the stall door securely bolted, I lowered the toilet seat, and took off my leather jacket. Removing my clasp knife from my trouser pocket, and starting under the left arm, I began to carefully pick away at the stitching that held the jacket's lining in place. Several minutes later I gave a gentle tug, and a section of it came free. Behind the original fabric lining was a double lining of polythene, and sandwiched between them was a layer of West German currency, 2,000 Deutsche Marks in total, close to £750. There was also an East German ID card, which I left where it was. With the East German police force and their secret counterparts, the Stasi disappearing at a fast rate of knots, the ID card had quickly become redundant, and if it were found on me as I was searched by a West German police officer it would probably cause more problems than it solved. Kafka had done me proud, and for a second or two I wondered what she was doing now – had she decided to stay put in Czechoslovakia or, like the majority of the people in the former Eastern Bloc, was she patiently waiting her turn to head west?

I put DM300 into my trouser pocket, and folding the remainder of the currency neatly I slipped it into the zipped pocket inside the jacket. I reached back into the lining. I knew that there was something else, something hidden beneath the armpit of the left sleeve. I knew it was there because that's where I had put it. It was my own piece of insurance – the British passport Scott had given me in Victoria Park. The one I had shoved down the front of my trousers in Kafka's apartment that night back in August. It was time to book into the motel.

I passed through the glass door and into a near-empty reception lobby. The floor was covered in durable dark blue carpet and dotted around the area was a selection of potted trees. All natural looking, but all plastic. Ahead of me I could see a lift and two doors. One was marked Bureau, and the other *Zimmers* (rooms).

As I approached the motel reception desk, I found myself silently repeating: *It doesn't matter what you look like; your money is as good as the next man's.*

In the end, I needn't have worried. The receptionist only smiled as she asked me for my passport, and exchanged it for a room key.

'There we are, Herr Butala. Room twenty-seven. It's on the second floor.'

'Thank you.'

However, instead of going straight to my room, I made my way first to the Spar shop attached to the petrol station, and then to the transport café adjacent to the main lorry park. I felt comfortable there, invisible among the grease and grime of the other drivers, and, with the taste of pickled vegetables still lingering in my mouth, I bought myself breakfast. As I lifted the large mug of real coffee to my lips, I began formulating a plan.

First I needed to contact Scott, find out why he had all but abandoned me behind the Iron Curtain. As for Metzger's black book, well I had no idea what I was going to do with that right now. I had initially taken it with the intention of passing it on to Scott and the SIS, but now, given what had happened, I thought that I might be better off hanging on to it, as an insurance policy against what I was sure would be the future repercussions of my time spent in East Germany.

Then there was Huber. I still didn't know whose side she was on, but I was not prepared to just let her die, not if I could help it. Once I had found out what Scott's problem was, I would head back to what was left of East Germany and try to find her.

It was just before nine thirty on Sunday morning back in the UK. Scott had given me his home telephone number during our meeting in Victoria Park, but with strict instructions that it was only to be used in an emergency, and that I was never to try and call him at Century House, MI6 headquarters.

Although I hadn't thought much about it at the time, now I'd been abandoned behind the Iron Curtain, I remembered my conversation with Thompson as we left Covent Garden.

And as far as MI6 are concerned I don't exist?

Exactly.

Maybe it was the fact that I was tired, or maybe my paranoia was raising its ugly head again, but the more I thought about it, the more I felt Scott had used me. As a result, I was asking myself, was there something else, something much more sinister, going on here?

The phone at the other end only rang once before it was picked up.

'Scott.'

'It's me.'

For the next few seconds, there was nothing but silence, then: 'Tom?'

'Yes.' I sensed surprise in Scott's voice, as though I was the last person he expected to call. 'Where are you?'

I was way past tired, but felt my body tighten at Scott's question over an open phone line. Then I remembered I was back in the West. Standing in a public phone box on one of Europe's busiest motorways, and that there was no way anybody would be monitoring our conversation.

'At a *Raststätte* – Kassel Ost. Northbound on Route seven, a few miles south of Kassel.'

'You're back in the West?' Again he sounded more than a little surprised.

My sarcasm gene kicked in. 'Yes, but no thanks to you.'

Scott ignored the remark. 'What's your room number? And what name are you booked in under?'

It would appear that not having slept properly for close to three months had in no way affected my survival instincts. 'Why?'

Scott hesitated. He obviously hadn't expected me to challenge him.

'Er . . . so that I can phone you . . . as soon as I've sorted out how to get you back to the UK.'

I glanced at the plastic key fob I was holding in my left hand. 'Andel Butala, room twenty-seven.'

The tone of Scott's voice changed; he now sounded like a man in a hurry.

'OK. Don't go anywhere. Not until I contact you again. Once I've sorted things out at this end.'

'Roger that . . . but hurry, I can't wait here for ever.'

Now I was back in the West, armed with a clean British passport and more than enough money, I could have just hopped on a train and headed north, back to my unit. In fact, I could have jumped on the first flight back to London and confronted Scott, found out why he had abandoned me, but as always when working with spooks nothing is ever as simple as it first appears. I believed that the only person who had all the answers I was looking for was Scott and, if I was right and he was playing some sort of game, now that I had told him my current location I hoped he wouldn't be able to resist turning up in person. I calculated it would take him six or seven hours to reach me.

Then there was Huber. I had no idea where she was, whether she was safe or even still alive, but I needed to find out.

Back in my room, I shaved and stood under the hot shower for close to fifteen minutes in an attempt to revive my exhausted body. I walked back into the bedroom, picked up the half-cocked Sig from the bedside table, and screwed the silencer on to the muzzle. With a towel wrapped around my waist, and the Sig nestled neatly under my right thigh, I slept uneasily on top of the bed.

An hour later, just after 13:30, I was woken by a blast of cold air from the open window on my right. Fearing someone had entered the room I automatically reached for the Sig and pulled back the hammer the last half click, but I was alone. I slipped on the jeans and polo shirt I had bought earlier that morning in the Spar shop attached to the garage. Then, placing the Sig – with the silencer still attached, along with the Makarov, far enough under the mattress so that they wouldn't be found, not even by a chambermaid as she made the bed – I headed for the door.

In the corridor I turned right, and walking slowly along it, I made a mental note of the rooms that were in the process of being serviced. I walked straight past the lift and headed for the stairs. This wasn't because I needed the exercise; it was because a set of lift doors opening in a hotel lobby always turns people's heads. Draws their attention to your arrival. If I was going to get away with what I was going to do next, I needed to remain almost invisible.

In reception, I helped myself to a copy of the *Die Zeitung*, West Germany's national newspaper, and found myself a comfy seat in a corner where I had a good view of anyone coming and going.

It was just after two when the fresh faces started to appear behind the desk. Thirty minutes later, satisfied that the shift change was complete, I walked back up to the receptionist.

'*Guten Tag.*'

The receptionist raised her head.

'Sir?'

'Do you have a room available?'

She scanned the register on the desk in front of her. 'Yes, sir. Is it just for one night?'

Her question made me smile. Why would anyone want to stay more than one night in a motel room on one of Europe's busiest motorways? It's hardly the place for a vacation.

'Yes. I don't suppose room thirty is free? It's just that I've been driving all night, and I've stayed in that room before. The bed is comfortable.'

I watched as she ran her finger down the left-hand margin. 'It is, sir. Can I have your passport, please?'

I handed my British passport over and watched as she checked my face against the photograph.

'The room is ready for you now, have a pleasant stay, Mr Marshall.'

'Thank you.'

I was just about to turn away when I remembered Metzger's notebook.

'Excuse me, miss. Do you have a book of international dialling codes?'

The receptionist spun on her chair and reached out to the desk behind her.

'Yes, sir. What country is it you are looking for?'

I reached into my pocket and lifted out the notebook. 'I'm sorry, I only have the number. Do you think you could find out which country it belongs to?'

As luck would have it, at that very moment a man and woman stepped up behind me.

The receptionist looked round me and handed me the book. 'Would you mind, sir? This is our busiest time of the day.'

I returned to my seat in the corner of the lobby and, with the directory sitting on my lap, I began to flick through it. It would appear that 0098 was the country code for Iran, and the next two digits, 21, meant that the number was somewhere in the capital, Tehran. I had one more to find, but this time I knew that 001 was the international dialling code for the United States, and after a short search I found out that 001-757 was McLean, Virginia.

I returned the directory to the desk and headed for the stairs. I was confused, to say the least. McLean is regarded as a sleeper area for Washington, but it also has the same zip code as Langley, home of the CIA. I could now assume that at least one of the London numbers, the one in Tehran, and some of the other numbers belonged to intelligence organisations.

As I unlocked the door of Room 27 and walked inside, it slowly began to dawn on me what it was that I might have. As I closed the door behind me, my mind rushed back to the night Huber and I were chased out of Dresden, the night she was shot. We had both assumed that it was members of the Stasi that were manning the chase car, but what if we were wrong? What if they were members of the RAF? However, that still didn't explain why the Russian patrol turned up that morning in Dresden and, instead of it being led by one of their own officers or NCOs, they were being led by Major Putin, the head of the KGB in Saxony.

It had of course crossed my mind before that Putin might have been part of the conspiracy to assassinate Gorbachev. After all, he was head of the KGB in Saxony, and as such ideally placed to help enforce the Soviet Union's orders, had Metzger and his men succeeded in killing the Russian president. However, at that particular time I had no idea why he kept turning up as often as he did.

I lay back on the bed. It struck me that if – and it was an awfully big if – Metzger's notebook was proof of a working relationship between the RAF, a communist-sponsored terrorist group, British intelligence and the American CIA, and it ever became public knowledge, then heads would roll . . .

I walked to the bathroom, ran the shower, soaked the towels and, like a slob, left them strewn across the bathroom floor. I ruffled the bed so that it looked as if it had been slept in, and retrieved the two pistols from beneath the mattress. I then transferred everything I had, which wasn't much, to Room 30, two doors down, on the opposite side of the corridor.

Monday, 13 November 1989

I T WAS 00:17, and I had just turned off the TV when I heard footsteps and muffled voices in the corridor outside. I lifted the silenced Sig from the end of the bed, moved to the door, and peered through the security peephole.

There were two men standing outside Room 27. As I watched, they checked both ends of the corridor before drawing their weapons, and using what appeared to be a key to quietly enter the room. Minutes later they reappeared, locked the door, and headed towards the fire escape at the far end of the corridor.

I looked at my watch.

00:24. I'll give them twenty minutes, then take a look.

It looked like my plan was working. As far as the motel staff were concerned the occupants of Rooms 27 and 30, Herr Butala and Mr Marshall, were two different people of two different nationalities with nothing whatsoever to connect them. It was evident that my visitors were looking for Andel Butala, but I had no idea who they were, who had sent them, or where they had got a key.

I opened the door of Room 27 and ran my eyes across it. I had seen the two men enter the room, so took it for granted that it had been tossed, but they had been careful, nothing was out of place.

Which means they will probably be back.

Back in Room 30, I placed a small armchair against the wall, under the window and directly opposite the door. Then I settled down for the night, the fully cocked Sig sitting comfortably in my right hand, resting lightly in my lap.

Although I had heard nothing, my subconscious must have registered a noise, and I woke with a start. I looked at my watch. It was 06:24.

I had been asleep for close to four hours. I began to panic and wondered what I'd missed, if anything.

I got up from the chair, walked quietly to the door, and looked through the peephole. In the half-light of the corridor, I could see a figure standing outside Room 27. It was Scott.

I slipped the silenced Sig behind my right thigh and quietly opened the door, but as I gently released the handle, the latch must have snagged on the edge of the lock housing. I was already in the corridor and heading towards Scott when it sprung free with a loud clunk.

Scott turned. He smiled, let go of the door handle on Room 27, slipped his right hand into his pocket, and began to walk along the corridor towards me.

'There you are. I thought you said you were in room twenty?'

I remained outwardly calm, almost relaxed. However, as Scott drew closer I raised my right arm to shoulder height and pointed the silenced Sig at his forehead. My instructions were both clear and unambiguous: 'Using your index finger and thumb lift your weapon clear of your pocket.'

Scott did as ordered, held the gun up in front of me. It was an Austrian-made Glock 17, a 9mm pistol.

'Now using the index finger and thumb on your left hand, take it by the barrel, and hold it out at arm's length. And just so we're clear, if you try anything, the mood I'm in I *will* kill you.'

With his weapon leading the way, I beckoned Scott to follow me and began to back up towards Room 30, but instead of going in, I gave the door a good shove so that it was wide open, I went another two metres past the room before stopping.

'Inside.'

There was no argument from Scott, and with the Sig still levelled at his head, I followed him into the room.

'That's far enough. Now, throw your weapon on the bed and sit down in the armchair.' Scott did as ordered. 'Now, interlock your fingers, place your hands on your head, and cross your ankles.' Keeping my eyes and the Sig on Scott, I used my foot to close the door.

Scott stared at the pistol aimed at his forehead and smiled. 'I see you got my little gift. But I didn't send a silencer, so I'm guessing that you got that from Captain Townsend – the BRIXMIS officer I coerced into being your only contact while you were in the East.'

I was in no mood for idle chatter or pleasantries. I had questions and needed answers. 'Why are you here?'

I gave Scott little time to respond before providing him with a ready-made solution: 'Is it to check that your two goons didn't miss anything when they were here last night?'

Scott looked surprised. 'I have no idea what you're talking about; I didn't send anybody.'

I lowered my weapon slightly, but kept it fully cocked. The safety was off, and my index finger was resting lightly against the trigger.

'So why are you armed?'

Scott raised his eyebrows. 'I could ask you the same question.'

I extended my arm again, pushed the weapon closer to him. 'I'm armed because I've just spent three months playing tag with the Stasi and KGB and, if you didn't send the two goons last night, I guess it's not over yet. So, once again why are you here?'

'As I told you on the phone, to make sure you get safely back to the UK, and just so we're clear' – there was now an air of arrogance in Scott's voice – 'I don't appreciate being pushed around.'

I glared at him. Scott was right. Holding an SIS controller at gunpoint was overstepping the mark, but given what I'd already done, I was way past caring.

'Don't push it. The mood I'm in they won't even find your body, and you still haven't answered my second question – why are you armed?'

Scott brushed the question aside. 'My hire car's downstairs in the car park. I can have us both on a flight from RAF Gutersloh later this afternoon. We could be back in London for supper.'

I needed to slow things down. So, tucking the Sig into the back of my trousers, I walked to the bed, picked up Scott's weapon, released the magazine and slipped it into my pocket. I then tried to eject the round in the chamber, but as I pulled back the top slide I could see that the chamber was empty.

Amateur.

I flicked down the slide release, felt the weapon shake in my hand as it flew forward, and threw it on the bed.

'You'll get the magazine back later, when I'm sure whose side you're on.'

Scott glared at me and then shouted, 'You can't be serious?'

I ignored his outburst and continued. 'London will have to wait. Kirstin Huber, a young female member of the Bewegung, was wounded as we made our escape from Dresden. By now both the RAF and what remains of the Stasi will know that she was with me. If you want me to go back to London, you'll have to help me get her out.'

'And if I refuse?'

I blew out heavily through my nose. 'No problem, you can either wait here, or piss off back to London, but get in my way and I *will* kill you.'

Scott said nothing; he just sat staring at me, which prompted me to expand on what I had just said.

'And let's be honest, given the current state of affairs, who's going to ask questions about another dead spook found in a German motel room? Shit, for all they know, you could be the leak; it could've been you who sold out Littman and the others to the Stasi.' Then to emphasise my position I added, 'And besides, given what I now suspect, I doubt that anyone back in London even knows I'm here.'

It was 10:42 when Scott lifted a rucksack out of the boot of a dark blue Opel Vectra and closed the lid.

I smiled to myself as I got into the Moskvitch.

Bright red. Very fucking covert.

More robust, and more reliable than the Moskvitch I had stolen a few nights earlier, Scott wanted to use the Vectra for our journey back to the East. It took me less than five minutes to talk him out of it, telling him that it would stick out like a sore thumb among the East German Trabants, Wartburgs and Russian Moskvitchs. Make us a target, and that it wouldn't get very far on the shit the East Germans call petrol.

As he walked across the car park towards me, I earthed out the ignition wires of the Moskvitch on its steering column. The engine started first time, and I looked at the petrol gauge.

Just over half full. If I put ten litres in now, once it's mixed with the

Eastern Bloc shit already in the tank, it shouldn't do too much harm. Besides it only needs to get us back here once I have Huber.

13:27 – Back in East Germany

The ease with which Scott had allowed me to take the lead and accompany me in my quest to find Huber had taken me a little bit by surprise. I thought he might have kicked up a fuss; tried to pull rank on me. But if he was on the level, maybe, having abandoned me earlier, he was somehow trying to make amends; perhaps he was even doing it out of some sense of guilt.

The return journey east, with most of the traffic now heading in the opposite direction, was problem free. Just to be safe, however, and ensure I could find the tiny village again, I retraced the same route Huber and I had taken. As I pulled the car off the metal road, through the narrow tunnel and on to the logging track, I sensed Scott turn towards me.

'By the way, where did you get the vehicle?'

I kept my eyes on the track as it wound its way through the forest. The last thing I needed right now was a follow-up encounter with the log fall.

'I stole it from outside a small *Gästehaus* about thirty clicks from here.'

The tone of Scott's voice changed, he now sounded like a teacher chastising a naughty child. 'And what happens if we get caught in it?'

I couldn't stop myself laughing out loud. 'East Germany is in utter turmoil. It has no properly functioning government and a large number of its citizens, including members of its police force, are currently heading west as fast as their clapped-out cars will carry them. While on the other side of a rapidly disappearing Inner German Border, West Germany is preparing itself for the largest movement of refugees Europe has seen since the end of the Second World War. Who the fuck is going to give a shit about a stolen ten-year-old Moskvitch?'

Before Scott had a chance to respond, I brought the car to a halt, looked around me, and got my bearings. We were outside the tiny rough-built house Huber had been taken into three days earlier.

Given how quickly things were happening elsewhere in East Germany, it seemed that little had changed in the tiny hamlet. Without a permanent metal road, street lamps or pavements, and plumbing that I suspect culminated in a large ditch somewhere behind the houses, it was like taking a step back in time, back to the fifteenth century. In fact, thinking about it now, the only thing that was missing was the stake where they burned the witches.

I turned my attention back to the house. Standing in the doorway was the old man who had helped Huber. He smiled and motioned me to come in. My heart quickened. Maybe she was still here? As I approached the house I sensed Scott a few paces behind me.

It was a small house and, as I crossed the threshold, I was reminded of the rows of terraced houses back in Belfast. Those where the front door opened directly into a small living room, which in turn led through to an even smaller kitchen, the only two rooms on the ground floor; the toilet housed in a small outbuilding in the back yard. However, these rough-built dwellings were nowhere near as lavish as their Northern Ireland counterparts.

As the three of us sat down around a small wooden table, the wife appeared from the kitchen with a pot of what passed for coffee in those parts.

I waited for her to sit down before speaking. When I did it was in German – I doubted the old couple would speak any English.

'*Wo ist mein freund?*'

The old man had a grave look on his face and I feared the worst. He continued in German.

'After you left, later that day two men came into the village. They were looking for you and your friend, but we managed to hide her.'

I immediately thought about the policeman we had encountered, the one who had shot Huber, and my two visitors at the motel the previous night.

The old man continued, 'That night, once it was dark, I rode a neighbour's bike into a nearby village and spoke to the local doctor who agreed to treat her.'

'Do you know where she is now?'

The old man still had hope in his eyes. 'The doctor collected her in his car. He promised to treat her wound and, when she was well enough, return her to her own people.' But as the words left his lips, I saw the hope rapidly disappearing from the old man's eyes. 'We haven't heard from either one of them since. Before she left she told me that if you returned, I was to tell you she was going back to the southern safe house.' The old man looked down at his cup sitting on the table. 'But she didn't tell me where it was.'

I rested my hand on his shoulder and squeezed. 'That's OK; I know exactly where she's gone.'

As we reached the front door, I paused and turned back to the old man. 'What happened to the policeman? Did he return to the village once I'd left?'

The old man smiled, raised his eyebrows, and slowly shook his head. '*Nein.*'

Scott was staring out of the side window when he asked, 'Where are we going?'

'Zinnwald. The southern safe house is in the Mining Projects. We agreed that if we ever became separated, we would make for there first.' But, now knowing that if Metzger had known about the safe house, then so would other members of the RAF. Maybe they were the people the doctor had been talking about?

Monday, 13 November 1989

Zinnwald

A s we passed the large yellow sign that announced our arrival in Zinnwald, I looked at my watch.

16:10.

I handed Scott the loaded magazine for his weapon, the one I had taken from him back at the motel, but instead of inserting it into the pistol grip of the Glock, he slipped it into the pocket of his coat and, pulling back the top slide, fed a round into the chamber.

I kept my eyes on the road.

'So, if you had a spare magazine, and have been armed all along, why didn't you turn on me the first chance you got?'

Scott turned away, towards the side window. 'I wasn't sure I could win.'

At the bottom of the main street, I turned left on to the service road that led to the Projects. As we passed the block where Metzger had lived, I saw the pitted and scorched tarmac where the grenade had exploded beneath his car. The windows closest to the blast were still boarded up. I was puzzled as to why there had been no mention of the explosion on the state news channel at the time, but as we crested a rise in the road, and it levelled out, Scott grabbed my right arm.

'Pull over. QUICK.'

I pulled the car to the kerb, slipped it in behind an ancient-looking Barkas minibus, and began searching for the cause of Scott's panic. Seventy metres away, on the opposite side of the road, was a slightly built man climbing out of a black Wartburg.

There was a note of surprise in Scott's voice. 'That's Franz Schneider.'

I didn't recognise the man. 'Who?'

'Franz Schneider, the agent who replaced Littman.'

Scott had never told me his name. He had only ever referred to him as 'Littman's replacement' during my initial briefing back in Victoria Park. So, to say I was surprised would have been an understatement. 'The agent you thought was missing – dead? The man who fed you the information surrounding Operation Konev?'

'Yes.'

For some reason, I began to panic. I don't know why. It was just one of those moments you get when you think you've missed something really obvious.

I was brought back to the present by a familiar face climbing out of the front passenger seat.

Scott sat staring through the windscreen. 'Do you know who that is?' he asked.

'Yes. His name is Peter Bonsack. He's the leader of the Bewegung in Zinnwald, and their car is parked outside the same block that houses the safe house.'

I sat and stared at the two men. If Schneider was the man who had fed Scott the information regarding Operation Konev, then where had he been for the last four months and, more importantly, what was he doing here now with Bonsack, the man everybody thought had been arrested in Leipzig on 7 October?

As Bonsack moved to the rear of the car, he took a quick look around before opening the door. I drew breath sharply as a second later Huber stepped out on to the road. Head bowed, her left arm in a sling and with Schneider walking close behind her, she followed Bonsack into the block of flats.

I sensed Scott was now staring at me.

'I take it from your pained expression that the petite blond is Huber – the missing girl?' A few seconds later he continued, 'So . . . if Schneider has been alive and well all along, why did he fail to keep in touch?'

I remained facing forward, but my sarcasm gene was beginning to kick in again. 'Surely the bigger question is, what the fuck is he doing here now with Bonsack? You told me back in Victoria Park that you didn't know anyone inside the Bewegung?'

Scott breathed in heavily through his nose. 'I had no idea Schneider was in contact with them. But we now have to assume that Schneider is a double agent. And given that he's now here with your guy Bonsack, I think we can also assume that they're both working for the other side.'

With my eyes fixed firmly on the entrance to the block of flats, I said, 'No shit, Sherlock?' I couldn't think of anything else to say. I was as angry as hell knowing that I had been played all along. But what was really eating away at me was, had Huber been part of the charade?

Scott broke the silence. 'So, what are we going to do now? We can hardly march in there and demand that they let her go. Besides if, as it appears, your girl Huber is also working with them, she might not want rescuing, which means we'd be outnumbered and they'll probably kill us both.'

I said nothing at first. I just sat there trying to make sense of what I had witnessed and what Scott had just said, while at the same time working out what I was going to do next. Close to a minute later I said, 'To stand any chance of getting Huber back alive, we need to get Bonsack and your man Schneider out into the open, but not here. Somewhere isolated. Somewhere that will give us the edge.'

It was beginning to get dark, but as I looked around me I could see children were still playing in the street. The last thing I wanted to do was to get into a firefight in a built-up area. Out here on the street.

No women, no kids.

I turned to Scott. 'The one advantage we have over Bonsack and your man is that neither of them know that you're here.' I reached into the inside pocket of my jacket, took out Metzger's notebook, and ripped out the front page, the one that contained some of what I assumed were Metzger's domestic, low-value East German contacts. Those who would probably never surface again. I began writing on it.

'Is that the NOC list?'

'Yes. I'm guessing it's what Bonsack wants, and if it wasn't you who sent the two men to the motel last night, they were his men and they were looking for the list.'

Although that doesn't explain how they knew which room I was in.

'But don't get any ideas. You were right.'

'About what?'

I began folding the piece of paper. 'You wouldn't win. Try to take the notebook before I'm ready to give it to you, or get in my way, and as I said earlier, I *will* kill you.'

With Bonsack, Schneider and Huber safely inside the block of flats, I got out of the car and called to a young boy who was kicking a half-inflated football against the end wall of one of the blocks. It is suggested that the language and vocabulary used by children, because of their age, is simpler, but unlike adults they sometimes don't have the ability to fill in the blanks, any words I might leave out. I just hoped my German was good enough to convince the youngster to help me. I took a deep breath, and asked him, 'Do you want to earn twenty Marks?'

The youngster nodded enthusiastically.

'Can you count?'

He looked at me as if I was an idiot. '*Naturlich, bis zu hundert.*'

'Good man.' I handed him the folded piece of paper and pointed to the block of flats. 'I want you to go to Flat 4 on the ground floor and give this to whoever opens the door.' Then taking an East German twenty Ost Mark note from my pocket, I first showed it to the youngster and then – to his horror – I tore it in two and handed him half. 'After you have delivered the note I want you to meet me at the end of the road to collect the other half of your reward. Do you understand?'

The young lad was still staring at the half note I'd given him. He was thinking about it, but after a second or two he nodded and, as I climbed back into the car, he headed towards the block of flats at a run.

As soon as he was out of sight, I slipped the car into gear, drove to the far end of the street, and backed it around a corner.

Scott was staring at me again. 'What are you doing? What was on that note, and why did you write it on a page from the NOC list?'

I felt myself grin, like a schoolboy who had just stitched up the playground bully.

'I told Bonsack that I have what he wants. I used the first page from the notebook so that he would know I wasn't bluffing.'

The tone of Scott's voice softened. 'Why give the boy only half of the twenty Mark note?'

I thought back to my childhood in the East End of London. 'You don't know much about kids, do you? If I'd given him all of the money before he delivered the note, there's a good chance he wouldn't have even bothered; he would have just headed off to the nearest shop with it. By giving him only half of the note he has to complete the task, that's if he wants to collect the other half. Half of a twenty Mark note is no good to anyone, and in a few days' time I suspect that even a whole twenty Ost Mark note will be pretty much worthless.'

'So, why drive to the opposite end of the street and park the car out of sight?'

I was beginning to wonder how Scott had managed to survive for so long and answered him without taking my eyes off the block that contained the safe house. 'In case Schneider or Bonsack try to follow the boy back to us.'

A minute later, as anticipated, the young lad came running out of the block laughing, like he was playing a game of 'knock down ginger', a game we used to play as kids. The one where you knock on a neighbour's door and then run like hell before they have a chance to answer it. Once the dust had settled and they had gone in and shut the door, you would repeat the process. It's the type of game that never stops giving fun. The youngster headed straight for the spot where he expected to find me, and collect the second half of his wages.

Seconds later Schneider appeared, at a run, and made no attempt to conceal the weapon he held in his right hand as he looked around for the boy.

I called to a young girl sitting on the kerb cradling a doll and, as she drew closer to the car, I asked, 'Would you like to play a new game?' I paused.

Shit, I sound like a fucking pervert.

I continued, 'At the other end of the street is a boy wearing a red jumper.' I held up the second half of the twenty OM note. 'He has the other half of this. If you can find him, you can share it.' I chuckled to myself as, dragging her doll by one leg behind her, she headed for the far end of the street at full speed.

'What's so funny?'

'That little lad is going to be so pissed off when he finds out he has to share his booty with her.'

With the engine still running, I slipped the car into gear and headed back towards the main road.

'Where are we going now?' There was a hint of frustration in Scott's voice.

'North-west. To Colditz.'

It was just after 19:00 when I pulled off Route 4 and into a petrol station halfway between Dresden and Klipphausen, and as I brought the car to a halt I turned to Scott.

'Stay here; I won't be long.'

'Where are you going?'

There was a note of concern in his voice. He sounded like a child who didn't want to be left alone, and it was then that it hit me. Scott was the mission commander, my controller, and as such he should have been the one calling the shots, but since disarming him back at the motel, he had been more than happy to follow, while I took the lead. At first, although it didn't sit easily with me, I put his subservience down to the fact that I was the soldier, and that the mission objective, along with the associated intelligence, had now changed. However, my experience while working across the water with those of Scott's profession, namely MI5, had taught me that his current behaviour was totally out of character. Spooks are traditionally 'know it alls', the type that will insist on doing things their way, regardless of whether they know what they're doing, or have the necessary experience.

I answered him as I opened the car door. 'To the shop beside the petrol kiosk, I take it you want to eat tonight?'

As I went into the shop and closed the door behind me, I paused and looked back through the glass at Scott. He was still sitting in the car but was so nervous his head appeared to be on a swivel as he turned first one way, and then the other. I had made a hasty decision back in Zinnwald, but now, alone for the first time since leaving the town, I had time to think about it. I turned away from the door.

I hope you know what you're doing. Because once the wheels are in motion, there will be no going back.

Five minutes later, having paid for our food, and an East German version of a Zippo lighter, I was back in the car, sitting beside Scott.

At the intersection with the A14, Scott's curiosity finally got the better of him.

'Why did you choose Colditz for the meeting with Bonsack and Schneider? Isn't there a town there? Won't there be lots of people about, witnesses, or is that what you're counting on?'

I kept my eyes on the road. 'It's only a small town, not much more than a village by Western standards, and now that the Wall's down it's practically deserted. Up until recently, it looks like the castle was being used as some sort of asylum – that was until, like the majority of East Germans, the carers deserted their patients, leaving them free to wander the castle grounds unsupervised. So, in answer to your question: yes, there will be people around, but hopefully not one credible witness.'

Monday, 13 November 1989

Colditz

I LOOKED AT my watch.

20:27.

I had parked the car in the woods, about a kilometre from the castle, and now, as we approached it, I looked up at its crumbling walls. They were white in the moonlight; without lights or any signs of life it reminded me of a scene from a 1940s black and white horror film. However, I knew that the horrors lurking behind these walls were incredibly real.

The rhythm of Scott's breathing began to match the sound of his footfall as he followed me through the castle gates and into the courtyard.

I caught a fleeting glance of a figure wearing the same sort of gown the young man in the cupboard had been wearing on my first visit – what appeared to be some sort of patient's medical gown – as it scurried across the open space to my left and disappeared into a building. I lowered my voice to a whisper as my eyes continued to scan the area for anyone else.

'Try not to make eye contact with anybody. We don't need any new friends; anyone getting in our way tomorrow morning.'

Without waiting for Scott to respond, I continued across the courtyard and entered the castle's West Wing. As I began to climb the spiral stone staircase in the pitch dark I felt something brush against my leg. Scott had shortened the distance between us.

A few seconds later he whispered, 'How do you know where you're going?'

I didn't answer, he would find out soon enough. Once again, he was merely seeking information, not demanding it, something that was totally out of character for someone of his profession and position.

As I entered the moonlit room on the first floor the strong smell of ammonia and stale urine that I had experienced on my first visit began to burn my nose and throat again.

A second later I heard Scott retch and then mutter 'Jesus' under his breath.

I handed him the bag of food I had bought at the petrol station shop. 'Go and sit over there – against the wall. But don't make any loud noises or sudden movements.'

As Scott headed for the other side of the room, I quietly approached the door of the cupboard set into the wall. I crouched down and, balancing on my toes, I whispered, '*Sind Sie dort, mein freund?*' Then again, 'Are you there, my friend?'

The cupboard door slowly opened and, as my eyes grew accustomed to the gloom, the face of the young man I had befriended three days earlier slowly began to take shape. As the malnourished, shaven-headed figure moved slowly forward and into the moonlight, I heard Scott gasp as he got his first sight of the pathetic creature who lived in the cupboard.

The young man flinched at the sound. I flashed Scott a look and stretched out my hand. The young man smiled sheepishly and, after some encouragement, eventually took it.

I glanced down and, in the moonlight, saw the dark patch of skin that was the tattoo on his right forearm: the lump hammer and compass surrounded by a wreath of rye; beneath it were the letters NVA – the only clue that this empty shell of a man had once been a soldier.

A few seconds later, with his eyes now firmly fixed on Scott, he allowed me to lead him across the room to where he was sitting.

My instructions to Scott were short, quiet and precise. 'Don't stand up. We don't want to frighten him. Now offer him your hand.'

Scott hesitated and in a whisper said, 'What? Are you mad? He's filthy!'

I grabbed hold of Scott's hand, placed it on the young man's and, holding on to them both, gently shook them. To some people this might seem to be something of a pointless exercise but hand shaking is a way of life for most Germans, something they do every day, as natural as saying good morning, and I hoped that it might trigger a distant memory in the young man's brain. Remind him that not everybody he came across was out to hurt him. Help him accept us as friends.

With the introductions over I sat the young man down against the wall, beside a very nervous-looking Scott. Opening the bag, I lifted out two bread rolls, a packet of processed ham, a bottle of water and offered them to him.

The young man's eyes widened as he snatched at the food and without a sound retreated quickly back across the room. Sitting on his own, his back against the wall and close to the imaginary safety of his cupboard, he began to tear at the food like a hungry animal.

Scott said nothing for a while. He just sat and stared at the scene being played out in front of him, a look of disbelief on his face as he tried to wipe the young man's dirt from his hands. It was close to a minute later that he lifted his head and said, 'What do you think you're doing? I thought you said we didn't want any new friends.'

This was exactly the kind of response I would have expected from him, which made his almost subservient behaviour up to that point even more confusing.

It had been less than a week between my visits but it was plain to see that, even during that short amount of time, the young man's condition had deteriorated. I was still staring at him when I eventually answered Scott. 'He isn't a new friend. The last time I was here he brought me food and provided me with company while I waited for it to get dark. I told Bonsack that if he wanted Metzger's notebook, the NOC list, he was to meet me here at eleven o'clock tomorrow morning and that he was to bring Huber with him. I don't think he'll risk turning up in the dark. My guess is he'll wait for daylight, until he can see what he's up against. But, if I'm wrong and he shows up early, then our friend over there is the perfect guard dog.' I glanced around the room. It was unchanged from my last visit and, to be honest, I would have been extremely suspicious if it had been.

Tuesday, 14 November 1989

A T FIVE O'CLOCK that morning, when I took over the watch from Scott, it was pitch black outside. As he dragged one of the soiled mattresses on to the floor and settled down to sleep on the bare metal springs, I made myself as comfortable as I could on the window-sill. I would probably have been more comfortable sitting on the floor but the window gave me a commanding view of the castle courtyard and main gate and it was from there that I began to formulate a plan.

Given my background, you will probably be expecting the meticulous type of planning that most people associate with Special Forces' operations and, under normal circumstances, when missions are planned at Division, Brigade, Regiment and, in some cases, Squadron level, detailed planning will take place. Especially when it comes to operations involving the Special Projects team – the squadron tasked with carrying out the Regiment's anti-terror and siege-breaking duties, such as at the Iranian Embassy and Mogadishu. Then, the actions of every man involved is planned in minute detail and rehearsed for a situation where the ultimate action will be short and extremely clinical.

However, get down below that, to Troop level (16 men) or lower still, Patrol level (4 men), and it just doesn't happen. It's all far more informal, especially where there are no outside agencies involved. We train together, live and work together, and together we make things happen.

Yes, the objective that has been set by the 'Head Shed' is always there and will remain the driving force behind the mission throughout but, once our boots are on the ground, our actions become totally responsive: action – reaction. As a result, the parameters of our mission – the nitty-gritty of the operation – will inevitably become much more fluid. We quickly learn to adapt to everything that is happening around us: the environment, the weather and the changes in the enemy's strategy. In some cases, even the attitude of the local population.

Take it down even further, to one man alone, without backup, equipment or the resources he needs, and the ability to improvise is crucial. The prime objective – which in my case was removing Huber from harm's way – and my secondary objective, to obtain the information I required from Bonsack, remained constant. But, while I had a loose plan in my head, it was only a guide, a sketch map for what would inevitably be a constantly evolving situation.

Back at the stable block in the farmyard at Schwarzbachtal, my initial plan had been very simple: get between Adler, his partner and their car; disable it and disappear. But when Adler's partner appeared unexpectedly from the barn, I instantly ditched that plan and let my training, knowledge and natural aggression take over. I was forced to adapt and I did. The situation in Colditz was different only in that here I was more familiar with the ground and the players involved. However, I still had no idea how many would turn out to be an asset, a friend, or a hindrance. I wasn't sure who the enemy was.

Unlike at Schwarzbachtal, I already knew that developing a single plan on the hoof and adapting it as things progressed was not going to be enough to get this job done. Whatever I came up with would need to cover every eventuality; every twist and turn that Bonsack might throw into the mix. I had to assume that someone like him – someone who had survived as long as he had – would be an intelligent and dangerous adversary and the more scenarios I could anticipate and plan for, the less chance there was of him countering them, which in turn would increase my chances of survival.

Picking Colditz for my meeting with Bonsack wasn't a random act or a decision I had taken in haste. The fact that, apart from the inmates, the castle had been abandoned and the local population was rapidly deserting the surrounding area made it ideal for what I had in mind. The isolated location also meant that there was little chance of being disturbed by an inquisitive local and, given the state of the inmates, there was no way they would want to venture up here to see what was going on. All of which meant that the only witnesses to what might go down here later this morning were the poor deluded patients.

Although I wasn't certain that he would bring Huber as I had instructed, I was pretty sure that when Bonsack eventually turned up he would not be alone. He would probably have Schneider in tow as backup but I had no idea whether he would bring anyone else, maybe Fischer and Mayer, his two minders.

Critical to my planning was that he had no idea that Scott was here with me at the castle. He would think that I was alone and he had a vital two to one advantage over me.

I was still staring out into the courtyard when the moon cast a fleeting shadow on the outer castle wall.

Someone's in the courtyard.

A few seconds later I heard the faint sound of footsteps on the stairs. Slipping off the windowsill I pulled back the hammer on Huber's Makarov and moved my silhouette from in front of the window, back into the shadows. It was the young man. For reasons only known to him, he had quietly left the room during Scott's watch.

He turned and looked at me as he crossed the threshold. Then, without a word, he disappeared into the safety of his cupboard.

As I watched the door close silently behind him I suddenly felt guilty. He had the body of a grown man but now, as a result of the horrors inflicted on him here, he was little more than a child.

A child I may be forced to use as a weapon later today.

On my first visit to the castle his kindness and the friendship we had shared was genuine. However, the food and drink I had given him the previous night had all been part of my preparation – building a possible Plan B, a much riskier alternative to plan A, that was rapidly coming together in my mind.

Under normal circumstances and based on your own experience, the enemy will normally only have one or two options, and as a result you will plan accordingly. It's a case of if they do one thing, we will implement Plan A. If they do something else, we will counter it with Plan B. So, if an unforeseen element is thrown into the mix – such as a larger than expected enemy force, or the sudden appearance of amor – and the world turns to shit, a Plan B can mean the difference between success and failure, life and death. Just as I had chosen Colditz as the venue for the meet, if Plan B became necessary, the young man in the cupboard might well become part of it.

I looked at my watch.

06:53.

I returned to my position on the windowsill.

Life had seemed relatively straightforward before Scott and I had arrived in Zinnwald the previous afternoon. We had only to drive back into the East, find Huber and leave again. However, the minute Scott identified Schneider as he climbed out of the Wartburg everything had changed.

If Scott was telling me the truth and the two men who had visited my motel room early the previous morning had not been his, then I had to assume that as Huber was now with Bonsack and Schneider, that she had told them where they could find me – at the Kassel Ost Raststätte.

I hadn't discussed my plans with her until we were chased out of Dresden, mainly because of what had happened over the previous few months. I had been finding it increasingly hard to trust her and, as a result, all such information was now on a strictly need-to-know basis, and up until that point she hadn't needed to know. I'd like to think that she hadn't given up the information without a fight – but then, almost immediately, I was hit with guilt as I realised what that might mean for her. But if I was right, and they had forced her to tell them where I was, then I also had to assume that the two men who had visited my motel room were two of Bonsack's men. And if that were the case then the only reason for him coming here this morning would be to recover Metzger's black book. The problem was, as I had never mentioned the book to Huber, the only way Bonsack could know that the book existed was if he and Metzger were a lot closer than it had first appeared? But how did he know that I now had it.

I was also becoming increasingly suspicious of Scott. Why had he turned up outside my room at the motel with his pistol drawn? He gave the impression that he was inexperienced when it came to fieldwork, but deep down inside I had the feeling that this was nothing more than just another part of the charade, that he was hiding something, and that maybe he had another, darker agenda. I had never liked him – not that liking someone has ever had anything to do with taking orders from them – but this feeling that he was not playing a straight game was now beginning to obsess me.

Then there was Huber. Although I still had my suspicions about where her loyalties might lie, even following her declaration of love that morning back in Leipzig, I had to admit that things between us had steadily improved. Up until the point where we'd been separated after she'd been shot, I hadn't thought about her as anything more than an asset; a means to an end. But since then, the longer I spent on my own without her, the more it became apparent that my feelings for her had grown and that she now meant much, much more to me.

Perhaps it seems strange that I didn't just take advantage of the situation. What harm would it do? Nobody would have ever known. But, in a world as dark and convoluted as the one I was living in, a world where loyalty counted for nothing and life had proved to be very cheap, for the sake of my own sanity I had to hang on to something good. Something right. And for me that something was my loyalty to my wife. Using Huber as some sort of stress relief toy meant losing sight of right and wrong. If that happened I knew I was lost. I would become nothing more than a hollow shell, one that would eventually be consumed by the darkness that surrounded me.

I was determined that Huber was not going to become yet another victim of whatever devious games were being played here. I was willing to risk everything to ensure that she had the chance to prove herself loyal and, if she were, walk away from Colditz. Not even this was simple though because, much as I had come to realise just how much I cared for her, my paranoia was once again in overdrive. Was Huber really just unfortunate, an innocent who believed in democracy and who had simply been trying to do her part to achieve it? Or was she working for Metzger, or the Stasi – had she been against me all along?

My mind suddenly jumped to another possibility. What if, like Littman and Schneider, Huber was part of Scott's organisation? Working at Dynamo Zinnwald at his behest? Then there had been her sudden appearance that morning at the railway station in Dresden; had she known I'd be there? Scott hadn't put up much of a fight when I had insisted on coming back into the East to find her. Why risk himself for someone he didn't know? But then, if she had been working for him all along, living and working in

Zinnwald, he could have sent her to find out what had happened to Littman. I knew that if I was to attain any form of closure on all that had happened, I needed to hear the truth from Huber.

But, regardless of what the truth would turn out to be and having no idea how events would unfold, the one thing I was certain of was that not everybody would be leaving Colditz alive today. My one hope was that if my suspicions about Huber not being on the level with me were correct, then it would be someone else, or bad luck, who would decide her fate and not me – *no women, no kids.*

Tuesday, 14 November 1989

08:04.

As I looked across the room to where Scott was sleeping, the first rays of the morning sun began to creep across the windowsill and on to the wooden floorboards. It was time to wake him. I pushed the Makarov into my belt, walked across the room, took hold of his left foot, and gently shook it.

As soon as his eyes were open, he sat up like a frightened child, threw his legs over the side of the bed, and looked like he was ready to run. Then his face dropped as he realised that it was not just a bad dream. It was real.

He ran his fingers through his hair and glanced around the room, ending at the cupboard.

'It would appear that you were wrong. While you were asleep, and having devoured all of the food you gave him, your pet dog upped and left.' There was more than a hint of 'told you so' in his voice.

I didn't respond. Scott was mistaken on both counts. Firstly, I hadn't been asleep. I didn't trust him and, as a result, I had only been dozing, aware of every move he made and everything that was going on around me. Secondly, although the young man may have left the room during his watch, I had seen him return and make his way to his cupboard a little before seven. That I would keep to myself. Scott didn't need to know any more than was absolutely necessary.

Leaving Scott sitting on the bedsprings I made my way back over to the window. Plan A was complete, although currently locked inside my head. It was also simple: two variations of a single scenario which I intended to work out in detail with Scott. In essence, I wanted him to kill Schneider as he left the car and came to join Bonsack. Then instead of Schneider, it would be Scott who walked into this room and Bonsack who would be outnumbered and surrounded, not me. But for now, while I waited for him to get his act together, I needed to prepare Plan B, something I would not be sharing with Scott.

I pulled the Makarov I had taken from Huber back in the village from the waistband of my jeans. Then, staring out into the courtyard, using my right thumb, I slid the magazine release catch on the heel of the pistol grip to the rear and felt the magazine drop into the palm of my hand. I pushed the weapon back into my belt.

Next, pushing down on the top round, I slid it forward and out of the magazine. I did the same with the following six rounds, but as my thumb slid over the eighth and final round (the magazine on this model of Makarov only carried eight rounds), I hesitated. I was fairly confident that if Bonsack was here for the book he would not risk opening fire until he had what he wanted. I was considering emptying the Makarov so that if I was forced to drop it, then it could not be used against me. Then the pessimist inside me took over.

But what if he just comes into the room and opens fire?

I dropped the seven loose rounds into my jacket pocket and, after pushing the magazine back into the base of the pistol grip, I pulled back the top slide. Holding it back slightly I allowed it to ease forward, feeding the last remaining round into the chamber as it went.

One chance, however slim, is better than no chance at all.

Sun Tzu, the famous Chinese general, once said, 'All warfare is based on deception.' If Plan B was going to stand any chance of success, I would need to deceive Bonsack into thinking he was close to winning; into assuming that, with Schneider lurking downstairs, ready to come up the moment he was needed, he was no longer under any pressure. And, in order to get Metzger's notebook, he would need to keep me on side by answering my questions, before, inevitably, trying to kill me.

However, if Bonsack opened fire the moment he entered the room, leading to a kill or be-killed shoot-out then, given my training, the countless hours spent in the Killing House, where only a head shot was acceptable, firing the one round I had left in the Makarov should kill him or, at the very least, cause enough damage to give me sufficient time to draw the Sig.

While an immediate shoot-out had to be a possibility to be planned for, I seriously doubted that Bonsack would try to kill me before he knew where Metzger's notebook was as I could have hidden it anywhere in the castle. Kill me and he risked never finding it. So, the odds dictated there would be a stand-off; one where, at some point, he would demand that I toss my weapon away. When that happened, and if I had no other choice – by which I mean no chance of a clear head shot which would not also risk hitting Huber – the crux of Plan B was that the young man in the cupboard would come into play.

Standing with my back against the wall, directly opposite the cupboard, if it came to a stand-off, and I was forced to put the Makarov down on the floor, I would try to slide it to a position somewhere behind Bonsack; out of his reach and line of sight – and near the cupboard.

My plan, my hope, was that seeing the Makarov – a familiar weapon to members of the NVA – lying within easy reach might encourage the young man to try and pick it up, coax him out into the open and, in so doing, make a noise and distract Bonsack. Force him to turn around to see what was happening behind him. That momentary distraction should, I reckoned, give me the chance I needed to regain control of the situation and, with only one round in the Makarov, it would also limit the collateral damage in the unlikely event that the young man opened fire.

Some of you reading this may think that even though I knew the young man in the cupboard had been a soldier and knew too that he had been abused and maltreated by the regime, that this plan was still a bit of a long shot, it being very unlikely that he would do exactly what I was hoping he would do, partly because there was no way I could be sure that he had even the slightest notion of what was going on.

You may also think it implausible that a highly trained soldier like myself would ever have risked life and limb on the slim chance of such a plan coming off. But the reality is, when you are faced with a ruthless killer who is armed – and I had no doubt would kill me as soon as he got what he wanted – you have to play the odds. And sometimes when your options are narrowing almost to zero, you will identify the most unlikely option, the longest shot, as the best of a bad bunch.

Besides, in reality, what was I hoping for? It's true that I was going to present the young man with a loaded weapon, an object that he was no doubt familiar with, but I didn't expect him to take up the fight in order to support me. No, as I say, I just hoped that if he reached for the weapon or made any kind of movement in response to its presence, any kind of noise, he would alert Bonsack to the fact that there was someone else in the room and create a momentary distraction. At which point my survival would come down to my Special Forces training.

I knew that in the split-second I would have to react, that with reflexes faster than those of anyone, even a murderous terrorist – someone who had not had the benefit of that unique and matchless training – that I could make that instant deadly decision and carry it out ruthlessly and without a fraction of a second's hesitation.

Yes, this Plan B, my emergency fallback strategy, *was* risky in many different respects. And even if it went the way it was intended it still might get the young man or Huber killed in the process . . .

As I brooded on this I decided there was no point in trying to explain my plan to the man in the cupboard. Apart from the fact that what I was intending to do would probably scare him to death, there was no guarantee that he wouldn't end up totally confused and be more of a hindrance than an asset. As always in such situations, when dealing with an unknown quantity – in this case the reactions of a mentally impaired young man – the final outcome can never be guaranteed.

Over the centuries numerous battles have been won and lost because one side has come up with a plan or counter plan that was totally unexpected; has broken with tradition, gone against what was considered at the time as the accepted military strategy. But this had become part of Regiment training, it was one of our greatest strengths, being able to improvise, change tack on the spur of the moment – because the most unlikely option is also the one that your opponent is least likely to anticipate.

What Plan B offered me was something that Bonsack could never have imagined: a simple distraction behind him that he would be forced to react to. The obvious flaw in the plan was that the young man might decide to stay silent and hidden, but if all my other options ran out, it was worth a go and, rack my brains as I might, I could see no other possible Plan B. Of course, come daylight, Bonsack might turn up mob-handed, or refuse to come up to the room. If that happened I would have to immediately adapt and come up with something different if I were to overcome and survive.

I slipped the weapon into the right-hand pocket of my jacket. A few seconds later I felt Scott brush up against me and, as he stared over my shoulder and out into the courtyard with its fresh covering of frost, I asked, 'How good are you with that Glock? Have you ever killed a man?'

I heard him swallow. 'No.'

I turned and gave him the type of look that asks 'Are you telling me the truth?'

'But I always get a good score on range days.'

I turned back to the window. 'I told Bonsack to be here at eleven o'clock. He won't wait that long.'

I sensed Scott turn and look at me. 'How do you know that?'

'Because I wouldn't. We need to be ready.'

I wished it were someone else standing beside me. Scott was an unknown quantity. I had no idea how he might react when the shit started flying, but beggars can't be choosers. If he were not up to the job, well . . . I'd just have to try and pick up any shortfall myself.

Satisfied that Scott at least knew which end of a Glock the bullets came out of, I took the silencer the BRIXMIS officer had given me from my jacket pocket.

'Has your Glock got a threaded barrel?'

Scott's voice was suddenly upbeat. 'Of course.'

I handed him the silencer. 'Then you'll need this.'

I watched in silence as he confidently screwed it to the muzzle and, pulling back the top slide, cocked the weapon. It was a nice smooth action, but I'd seen it all before. Men who would give a flawless performance of weapon handling and attain a near perfect score on the range, but were not able to hold the gun steady when the rounds started heading in the other direction; back towards them. However, in the end, only time would tell.

'Right. Here's the plan,' I said.

Tuesday, 14 November 1989

10:07.

I stared at Scott for a moment or two before speaking.

'OK, here goes. Plan A. If Bonsack follows my instructions and brings Huber with him, the first thing we need to do is try and separate him and Huber from Schneider.'

Scott tilted his head to one side. 'Why not just jump them in the courtyard? As they drive through the gates?'

I shook my head. 'Because I need Bonsack alive. I have questions that need to be answered. Besides, if Bonsack doesn't bring Huber, and if I am going to stand any chance of finding her once this is all over, I'll need him to tell me where she is.'

He will also have to be alive if I am going to have any hope of discovering what has really been going on for the last three months.

Fail to establish either one of these and, given the fact that by killing Metzger I had helped prevent Gorbachev's assassination and ensured the fall of the Berlin Wall, I suspected I would be looking over my shoulder for the rest of my life. I'd spend each day waiting for payback; a bullet or bomb from the vicious remnants of the RAF, or a visit from the dark, vengeful powers that lurked in the shadows back in Moscow.

Assuming that Scott had some basic knowledge of infantry tactics, I inclined my head in the direction of the window and confirmed to him what I already knew.

'There's too much room down there. We have no idea where anyone will be sitting in the car. That means that at least one of them will be able to use the car for cover.'

The pitch of Scott's voice changed, he suddenly sounded excited. 'Not if we come at them from both sides.'

I stared at Scott in disbelief. His comment seemed to show a complete lack of basic combat training and experience. I shook my head again.

'No. Apart from the fact that launching an ambush from both sides means we run the risk of shooting each other, and killing Huber in the process, if we launch our attack from the same side we could get dragged into a running gun battle that might lead us through areas of the castle we are unfamiliar with. Also, the sound of prolonged gunfire might encourage one of the locals in the village to report it to the authorities. If they come to investigate we'll have no option but to run. Then there'll be no way I'll get what I need out of Bonsack . . . or you, Huber and me out of East Germany.'

Scott dropped his eyes to the floor. 'So, what are we going to do?'

'At the bottom of the stairs there are two doors that lead into other parts of the building. I need you to pick one and hide behind it. If Bonsack brings Huber, I'm going to try and separate him and Schneider. Given the visit I received from the two goons back at the motel, we have to assume that Bonsack is coming here to recover Metzger's notebook – if not, why else would he have agreed to the meeting? With the Wall down, he no longer needs my assistance. Which means he'll probably try to humour me – meet me halfway. At least, at first. Until he gets exactly what he wants. I'm going to try to insist that he leaves Schneider in the car while he and Huber come upstairs. If I'm right and he does humour me, he'll tell Schneider to stay put. However, whatever happens, whether he follows orders or not, I will need you to take care of Schneider.'

I saw Scott swallow. 'What? Kill him?'

I felt my eyes narrow. 'If, once they're separated, Schneider tries to follow Bonsack and Huber up here . . . Yes.'

Scott was still staring at me. 'Then what?'

'Once you're sure Schneider's dead, make your way up the stairs. With Bonsack sandwiched between us he shouldn't prove to be too much of a problem. But, unless it can't be avoided, let me do the shooting up here. I don't want him or Huber dead.'

Scott stood in silence for over a minute, clearly thinking over my plan, before speaking again. 'And if Bonsack doesn't bring Huber? Or, even if he does and Schneider refuses to remain in the car?'

I turned back to the window. 'That's a game changer. Even if he does bring Huber, as you say, there's still a possibility that, however much I insist, Bonsack and Schneider will come up here together. If that happens, allow them to pass your position and climb the stairs. Once they're out of sight, follow them up. As soon as you have a clear shot at Schneider, take him out. In the back if need be. I'll take care of Bonsack.'

Scott turned his back to the window and rested against the sill. Given what I had just told him, along with what I was now expecting him to do, he showed no signs of anxiety. In fact, he looked almost relaxed.

Something's not right here.

A few minutes later I saw Bonsack's black Wartburg pull through the castle gates. I looked at my watch.

10:16. Early, just as I suspected.

With one eye on the Wartburg I looked back to the gate, but nothing else appeared.

And only one vehicle. So no reinforcements, thank God.

I turned to Scott. 'You need to get a wiggle on. Our visitors have just arrived. If it pans out the way I think, you'll only get one chance at this. For all our sakes, don't fuck it up.'

Scott said nothing as I watched him pull the silenced Glock from his belt and head quickly towards the door.

As the front passenger door of the Wartburg opened and Bonsack climbed out I drew the Sig from my belt and moved to the left side of the window.

The Sig had long been my weapon of choice. It had a smooth action and was more accurate than the Makarov. I was comfortable with it. Like a favourite tennis racket, I felt it improved my performance. But using a sleek Western-made weapon would definitely draw attention to you in a communist country, so sometimes it was wiser to use the Makarov.

I doubted Bonsack would take the shot, not before he had what he wanted, but there was no point in providing him with an easy target.

He took a good look around, walked to the rear passenger door, opened it, and reached inside. As Huber stepped out of the car I felt my pulse rate rise. It was at that very moment that I admitted to myself that, whether it came to Plan A or B, everything I was planning was geared to keeping Huber alive. Seeing her in the courtyard I realised that I was now deeper into this woman than I would care to admit. Were it not for her I would have simply shot and wounded Bonsack as he walked into the room – something I was more than capable of doing – leaving Scott to deal with Schneider while I got what I needed out of Bonsack. There would be little need to risk falling back on Plan B.

But what was winding me up most of all was that I still couldn't make up my mind whether she was really Bonsack's prisoner – or his accomplice. It wouldn't be long before I found out.

With my body shielded behind the castle's ancient brickwork, I called down to Bonsack. 'Come up to the first floor. Bring Huber with you. But tell your friend to stay in the car.' Although Scott had told me Schneider's name, I couldn't use it, because it would have made Bonsack wonder how I knew.

To my relief, Schneider did as I asked and stayed sitting behind the wheel. As I watched Bonsack guide Huber across the courtyard towards the west wing I pushed the Sig into my belt behind my back and, after covering it with my jacket, lifted the Makarov out of my jacket pocket.

A few seconds later I lost sight of Bonsack and Huber. Next moment I heard the outside door crash against the wall of the lower hallway. They were inside the building, on their way up the stone staircase. I moved away from the window and took up position on the other side of the room. Having spent close to four months being around Bonsack, attending meetings, I knew that the one thing he loved to do was talk. If I could get him to relax, even a little, I hoped he would tell me everything I needed to know.

The room was approximately twenty feet long by fifteen feet wide; I took up position in the centre of the wall, on the opposite side of the room to the door, practically opposite the young man's cupboard.

Given what would possibly happen here during the next few minutes, I believe that it's now important for you to get a better feel for the room. To make it easier to explain I'm going to use the military clock system. The theory behind this process is relatively simple. Firstly, in this case, imagine me as the centre of the dial. Secondly, given my current position, close to the centre of the room with my back literally against the wall, we will only be concerned with the numbers on the top half of the dial – from 9 o'clock, through 12 o'clock and on to 3 o'clock.

At 3 o'clock – to my immediate right - were the only two pieces of furniture in the room: two military-style bedsteads complete with heavily soiled mattresses, which were the source of the strong smell of ammonia filling the room, still slightly burning my nose and throat. I stared again at the three sets of leather straps that stretched across each bed and thought of the injuries that must have been inflicted on the young man in the cupboard.

The two beds were less than seven feet long and around three feet wide and with their heads pushed up tight against the wall, the area to my front, what might become the killing ground, was clear of all obstructions. Leaving nowhere and nothing for anyone, including me, to shelter behind.

Between 12 and 1 o'clock, slightly to my right, was the young man's cupboard. It was five feet high and around three feet wide, something resembling a UK airing cupboard. It was without shelves, although the wooden rails that had supported them were still fixed to the side walls, and it was obviously deep enough for a man to hide in. It had been built into the wall, probably as a much later addition, and its plain wooden door, when it was closed, sat flush with the brickwork.

Situated in the top left-hand corner, at my 11 o'clock and on the same wall as the cupboard, was the main doorway: eight feet high and four feet wide, but minus what I assumed had once been its heavy wooden door. The only other exit point was set into the left-hand wall, between my 9 and 10 o'clock: a tall, rectangular window. Behind it there was nothing but a twenty-foot drop on to the rock-hard dirt floor of the courtyard and, as such, using it as an escape route was hardly a viable option.

From my current position, I had a clear view of the door, the young man's cupboard and the room's only window. All I could do now was wait for Bonsack and Huber to arrive.

As I waited, hearing nothing, I began to wonder what Bonsack and Huber were doing downstairs. I glanced around me again. Knowing what might happen here shortly, the room now looked a hell of a lot smaller than it had on my earlier visit or, even, that morning in the half-light.

Set against that I, unlike Bonsack, had spent endless hours rehearsing various room combat scenarios using live rounds in the Regiment's Killing House and, with a room of this size, even armed with only one round, I was reasonably comfortable that my capabilities would pull me through. Unless, that is, he was a former member of Diensteinheit IX, a special and covert counter-terrorism unit of the GDR's Volkspolizei, the closest thing the communist state had to the Regiment. But I very much doubted this. For starters, he was missing that air of confidence that comes with being a highly trained and experienced Special Forces soldier. My guess was that, even if he was some sort of trained agent, unlike the James Bond 'secret agents' so loved by Hollywood, most of them couldn't shoot for shit in a real combat situation, being far too busy being sneaky to put in the endless hours needed on the range to turn them into someone like me.

I decided Bonsack was taking his time probably because he feared some sort of ambush on the stairs. Meanwhile, as I waited, my eyes flashed across the floorboards – unpolished, but worn smooth by years of constant use.

Which will make it easier for me to place the weapon exactly where I want it.

Then my eyes went up to the ceiling, which hung ten feet above the floor. Off centre, to the left and closer to the door than I was, hung a single hanging light fitting, still minus the bulb. And that was it. I focused back on the door, readying myself for what must happen next.

It was a full two minutes before Huber appeared in the doorway, her dishevelled hair hanging in front of her face. Bonsack was standing directly behind her. In his right hand, resting on her right shoulder, pushed into her neck, was the muzzle of a fully cocked Makarov, while the fingers of his left hand were digging into her injured left shoulder.

As the pair stepped out of the shadowed doorway and entered the room I raised my weapon.

'That's far enough.'

If I was forced to revert to Plan B I needed to stop Bonsack before he walked across the room and reached the cupboard, perhaps even positioned himself in front of the door and, in so doing, blocked it from opening. But I also needed him far enough into the room to stop him using the doorway as cover.

Bonsack was six feet from the door, three feet off the wall opposite, and ten feet from me, when he eventually stopped.

He had changed. The once gentle, friendly individual who would do anything to keep the peace now had an unpleasant arrogance about him. He seemed to feel relatively safe standing behind Huber, but it didn't stop him from pulling her closer when he saw my weapon.

'It's good to see you again, Butala, or whatever your real name is. Don't do anything stupid. Where's Metzger's notebook?'

I forced a smile. Bonsack's impressive command of English would make this much easier.

'Relax. Give me some credit. It's in the vicinity, but obviously not in the room. I need to make sure you won't just kill me and make off with it. If you want the notebook we'll have to work something out.'

Bonsack let go of Huber's shoulder and, taking a handful of her long blond hair, pulled her head back so that I could see her face.

Both of her eyes were swollen; the right one almost closed. Her lips were heavily bruised and the trail of dried blood that ran down her chin and on to her neck told me her mouth had been bleeding. Although it was obvious that she had taken one hell of a beating, at least she was alive. I breathed a silent sigh of relief.

Prisoner it is then.

Bonsack smiled at me. 'I'm sorry my men missed you at the motel last night,' he said, obviously enjoying the moment. 'But, as you can see, it took Fräulein Huber a little longer than expected to remember where you might be.'

'And if I'd changed my mind? Gone somewhere else?'

'Then we would have lost you, had no idea where you had gone, or how to find you.'

If I'd been on my own I would have had one ear on the court-yard downstairs, listening for the sound of a car door opening or closing, but that was no longer my problem if Scott played his part. What was more, given that Schneider had gone to ground and misled Scott, I reckoned that when it came to it Scott would have no compunction about taking him out.

My main concern now was Huber. She was in a bad way and I was desperate to know that she was OK – offer her support, comfort – but there was no way I could let Bonsack see just how much she meant to me. If he had the slightest suspicion he would use it against me; extract maximum use from her as a hostage. My apparent lack of any interest in her welfare might just save her life. I just hoped she would understand.

He let go of Huber's hair and, as she lowered her head, I saw him dig his fingers deep into the bullet wound in her left shoulder again.

Her legs buckled with the pain, but Bonsack had a tight grip of her. He needed her as a shield and so he stopped her falling to the floor. Instead, he screwed the barrel of his Makarov hard into her neck. Just below her right ear.

'Throw your weapon over here or I'll kill her . . .'

He paused and his face changed. The only way you could describe it was evil.

'In fact, it might be better if I do. Get it over and done with right now. That way the two of us can conduct our business without further distraction. Man to man, so to speak.'

Bonsack's statement confirmed what I already knew. That once he had what he wanted he intended to kill us both. With my weapon already raised, pointing directly at him, I toyed with the idea of taking the shot but, as my finger drifted on to the trigger, as if he was reading my mind, he stepped to his left, positioning Huber directly between us again, forcing his weapon deeper into her neck.

The fact that up until that point Bonsack had not once pointed his weapon at me told me that, much as I had suspected, he lacked confidence in his own ability with a pistol. He was obviously hoping that I would not open fire and risk him shooting Huber.

He was right to hope, because even if I shot with complete accuracy there was always a risk that his trigger finger would tighten, possibly even as a reaction to me firing my weapon, and Huber would be dead.

I left my finger where it was, resting lightly on the trigger, and shook my head. 'I don't think that would be a good idea. Without Huber as a shield, and your friend still sitting in the car downstairs, I doubt you would win the resulting shoot-out once we were, as you say . . . "man to man".'

I saw Bonsack's lip curl. 'So, where's Metzger's notebook?'

I stared at him for a second or two and then said, 'I'll trade you the notebook for some answers. After all, outnumbering me two to one, what have you got to lose?'

Bonsack thought about it. 'OK. But be quick. I'm a busy man. What do you need to know?'

'When did you first realise that I had Metzger's notebook?'

Bonsack's expression quickly changed. For only the third time since I'd known him he lost his upbeat attitude.

'The morning you murdered him. I was due to pick up Metzger and his family at ten o'clock that morning. Before his men made their attempt on Gorbachev. We were going to head south, cross the border into Czechoslovakia and lie low. Wait for the dust to settle and for everything to return to normal. But then I got the news about the bomb attack in Zinnwald.'

He paused before continuing and I saw his eyes flick momentarily, up and to my right. He was recalling the events of that day.

'So, telling Huber I had somewhere to go, I left the house and headed for Zinnwald. When I arrived at the Projects the place was still crawling with police. A neighbour confirmed what I already suspected, that Metzger had been killed in an explosion. However, I still had no idea who had carried out the attack and immediately headed for his cousin's bar to retrieve the notebook. But, when I arrived, Metzger's cousin told me that it was gone, that someone had broken into the bar earlier that morning, attacking his wife in the process. When he told me that, instead of finding her dead, although she was groggy, she was otherwise unharmed, I knew that it had to be you.'

I stared at him. 'Why me? It could have been anybody. Other members of the RAF, the Stasi, anybody at all.'

Bonsack grunted. 'No. If it had been someone from within the RAF who killed Metzger they would have also murdered his wife, and possibly even his son. Then there is his cousin and his cousin's wife.'

I felt my eyebrows rise involuntarily. 'Why? What's happened to all that student idealism?'

'Things have moved on. We, the new, third generation, have much more to lose now. It's true that we live here in East Germany with a certain amount of protection provided by the state, but even East Germany has rules, laws, and there are limits as to what we can get away with. Sometimes people have to be removed to avoid being betrayed.'

'And if it had been the Stasi?'

'They would have simply arrested him, along with every other member of the RAF they could find – dealt with them at their own convenience. Conversely, given your misguided sense of fair play and your refusal to involve the innocent . . . What is it you say, "no women, no kids", it had to be you.'

It would appear that my plan was working. I had Bonsack talking.

'It's a shame that you find it impossible to leave things alone. If you had, the Monday evening rallies might never have grown as quickly, or to the size they did. And without a means of expressing their frustrations the people would have been pushed into a series of uncoordinated riots, which in the end would have escalated into violence. Giving the authorities the excuse they needed to open fire. Metzger's men would have tried to kill Gorbachev and, succeed or fail, the Russians would have had the excuse they needed to retake control of East Germany, the Berlin Wall would not have fallen and, more importantly, we wouldn't be standing here now. Before you got involved, shared the fact that you had a radio and were willing to help in any way you could, the Monday night rallies being held in Leipzig were small, some nights only ten to twenty people might turn up. It was never my intention to help make the rallies the success they later became. In fact, that was the last thing I wanted.'

I cut in. 'So, why not just lie low, carry on with your life? It's not as if anyone was going to point the finger at you. As far as the East German people were concerned you were one of the good guys.'

Bonsack's tone was somewhat regretful, like a relative delivering bad news about the demise of a family member. 'The minute I heard Gorbachev's veiled warning to Honecker that "life punishes those who come too late". Meaning that he and his government could no longer rely on the Soviet Union to keep them in power. I knew then that it was over. That it was only a matter of time before the East German government collapsed, the Stasi disappeared and we, what remained of the RAF, would be left to the mercy of the Western authorities. And, if that happened, the only way we were going to avoid spending the rest of our lives behind bars was to have something to bargain with.'

I raised my eyebrows. 'And?'

'After leaving Zinnwald I headed south into Czechoslovakia. I needed time to work out what I was going to do next. By the time I returned to Leipzig you and Huber were already gone. It took what was left of the RAF network, those that hadn't just disappeared into thin air, close to a month to find out where you had moved to in Dresden. But, as we pulled into the street where you were staying, we were stopped by a Russian patrol. The KGB officer in charge told us that the road was closed, that they were searching for a fugitive, and we would need to find an alternative route.'

I smiled to myself. I already knew the answer to the question I was about to ask, but couldn't resist the temptation to irritate Bonsack. 'So, what happened? Why didn't the Russian just let you through? I thought you – the RAF and KGB – were best buddies.'

Bonsack practically spat out his answer. 'We are . . . were . . . supported by the Stasi, not the KGB, although Metzger had powerful contacts in both organisations. In fact, if he'd been with us that morning maybe things might have turned out differently . . . I, like every other East German, hate the Russians.

'I knew that you would try to get the notebook back to your masters in the West but, unable to get past the Russian patrol, we were forced to retreat and wait for you to make your next move. It was pure luck that we were parked at the petrol station on Bautzner Straße when you stopped to pick up Huber.'

I often wondered why Bonsack had been sitting at that location that night. It wasn't until a few months later, when the euphoria connected with the fall of the Wall had started to dissipate, that the true events of those lost few days started to be revealed. As soon as the Wall fell both the Russians and members of the Stasi did their best to hide the true nature of what had been going on in East Germany for years. They attempted to remove or destroy any files which contained the names of those who had been working as informants for the Stasi and KGB. Maybe that's why Bonsack was parked opposite Stasi HQ on Bautzner Straße. Maybe he was trying to find a way of removing or destroying his Stasi files, but once again, as it had been with Putin, it was nothing more than supposition.

I felt myself smile. 'And I suppose you were just going to ask me politely to give the notebook back?'

Bonsack sneered. 'Not exactly. I decided that we would follow you to the outskirts of the city and, once you had joined the auto-bahn, we would run you off the road. However, all that changed when that idiot downstairs, Schneider, forgot to check the fuel gauge on the car before setting off. We ran short of fuel and were forced to abandon the chase.'

Hindsight, or having access to additional information, is a beau-tiful thing. If I had known that Bonsack was running short of fuel that night there would have been no need for us to leave the autobahn and end up crashing the car. We could have just continued merrily on our way to the West.

I smiled at Bonsack. 'Of course, none of that is important right now. How did you find Huber?'

Bonsack took a moment or two to answer but, when he did, once more there was a tone of regret in his voice. 'The doctor who treated her bullet wound was a member of the Bewegung. A good man.'

Was?

I didn't need to know any more; I could work the rest out for myself.

My right arm, the one holding my weapon, was growing tired and in an attempt to relieve the pressure I lifted it an inch. I imme-diately saw Bonsack flinch.

'I don't recognise your friend downstairs. Who is he and what's his role in all of this?'

Bonsack's reply bordered on dismissive. 'Schneider? He is – was – Metzger's second-in-command.'

As Metzger told me back at the church in Zinnwald . . . 'I'm Klaus Metzger – his second in command . . .' Which makes you the top dog.

I smiled before sharing my next piece of information. 'You do know that he's a double. He works for British Intelligence?'

Bonsack grinned sarcastically. 'No. He *is* a double, but he works for us – the RAF and indirectly the Stasi.'

Bonsack's revelations were hardly ground-breaking news. By the mid-eighties intelligence agencies in the West were already coming to the conclusion that the RAF was, to all intents and purposes, an East German dog of war, a vicious and unruly beast that was kept on a very short leash until a high-value opportunity in the West presented itself.

It was just a simple matter of deduction really. During their long campaign of bombing, kidnapping, robbery and murder, and although they were being hunted by just about every police force in Europe, practically each and every time they managed to disappear without a trace. The only logical conclusion was that they were being allowed back into the East and, as nothing happened in East Germany without the blessing of the Stasi, it hadn't taken the Western intelligence community long to realise that the East German secret police were their current protectors and controllers, allowing the group to travel back and forth across the Inner German Border in order to cause mayhem whenever and wherever it suited them.

'Well, if that's true, if he's working for the RAF, why did he pass on information about Operation Konev, the plan to assassinate Gorbachev, to his British handler?'

Bonsack lost his grin. 'Ah, that was Metzger's idea. He knew that if Schneider fed the British information about a Soviet operation then, given the tension that currently exists between East and West, if he mysteriously dropped out of sight immediately after sharing it, London would be forced to send someone to investigate. Whoever they sent would need a way of reporting back. Metzger was obsessed with obtaining your radio. But, of course, you already know that.'

Improbable as this had first sounded back in the stable block at Schwarzbachtal, now that Bonsack had explained it, I could almost understand Metzger's infatuation with getting hold of a Western military-grade radio, especially something like the Clansman 319. Given what he had planned for Gorbachev, along with the almost inevitable fallout such an event would cause, such a radio would be invaluable to him if he wished to maintain communications with his contacts in the West.

Furthermore, if, as I now suspected, Metzger's personal contacts – the contacts listed in his black book – included members of the Western intelligence community then, given he did not have any way of contacting them when he was in the East, any information he had given them in the past must have been passed on while he and the RAF were conducting terrorist operations in the West.

My suspicion was that, knowing East Germany was about to take a step back in time, Metzger had been trying to build himself the option of a more comfortable future in the West. It was a known fact that some intelligence agencies would do almost anything to strike a deal, dishonest or otherwise, in order to obtain the right kind of information.

In reality, these people should have been neutralising the likes of Metzger and the RAF, not trading information with them. Once the Russians retook control of East Germany and closed the borders, the 319 would give him the ability to continue this sick trade, speak directly to these agencies, all without the knowledge of his current masters in Moscow, who would most certainly have stopped him had they known what he was up to on the side. The KGB and Stasi were paranoid about betrayal and keeping total control.

In fact, and the reason Bonsack's explanation made sense to me was that, faced with the same scenario, I would probably have done something similar. I would not have trusted the Stasi, or in Metzger's case the KGB, as far as I could kick them and would have had little doubt that, had it suited them, they would throw me to my enemies or, at best, 'disappeared' me into some deep, dark hole. Metzger had obviously come to the same conclusion and, like any terrorist with a strong survival instinct, had tried to do something about it. In feeding British intelligence information about a mythical 'Operation Konev' he had succeeded in getting the HF radio he so desperately wanted delivered to East Germany. However, he had also succeeded in summoning me: a fatal error as it had turned out.

So, while the part of Metzger's plan that involved getting hold of my radio now made a certain amount of sense, I was still confused about the rest of the plan.

'But why give away the plot to assassinate Gorbachev?'

There was a hint of frustration in Bonsack's voice when he answered.

'Metzger thought that if he created a fictitious Russian operation and gave it a high-profile name like "Konev", it would create even more interest within British intelligence. Marshal Konev is a national hero in Soviet Russia. The military view him as some kind of Superman figure.

'But Operation Konev had nothing to do with Gorbachev's assassination, or the Kremlin's Old Guard and KGB plan to oust Honecker's government and retake complete control of East Germany. In fact, they were so paranoid about being found out that I don't think they gave their plan a name. Metzger's only reason for fabricating

Operation Konev was to get British intelligence to send an agent into the East. He knew that whoever they sent would need a powerful HF radio to report his findings back to London. Getting messages across the border any other way would just be too high risk. Too open to interception. Metzger's mistake was that he hadn't counted on you putting your own unique twist on his story and then linking it to Gorbachev's assassination. I told him he was underestimating the British. That he was taking far too many risks . . .'

'So, Operation Konev wasn't the plot to assassinate Gorbachev?' I asked, trying to get my head around what Bonsack had just told me.

He practically barked his answer at me. 'No. As I've just said, it was something dreamed up by Metzger and Schneider. It was only you who connected the two, made it real.'

I thought about pressing Bonsack for more information – like why Metzger had used 7 October, the actual date of the assassination attempt, instead of something fictitious, a different date, something totally unconnected? But then I dismissed it. Metzger would have needed to come up with a date that made it necessary for Scott to send someone in when he did – to make sure that the radio was already in Metzger's hands when Gorbachev was assassinated and the world turned to shit – and, let's be honest, 7 October, the day that was probably going to throw Europe and the rest of the world into chaos, must have been at the forefront of his mind. Add to that the fact that the date was only a matter of two months away at the time Scott was informed, and the pressure would be on.

Thinking back later, I had to admit that there was no way the Kremlin Old Guard or members of the KGB, those who had planned Gorbachev's assassination, would have given such a plan an operational name – something that might link it back to Moscow. After all, they would want to disassociate themselves from any such event if anything had gone wrong or it had been discovered. But in the end it would appear that Metzger had simply tried to be too clever for his own good and, in trying to fool his own KGB and Stasi bosses as well as British intelligence, had not only led to the Moscow Old Guard plot being discovered and stopped by me, but also to his own death. It had its own obscene logic I suppose, and also its own unlooked-for outcome.

'So, what about you and Metzger? You were on opposing sides

within the Bewegung. Metzger was all for starting an armed struggle whereas you were seeking a peaceful, non-violent solution. And, what's more, you were winning.'

Bonsack laughed out loud. 'That was also part of the charade. As Napoleon once said, "divide and conquer". Metzger and I were both after the same thing. Using ordinary East German people, I was to build the Bewegung into a viable threat to the East German government. Then, when Metzger's men tried to murder Gorbachev on East German soil, Honecker would have naturally blamed the Bewegung. After accusing Honecker and his party of losing control, the Russians would have retaken control of what, to all intents and purposes, was a Soviet state on the brink of revolution.'

You and Metzger were playing everyone.

I thought back to the night of 2 October and the rally in Leipzig.

'Which is why you looked so disappointed when thousands turned out and, despite an enormous amount of provocation from the East German authorities, the demonstration passed off peacefully. That's when you realised that your part of the plan had failed.'

Bonsack practically snarled at me. 'You had to get involved and help the Bewegung achieve its aim . . . peacefully.'

I changed the subject again, although this time I already knew the answers to the questions I was about to ask.

'So, I assume it was you who told Metzger's men where they could find Huber and me that night in Leipzig?'

Bonsack nodded.

I felt a smirk creep on to my lips. 'With the Wall already down, what do you hope to gain by possessing Metzger's notebook? Apart from the fact that you can't risk it getting back to either the West or Moscow.'

Bonsack's facial expression changed. He looked excited.

'As I told you earlier, with the Wall down and our benefactors, the Stasi, all but disappeared, given what we've done in the West over the last ten years – the bombs, bank robberies, kidnappings and murders – every law enforcement agency in Europe will be across the border hunting for what remains of Baader-Meinhof and the RAF. Metzger's notebook and the information it contains – the names and contact details of those he was working for or with – will give me enormous bargaining power. I suspect that some of those in the book are their agency's most powerful individuals. The last thing they'll want is for their world to disintegrate, their careers to be destroyed, perhaps even making them criminals in the process. And, if those names aren't enough to keep me out of prison altogether, it should ensure that I don't die behind bars. Now, where *is* the notebook?'

I now sensed Bonsack wanting to bring the meeting to a close. But I needed more time. Time for Schneider to leave the car. I was becoming increasingly anxious that this had not yet happened. I had anticipated that Bonsack would have told him to come upstairs after a certain interval, so giving Scott the chance to kill him and head up the stairs. But, if that didn't happen, I needed Bonsack to remove his weapon from Huber's neck and to create some space between them. That was if I was going to have any chance of taking the shot.

'I'm not finished,' I said. 'I have more questions.'

A thin grin crept across Bonsack's lips as he slowly screwed the muzzle of his weapon into Huber's right ear.

'I could just shoot her. Perhaps watching her die will make you more compliant?'

It was obvious that Huber had done all she could to protect me and in doing so had been severely punished for her trouble. There was no way I could now allow Bonsack to kill her. However, I knew for certain that once Bonsack had what he wanted he would do his best to kill us both and simply disappear and, with East Germany now in chaos, he would probably never pay for what he had done. The only way this was going to stand any chance of a happy ending, of Huber and I coming out of it alive, was if I followed my plan to its conclusion.

I slowly shook my head. 'You won't do that. Deep down inside, you know that if you kill Huber you'll be dead before her body hits the ground. Even if I miss with the first shot, which is extremely unlikely at this range, you'll never see the notebook again. Even if you come out on top, it won't matter how much pain you and your friend downstairs inflict on me. With my training it will be days before I give up the location of the notebook and I don't think you have days. Do you?'

Bonsack's expression changed, his attitude was now businesslike. I watched as he screwed the muzzle of his weapon into Huber's neck once more.

'Maybe not. But, before I answer any more of your questions and, if you don't want to watch her die, you need to throw your weapon over here.'

It had taken Bonsack longer than expected to get to the point where he demanded that I throw away my gun. But, now that it had finally happened, if I was going to stand any chance of removing Huber from harm's way, it looked as if I had no other choice. I would have to move to Plan B.

This was the moment I had been hoping to avoid. I had what I wanted from Bonsack and I had no further need or desire to keep him alive. However, even though I was confident that I could now kill or neutralise him with the single remaining bullet in the Makarov, I also knew there was a good chance that Huber could die or be badly injured if Bonsack managed to squeeze his trigger as I fired. Looking at her standing there, brave but terrified, I could not risk that happening. She had taken a severe beating in order to protect me a few days earlier, now it was my turn to take the risk in order to protect her.

While I had initially wanted to keep Schneider downstairs so that Bonsack and I could have this discussion, I now needed him dead and Scott up here in the room so that we outnumbered him as a matter of urgency.

Just what would happen next though depended on Bonsack. I had no idea what was going through his mind as he tried to work out how to neutralise me and still get what he wanted without killing Huber – losing his shield.

What I was about to do may seem foolhardy – irrational to say the least – but in such situations, situations where the well-being or life of a close friend or loved one hangs in the balance, the decisions we make are rarely rational. They are the product of a rapidly deteriorating situation; they are taken on the spur of the moment in order to save that life. Foolhardy yes, maybe even stupid, but they are the best decisions we can come up with at that confusion-filled moment in time.

However, I still felt confident that Bonsack wouldn't risk killing me until he had what he wanted: the black book. Everything he had told me up until that point confirmed that it was essential to his future survival, even more so now that the Wall was down, the

Inner German Border was rapidly disappearing and East Germany collapsing.

He had already proved, when he dug his fingers into Huber's injured shoulder, that he did not care about hurting her and also that he was more than capable of keeping her on her feet. By wrapping his forearm under her chin, pulling her into his chest, he could shoot her through the elbow joint and, although it would be incredibly painful for her, he would still be able to keep her upright in front of him.

What I needed instead was for Bonsack to feel confident enough to call Schneider – something I would have done ages ago had I been him. But once that happened, Scott would kill Schneider as soon as he entered the building. Then, discovering that he was now outnumbered and sandwiched between Scott and me, I had to assume that Bonsack would become more amenable. He would know that, once Scott appeared, killing, even wounding, Huber would do nothing more than sign his own death warrant. Nor did I think he would risk shooting at me, to wound or disable me. Forget the dramatic cowboy-type shoot-out. Shooting a pistol from someone's hand is something that only happens in films. Yes, members of the Regiment are trained to shoot to wound in some combat situations, as I had been back at the stables. In reality, though, given the speed of modern bullets, there is no guarantee that the round won't become what we call a 'bone creeper'. One which hits the target, say in the arm or leg, makes contact with the bone and immediately deflects, travelling along the bone at incredible speed until it either hits something large enough to stop it or is deflected in yet another direction, perhaps severing an artery or some vital organ as it goes; either of which will kill the target.

I knew I could take a head shot and kill or incapacitate with only one bullet, but even well-trained members of the normal green army – and doubtless ninety-nine per cent of terrorists too – are only ever taught to aim at the centre of the visible mass, the stomach or chest, in the hope that they hit something. In the stress of the moment most soldiers will miss with their first shot even at a distance of ten feet. As a result, I was confident that Bonsack wouldn't risk shooting at me until he had what he wanted. If he did shoot and he killed me then he had travelled to Colditz for nothing. In fact, while Bonsack thought he was the one in charge as he stood there, gun in hand, in reality he only had one meaningful play and that play – shooting Huber and/or me – was the one thing he could not do until he had the book.

The other thing I had in my favour was that Bonsack, the terrorist leader, doubtless considered himself a killer barracuda as he moved among his intended targets and members of the public. What he did not realise was that he was now trapped in a small pond with a Great White; a far more clinical and capable killer. I had to play for time until Scott arrived, but in order to do that I needed to switch to Plan B. So, feeling quietly confident, I decided it was now time to take the risk. If it worked it would be a stroke of genius. If not, then Huber and I, and probably Scott as well, would all be dead. I just hoped I hadn't misread the signs. I was about to play the biggest gamble of my life.

I lowered my weapon and, masking it from Bonsack's view behind my right thigh, I slid my thumb across the safety catch on the slide cover. Confirmed that it was fully 'up' – in the safe position. I couldn't afford for it to fire by accident. Next, I slid my thumb into the gap below the rear sight, between the slide cover and the hammer. It was all the way back. The weapon was cocked. Bending at the knees, I laid it on the floor.

Easy does it. Push it too hard and, even with the safety on, it could still fire as it hits the wall. Too soft and it will come to rest in front of Bonsack.

I held my breath as I watched Bonsack's eyes follow the Makarov as it bumped its way across the wooden floorboards. I needn't have worried. I had judged the distance well and breathed a sigh of relief as it came to rest against the wall, in a near perfect position; behind and to the left of Bonsack, but too far for him to reach for it without letting go of Huber and, in so doing, not only losing his shield but taking his eyes off me. Either of these would have given me the edge I was looking for and the opportunity to overpower him. However, I suspected Bonsack was too experienced to make such a fundamental error. At least not yet. Not until he had a good reason to do so.

Instead he did what was sensible. He kept pushing his gun deep into Huber's neck and turned to glance over his left shoulder to confirm the exact position of the Makarov. As he did so, I edged to my left. Like a goalkeeper facing a striker, I was narrowing the angle. I moved just far enough to my left, Bonsack's right, to place him and Huber directly between me and the discarded Makarov.

I was fairly confident that Bonsack wouldn't insist on searching me for an additional weapon. If he did, he would first have to release Huber and cross the room, a distance of at least ten feet. That or call me over to him. But both these scenarios were extremely unlikely. Bonsack knew that if I got close enough for him to do a search, I would also be close enough to turn the tables and reverse our positions.

As Bonsack turned back to face me he knew something had changed but, instead of questioning it, he simply adjusted his own position and moved Huber a pace to his right, putting her once again between the two of us. Now, with the weapon almost directly behind him, there was no way he could see it, not without turning his back on me.

I glanced down at my watch.

10:38

Bonsack and his party had been in the castle for a little over twenty minutes. I saw him loosen his grip on Huber's left shoulder.

I glanced past him to the cupboard. The door was still closed and not a sound was coming from inside. Maybe the young man had fallen asleep, although I doubted it.

It would appear, instead, that I had misread Bonsack. I had been certain that as soon as I was unarmed, he would call for Schneider, take full advantage of the two-to-one situation, but for some reason he hadn't. I needed to keep him talking.

'What about Huber?'

Bonsack was rapidly losing his patience. 'What about her?' he snapped at me.

'Is she working for you – the RAF, KGB or the Stasi?'

Bonsack looked confused. 'As far as I know, she isn't working for anybody.'

That was all I needed to know. Bonsack had no reason to lie. In fact, if Huber had been working for the East Germans, Soviets or RAF, he would have taken great delight in first telling me, and then rubbing it in.

I looked him in the eyes. 'So, what happens now?'

Tuesday, 14 November 1989

10:42.

Obviously feeling more confident and now keeping his weapon trained on me, instead of buried in Huber's neck, Bonsack turned his head slightly towards the window and shouted, 'FRANZ, COME UP HERE.'

I smiled to myself. It now didn't matter that the young man had failed to get involved. We were back to my Plan A. In two to three minutes, if Scott played his part, as soon as Schneider entered the building he was dead. Scott would then make his way upstairs and, in doing so, turn the odds in my favour. It was all beginning to come together.

I heard a car door slam, the sound of footsteps crossing the courtyard, the outside door swing back against the wall of the entrance hall and the faint but unmistakable sound of two rounds being fired through a silencer. A second later I heard a muffled crash as what I assumed was Schneider's body fell to the floor. A few seconds after that came a third shot from Scott's silenced Glock.

My eyes were still on Bonsack. It was clear that, like me, he had registered the same seven sounds. A silencer's job is not to entirely eradicate the noise of the shots, only to muffle and disguise them, confuse the listener. It had done its job.

I breathed a sigh of relief and, knowing that Scott would soon be arriving, as my confidence grew I watched the fear grow in Bonsack's eyes. The colour slowly drained from his face; his eyes narrowed. Then he squinted, trying to put into perspective what he had just heard. The muzzle of his Makarov switched away from me, back to Huber's neck. He was starting to panic.

'Who's downstairs?'

Without any return of fire to Scott's first two suppressed shots, and then having heard a third shot fired through the silencer, I was confident that he had completed his task uninjured.

'Schneider's dead. You're alone now.'

Bonsack was still frantically trying to work out the implications of what had just happened and he was becoming more and more jittery. My one fear now was that, under extreme threat and as his panic increased, he might start shooting before Scott arrived.

I glanced at my watch.

10:48.

Then I looked to the open doorway. Scott should be here at any minute. But, as I turned my head to Bonsack, I saw the cupboard door behind Bonsack slowly move. I knew that the young man had returned to the room but what I wasn't sure of was if, when the time came, he would be capable of playing the role I had planned for him. In fact, by this point I had all but given up hope that he would participate in the plan at all.

But, it would appear that the sound of Bonsack's raised voice when he shouted down to Schneider had awoken something inside him. Seconds later I saw his emaciated hand emerge from the cupboard and, like a scene from a third-rate horror film, its fingers begin to walk slowly across the floorboards towards the Makarov. I felt my pulse rate rise as he carefully took hold of the discarded weapon resting against the wall. But, instead of making a noise and acting as a distraction as I had hoped he would, I watched in disbelief as both the hand and the weapon disappeared silently back into the cupboard.

Fuck!

Had I got it wrong? Had the kindness I had shown the young man on my earlier visit and the previous night failed to forge even the slightest of bonds? In his confused state, had he simply taken the weapon as some sort of childish prize? But I told myself the fact that the young man had failed to get involved no longer mattered. With Schneider dead, Scott would make his way up the stairs, enter the room and create the distraction I needed. I glanced at my watch again.

10:51.

Schneider had been dead for close to four minutes. Even if he was being careful, it would have only taken Scott two minutes at the most to climb the stairs, so, where was he? Had my suspicions been correct all along, was Scott playing his own game?

If Scott didn't appear soon the only option left to me was to go for the Sig and pray that I was quicker than Bonsack. It was a sobering thought to now realise that I was alone, with a hardened terrorist pointing a gun at me and out of options. I was about to start winging it.

Of course, the fallback plan – Plan B – was hardly foolproof and had been a long shot. But, a little more than twenty minutes earlier, when Bonsack's car had pulled into the courtyard, I had had no idea whose side Huber was on, how the young man in the cupboard might react, or if Scott was working to his own private agenda. It now seemed that, with the exception of Huber, who was an innocent after all, my worst fears had all been realised. I had nobody I could count on. It was time to trust in my training.

But, even as I rehearsed the action I was about to take in my head, to slip my right hand inside my jacket, behind my back and draw the Sig; roll to my left and try to create some space between Bonsack and Huber, I saw the cupboard door begin to open. I paused and held my breath.

The young man was now standing, half-hidden in the darkness. The Makarov, which sat in his bony hand, was pointing directly at Bonsack and Huber.

All you have to do now is make a noise – push the door open a little wider – anything.

I saw Bonsack's eyes narrow. He had heard something, but was unsure of what it was or where it had come from.

He turned slowly to his left. As he did so he began to open up a gap between himself and Huber. Bonsack's weapon was still pointing at me, but his eyes and focus were now somewhere else; somewhere behind him.

A moment later he saw the young man and the weapon he was holding.

The young man had created the diversion I needed.

Even as I reacted, lowered my profile, bent at the knees and, reaching behind my back with my right hand, drew the half-cocked Sig from its hiding place in my belt, I saw the young man's right thumb flick the safety down. The weapon was now fully armed.

As my hands came together, my weapon reached shoulder height and I was about to fire, I heard a single shot.

I couldn't believe it. The sight of the discarded Makarov had obviously awoken something inside the young man. Even in his confused state his military training had kicked in and he had pulled the trigger. In near panic my eyes flashed across the room to Huber.

She was bent at the waist in a half crouch, her left arm raised as high as it would go, her hand shielding her face, while her right was wrapped over her head.

Then I saw Bonsack stagger and I breathed a sigh of relief.

With only eight feet between them the round from the Makarov had miraculously missed Huber before punching hard into Bonsack's left shoulder, rendering it virtually useless.

I saw his grip on Huber loosen, his hand slip off her shoulder and hang limply by his side, but he was by no means finished.

With his mind focused elsewhere, Bonsack hadn't seen the weapon I was now holding and, believing I was still unarmed, he rotated to his left, dropped his right hand, the one holding his Makarov, from Huber's shoulder and slid it smoothly through the narrow gap between his chest and her back. As it came out the other side he raised it again to shoulder height and aimed at the young man who was now rapidly retreating into his cupboard.

I shouted at him, 'BONSACK!'

Startled, he turned his head towards me.

I needed to stop him firing his weapon. Selecting the largest body mass I could, I squeezed the trigger of the Sig and heard it bark. Still looking over the sights, as if in slow motion, I saw the top slide pop back, the red-hot cartridge case fly away to my right, and felt my hand shudder slightly as the slide flew forward, feeding a fresh round into the chamber.

The bullet hit Bonsack in the side of his chest, just below his outstretched right arm. The force of the impact knocked him off balance and, still looking at me, he began to stagger sideways across the room to his left, towards the wall beside the cupboard.

As he struggled to regain his balance, working on instinct, I squeezed the trigger a second time and the Sig barked again.

The round passed through Bonsack's right eye. With only soft tissue to slow it down, a millisecond later it punched through the back of his skull and exploded out of his head, spraying blood and brain matter on the wall behind him.

It was over.

With the Sig still trained on Bonsack, I walked slowly towards Huber.

She was terrified. Her fear had somehow overridden the pain of moving her wounded left shoulder and now both her hands were clasped behind her head. Her forearms covered her ears as she tried to block out the noise. As I reached her, her legs buckled and, before I could catch her, she fell at my feet. Now down on her knees, with her hands still on her head, she fell face forward on to her thighs, sobbing.

I looked into the cupboard. The young man was lying on the floor in the foetal position; his arms folded protectively around his face and head, with the now empty Makarov lying on the floor beside him. He had been an unwitting player in a deadly game but had performed his role perfectly. As I walked past Bonsack on my way to the cupboard, I picked up his weapon and slipped it into my jacket pocket.

Down on my haunches, I lifted the rear of my jacket, pushed the Sig back into my belt and lifted the Makarov from the floor of the cupboard. Having fired the last round in the magazine, the top slide had remained at the rear. I pressed down on the slide release with my right thumb, and with my left hand covering the slide cover eased it forward.

The young man was now humming, rolling gently backwards and forwards. I decided to leave him where he was. There was no point in trying to coax him fully out of the cupboard. He felt safe there.

As I stood up and turned back to Huber, Scott appeared in the doorway. However, instead of immediately entering the room, he stood motionless on the threshold, his eyes fixed momentarily on Bonsack's body.

My adrenaline was still in full flow and I barked at him, 'Where the fuck have you been?'

Scott said nothing as his eyes flicked first to Huber, then to the young man and eventually to me. The extremes of emotion typically displayed by someone who has just killed for the first time – the joy of having survived the contact, mixed with the regret of having taken a life – were absent. His eyes were missing that haunted, glazed look. They were clear, and his demeanour showed no signs of remorse. He would have been no more than six feet from Schneider and looking him square in the eyes when he squeezed the trigger of the Glock. To look at him now you would think it was just another day at the office.

I walked towards the window and, as I passed Scott, I handed him the Makarov I had just taken from the young man.

'Here, stick that in your pocket. Now, I need you to take care of Kirstin and our friend over there until I get back.'

I sensed him turn towards me. 'Where are you going?'

As I stared out of the window and watched a small group of the castle's inmates, evidently drawn by the noise of gunfire, begin to gather in the courtyard, I answered him. 'I need to tidy up. We can't just leave Bonsack's and Schneider's bodies where they are and walk away.'

I made my way back across the room, took hold of Bonsack's right arm and heaved his body up to the standing position. Then, in a single movement, like an Olympic weight lifter, I dropped into the squat position, let Bonsack's body fall over my right shoulder and stood up. I paused as I reached the bottom of the stairs to stare at Schneider's body.

He was lying flat on his back. His brown eyes were wide open but lifeless. On the left-hand side of his chest, just above his heart and no more than three inches apart, were two bullet wounds. There was a third in the centre of his forehead.

I nodded my head.

Nice. Could have been a professional hit.

My reaction – my almost flippant thoughts about the dead man lying in front of me – shocked me. It was totally out of character. That moment of arrogance is something that has stayed with me since that day. If I ever write a list of things I regret, uttering those words to myself will be close to the top.

I stepped over Schneider's body and made my way out into the cold winter sunlight of the courtyard.

As if they knew where I was going, the ten or twelve inmates parted, cleared a path to the rear of Bonsack's car, but all without murmuring a sound.

I flicked the catch on the boot of the Wartburg and watched Bonsack's body tumble off of my shoulder and into the empty space. After slamming the boot lid shut I made my way back towards the building.

A few minutes later I repeated the journey, only this time the body I was carrying was Schneider's. With the Wartburg's boot already full, I loaded it into the front passenger seat.

Tuesday, 14 November 1989

11:03.

I brought the Wartburg to a halt in a small clearing a kilometre from the castle. Away from the village, but close to where we had left the Moskvitch.

I opened Schneider's coat, ripped off a piece off his shirt and, walking to the rear of the car, removed the petrol cap. As I stuffed the piece of rag into the neck of the petrol tank my nose began to fill with petrol fumes. I flicked the wheel of the Zippo lighter I had bought in the garage shop on our way from Zinnwald and held the flame to the rag. As the fire took hold and the flames began to grow I knew that it was time to leave.

I heard the Wartburg's petrol tank give a loud hiss, as one hundred metres away I unlocked the driver's door of the Moskvitch. The tank was about to blow.

As I pulled the car on to the track and headed back towards the castle I looked into the rear-view mirror and saw the fireball that, up until a few minutes ago, had been the pride of the East German automotive industry.

I parked the car nose out, pointing towards the castle gates, on the left side of the courtyard, reached under the driver's seat, removed Metzger's notebook and slipped it into the inside pocket of my jacket. As far as I was concerned my mission was over. All I had to do now was get Huber back to her family, if that's where she wanted to go, and head west.

However, I still had no idea what I was going to do about the young man in the cupboard or the rest of the poor unfortunates abandoned in the castle. It was not as if I could just roll into a local police station or any other government office and report what I'd found. Not without having to explain what I was doing there in the first place. Then there were the two charred bodies, those of Bonsack and Schneider, in the burnt-out Wartburg. It wouldn't be long before someone discovered them.

I crossed the blood-stained entrance hall and began to climb the stairs to the first floor. The silence was deafening. I would have expected to hear something. The sound of the young man droning, or Huber's crying, but there was nothing. Not a sound.

I took the Sig from the back of my belt and climbed the remaining stairs two at a time. With both hands gripping the weapon I raised it to shoulder height and, with my back sliding along the wall that ran past the window, I entered the room. Huber was still on her knees but had fallen face forward on to the floor. Blood was pooling around her head.

To her left, lying on his back, half in and half out of his precious cupboard, was the body of the young man. A single bullet wound in his right temple. The lack of blood told me that it had been a clean kill. He had died instantly, felt no pain. But there was no sign of Scott.

At that moment, and for the first time in my life, I felt the blood draining from my legs. For a split-second I feared that they might give way altogether. Then, as the adrenaline began to course through my veins and my mind cleared, a feeling of what can only be described as pure evil came over me. It was like nothing else I had ever experienced before. It was nothing like the feeling I got before or during combat. That was my job, a way of life, nothing personal. Whereas this was dark. Very dark. I've thought about it time and again over the years. The feeling I had that day; how in a heartbeat it left me totally empty – a shell of a man – one who was hell-bent on revenge. Someone capable of killing for pleasure.

'Drop the weapon on the floor and turn around . . . slowly.' Scott's voice was calm. There was no anxiety, no panic. He could have been ordering a beer at a pub in Knightsbridge.

I flicked on the safety and, after dropping the Sig on the floor, I slowly turned around.

Scott was standing in the doorway. It took me a few seconds to work out that after murdering Huber and the young man he had quietly made his way up the stairs towards the second floor, where he had waited for my return.

However, instead of the silenced Glock he had apparently used to kill Huber and the young man, and which he now held in his left hand, hanging beside his thigh, I was staring down the barrel of the Makarov I had given him just before leaving the room.

Scott was the first to speak. It was as though he was reading my mind. Without waiting to be asked he answered the obvious question. 'Because it had to be done. They had served their purpose and no longer had a part to play in the game.'

I glanced at Huber's body, then back at Scott. My blood was boiling. I was raging inside but knew that losing my temper now would gain me nothing, except maybe a bullet in the head. I took a breath. 'And what game would that be?'

Scott said nothing at first but then, as a sort of afterthought, said, 'My game. I have long suspected that there is a mole within Century House. I just couldn't prove it, but when the BRIXMIS officer told me what you had acquired I knew that if I could get my hands on it – the NOC list – well, anything was possible.'

I nodded at Huber. 'That still doesn't explain why they had to die.'

'If you're right and that notebook contains the information you say it does, the information you told the BRIXMIS officer to pass on to London that night in the Dresdner Heide Forest; the night you found out that you were not going to be extracted, then the fact that I have it needs to remain a secret. That way, once I manage to decipher the names, which will be a lot easier with the attached telephone numbers, I will know who is running agents for the other side. More importantly, I will also know if they are members of the British, American, or West German intelligence communities and I will then be able to identify the mole. Once I know that, and have secured my future, the powers that be back in London will make sure that these people continue to pass information to their opposite numbers in the East. But, from then on, it will only be the information we want them to have.'

Scott now had the look of a cat that had not only got the cream but had also stolen the keys to the dairy. He continued, 'And, as you know, a secret is only a secret until somebody else knows. Once it's out in the open it's no longer a secret and has no value to the holder.'

I shook my head. 'And you couldn't risk anybody else, specifically

Huber, opening her mouth and revealing the existence of the book at some time in the future?'

Scott smiled, but it wasn't a happy smile. 'Smart lad.'

I didn't know what Scott had planned for me but, given what he had just told me and what had happened to both Huber and the young man, I suspected it wasn't going to be pleasant. 'So, what happens now . . . ? To me?'

A look of regret began to creep across Scott's face. 'Well, given what you now know and what I've just done I can hardly let you return to your regiment and risk you telling either your commanding officer or someone back in London about what happened here. The original plan was to bring you in and, after a short, private de-brief, simply let you return to your regiment. But when Townsend, the BRIXMIS officer, told me about the NOC list, I realised it wasn't going to be that simple. So, I decided to leave you where you were while I worked out what to do next. Stranded alone behind the Iron Curtain with no way of getting out. It's not as if you were going anywhere.'

I all but growled at him. 'But then the Wall came down and I was no longer reliant on you to extract me?'

He pressed his lips together. 'Exactly. I had planned to find you, take the notebook and leave your dead body in the motel room. But then you turned the tables on me and came up with this ludicrous idea to save Huber. Killing you here, on East German soil, and removing all knowledge of the notebook's existence suddenly seemed a much better idea.' Scott glanced down at the bodies of Huber and the young man. 'And, as you told me earlier . . . now there are no credible witnesses to say otherwise.'

I wasn't done yet. 'And how exactly are you going to explain my death, or disappearance, to the powers that be back in Germany and London?'

Scott couldn't help himself and laughed out loud. 'Nobody knows that you're working for me, or that you're even here in East Germany.'

'What about Thompson and my current CO?'

Scott slowly shook his head. 'Nobody. Thompson has no idea that this mission is even taking place. Your current colonel thinks you're working for the Luge Association who are currently in Austria, as an army observer.'

Scott lifted the silenced Glock, slipped it into the left-hand pocket of his coat, rolled his wrist and glanced at his watch. 'This has all been very nice, chatting with you like this, but I need to go now.'

I had no idea why Scott had decided to use the Makarov but, given what he had just told me about my apparent non-existence – the fact that no one 'official' even knew I was here in East Germany – I can only assume that if he killed me using Soviet ammunition, fired through the Makarov, and placed the Glock in my dead hand then, if, or when, our bodies were found here, I would take the blame for killing Huber and the young man and Scott would be home free.

I watched as he raised the Makarov to shoulder height. The hammer was all the way back – in the fully cocked position – and all of a sudden I realised I couldn't remember if I had squeezed the trigger after releasing the slide before handing it to him. If I had done so that would mean Scott had reloaded the weapon and re-cocked it himself – something any half-decent soldier would have done. I heard a faint click as he flicked off the safety and I began to panic.

Is it loaded or empty?

'W . . . what about the notebook?' I asked, still playing for more time while I tried to work out a way of stopping him from squeezing the trigger.

Scott shrugged his shoulders. 'Don't worry, I'll find it eventually. It has to be either on your person or hidden somewhere in the car.'

As calmly as I could I began to reach into the right-hand pocket of my jacket.

Scott raised the muzzle of the Makarov another inch. It was now pointed at my head. He stretched out his arm. 'Don't.'

I smiled at him, but inside I was bricking myself as I continued to lift Bonsack's Makarov out of my pocket. 'Go on,' I said, as calmly as I could. 'Pull the trigger. It's empty.'

Scott's expression told me everything I needed to know. His eyes narrowed and were questioning. He wasn't sure; he hadn't checked. If he had known that the gun was fully loaded – if he had checked – he would probably have burst out laughing as he pulled the trigger. But he didn't.

I have often wondered how a trained assassin like Scott – because, given the cold-hearted way he'd killed Schneider, Huber and the young man, that's exactly what he was – failed to realise there were no bullets in his gun. Then again, and unlike me, he had not been carrying a Makarov around for months. Weighing 730gms empty, the Makarov is slightly heavier than a Glock 17. Given that Scott had already fired five rounds, combined with the added weight of the silencer, may well have been what confused him. I would have known just by picking it up that it was empty. And, as I did when Huber first handed me the weapon down in Zinnwald, whether it was loaded or not is something I would have immediately checked. That is what trained soldiers do.

I swear my heart stopped beating as I raised my pistol and watched Scott give a nervous smile as he squeezed the trigger. There was nothing but a hollow click as the firing pin failed to make contact with a firing cap.

I would like to say that handing Scott the empty Makarov had all been part of the plan – but it wasn't. It was pure fluke. No Special Forces soldier would ever put his primary weapon in his pocket, there's too great a chance of it getting snagged if you needed to draw it in a hurry. That's why I kept the Sig in the back of my belt. Moving Bonsack's loaded Makarov away from his body was done on pure instinct. Even though I knew he was dead, my training dictated the weapon still had to be made safe and moved out of his reach. Without thinking and not wanting to leave it lying on the floor – again, simple good housekeeping and basic training – I had slipped it into my pocket. When I then picked up the second empty Makarov, the one used by the young man, with the Sig returned to the back of my belt and one pocket already heavy with Bonsack's pistol, I had, without thinking, handed it to Scott to look after. Which is how he now came to be pointing an unloaded pistol at me.

Initially not a word passed between us as we stood staring at each other across the sights of our respective weapons. I was so angry that I toyed with killing Scott there and then.

As Scott realised his gun really was empty he went to reach into his pocket for the Glock.

I raised the Makarov an inch higher, to a spot on his chest, just below his throat. His hand dropped back to his side.

'That's the Makarov I gave the young man. I didn't know whether he would do what I wanted him to do or not, or what he might do when it was all over. So, I only put a single round in the chamber. The magazine is empty. Any half-decent soldier would have checked that the weapon was loaded before threatening to use it. However, just so we're clear and to avoid any confusion, this one is loaded. If you *had* managed to get your hand into your pocket, your Glock would have never seen the light of day. I would have killed you without giving it a second's thought. And, believe me, given what I know now and what you've just done, it would have been neither quick nor painless.'

To be honest, that's exactly what I wanted Scott to do: give me an excuse to kill him. But, as you would expect, faced with less than a 50 − 50 chance of winning, he resorted to type and backed down.

'Drop the Makarov on the floor.'

The weapon may have been empty but, in the right hands, it could still be deadly. I was staring into his eyes when I heard it bounce on the floorboards.

'Now, using just the thumb and index finger of your left hand, do the same with the Glock.' I took a step forward and extended my right arm, emphasising the threat. 'Slowly.'

I was moving before the Glock had completed its journey to the floor. I saw Scott's eyes widen as I leaped forward, closing the distance between us. A fraction of a second later a perfect left hook connected with his chin and there was a loud crack.

Scott followed the Makarov and the Glock to the floor.

Given the crack, I suspected his jaw was broken, but I was nowhere near done. However, it was only as I shifted the weight on to my left leg and prepared to kick his head off his shoulders with my right that I realised he was out cold, and there is nothing to be gained by beating a man who can no longer feel pain.

I pointed Bonsack's Makarov at Scott's forehead but, as I took up the first pressure on the trigger, I stopped. Him being unconscious had saved his life; robbed me of my excuse and opportunity to kill him.

Ten minutes later, as I drove through the castle gates, I looked in the rear-view mirror of the Moskvitch. Scott had regained consciousness and, using the doorposts for support, he was now standing at the entrance to the castle's west wing, staring.

He would know that he was lucky to be alive. There was no way he was going to call me back and risk me finishing the job.

It was as I drove out of the castle, through Colditz itself, and on to the road that led first south to Route 4, then west towards Herleshausen and what remained of the Inner German Border, that I began to wonder what it had all been for? I had spent four months living on the edge — literally running to live. But why? What if, once I had made it back to the West, was safe in the motel at Kassel Ost, I had just left it alone. Would Huber still be alive? That feeling of guilt that was now washing over me — that my arrogance, my belief that I could sort it all out, save the day and her, had somehow contributed to her death — was something that, even today, thirty years later, I have been unable to shake.

Going Home

M Y JOURNEY BACK, across to what to all intents and purposes was still East Germany, was one of the most traumatic journeys I have ever made. Not because it was filled with danger, or even that my life was at risk, it was all about what had gone before.

My mission was over, although, given what Scott had told me in Colditz, I doubted that anybody would ever know it had even taken place. What had happened, or what the ramifications would have been if things had not worked out the way they did – if Metzger's men had managed to assassinate Gorbachev – were beyond my comprehension. However, the body count for what had begun life as a peacetime 'sneak and peak' was staggering. Seven people were dead, four of them killed by me; and in circumstances I still have trouble justifying to myself today, even though, at the time, I considered my actions unavoidable, committed in self-defence, in a kill or be-killed situation. However, that doesn't make them any easier to live with, not even close to thirty years after the event.

As I travelled west along Route 4, I spotted what I assumed was the River Werra. I pulled off at the next exit and stopped in a small *parkplatz*. Standing beside the car, I removed the Sig from my jacket pocket. If everything Scott had told me back in Colditz was true, then I needed to get rid of the weapon before re-entering the West, but I couldn't just throw it into the river – what if it was found and linked back to the three people I had killed with it? My paranoia was now back in all its glory, and I quickly began to disassemble the weapon. First I removed the magazine and emptied the rounds into my pocket. Pulling back the top slide, I locked it in place and removed the slide stop. As I started to take it apart I looked at the metal frame beside the trigger guard. The serial number had been filed off.

Scott wasn't taking any chances.

With the weapon now in bits on the car bonnet, I lifted the barrel and slipped it into my pocket, then gathering up the rest of the weapon I set off towards the river. As I walked along the riverbank, I threw the individual pieces of the dismantled weapon and the remaining rounds into the water. Spread them out over a total distance of two hundred metres or more, but I held on to the barrel. That could still tie me to the bodies so I would dump that somewhere else. The Makarov wasn't so much of a problem. There was no way it could be traced back to me, so I would hang on to it until I was safely back across what remained of the Inner German Border before disposing of it. Ten minutes later I was back in the car and once again heading west along Route 4 towards the Herleshausen crossing point.

It was as I approached what was left of the Inner German Border that the realisation of what Scott had done, and how he had used me, began to kick in.

It would appear that the last three months had been nothing more than an elaborate charade, put together and then stage-managed by Scott. I remembered our first meeting in Covent Garden, the one I had attended with Thompson. The way Scott had jumped in and told me his name before Thompson had a chance to introduce him, and that from that point on Thompson never referred to him by name. Furthermore, given the fact that my paranoia was now running rife, I had no way of knowing, or ever finding out, whether 'Scott' was his real name or not. Whether there really was a mole within the SIS – or maybe could it even be the case that Scott was the mole? I would be lying if I said that the thought had never crossed my mind.

I also had no way of knowing what was waiting for me on my return to my unit in northern Germany. If Scott was telling the truth back in Colditz, and my commanding officer believed I was working as a military observer with the British Luge Team in Austria, then my return, although earlier than expected, would be relatively problem free. However, for all I knew, Scott could have been lying through his teeth about this as well and I could have been reported AWOL for close to four months and now be subject to immediate arrest and court martial. Given what I had learned at Colditz there was nothing I would not have put beyond Scott.

As I reached the border crossing at Herleshausen, waited my turn in the queue of cars, filled with family, friends and everything they could carry, all heading to what they believed would be a better future in the West, the rest of the free world was still celebrating the fall of the Berlin Wall, an event they considered to be one of the ordinary people's greatest triumphs over oppression,

However, as I took the slip road off Route 4, joined Route 7 and headed north past the Kassel Ost services, I came across the first casualties of what would soon become known as German reunification.

The hard shoulder was littered with the carcasses of abandoned or wrecked Trabants, Wartburgs and Barkas, the East German version of the Volkswagen minibus. Treasured vehicles whose engines had blown up, and then been abandoned shortly after having their tanks filled with what their primitive two-stroke engines considered the rocket fuel, which was being dispensed by the pumps at West German petrol stations.

Then there were those that were driven by individuals who had no comprehension of what a two and a half tonne Mercedes-Benz travelling at over 200kph will do to a motorised egg box that decides to change lanes at the very last moment. Sadly, the noise of ambulance sirens provided a lot of the soundtrack to my journey north that day.

The Moskvitch finally gave up the ghost in Dortmund, and to be honest, I was surprised it got me that far. I dumped it in a Ratios supermarket car park in the early hours of Wednesday morning and, as I made my way to the Hauptbahnhof, Dortmund's main railway station and a train that would take me further north, once again I prepared myself for confrontation.

Post Op (Post Operational) De-Brief

ALTHOUGH I WAS ready for whatever was going to come at me upon my return to my unit in northern Germany, I needn't have worried. But my colonel's look of surprise as I walked into regimental headquarters on that Thursday morning was an absolute picture. After a moment's silence, during which time I assume he was trying to work out where I had come from, he asked, 'What are you doing here, Mr Shore?'

I smiled. The term was not meant as some sort of put down. It's a tradition in some regiments, especially the older, more traditional ones, that commissioned officers use the term 'Mister' when addressing a senior warrant officer.

His question was understandable. I had returned to the unit unannounced.

'I work here, Boss.'

Around that time, the phrase 'Crash Out' disappeared from the active vocabulary of the British Army on the Rhine. It had referred to a regiment or brigade being suddenly ordered to leave barracks, often in the middle of the night, in order to take up positions to counter the combined armies of the Warsaw Pact – no longer deemed a threat. Apart from that, life pretty much returned to normal as far as I was concerned.

By Christmas I had still heard nothing from Scott and I wasn't surprised. After what he had done he was probably spending every waking minute, and hopefully some while he slept, wondering if, or when, I would contact Century House. If I did, the end of his career would probably be the least of his problems.

It's a well-accepted fact that every secret service organisation in the world appears to operate above, and for the most part outside, of the law. Given what Scott had told me that final morning in Colditz, along with the fact that he had murdered two innocent civilians, one of whom (the young man in the cupboard) posed no threat to him or anybody else on the planet, I now suspected that the whole mission had been Scott's idea from the very start. I decided he had somehow been 'off the reservation', operating outside the system and without the knowledge of his superiors at Century House. Of course, this meant that everything I had done 'for Queen and Country' had in turn been unsanctioned and unofficial.

But that didn't stop me from spending the next two years, my final two years in the military, waiting for the call that would have summoned me to the CO's office to be confronted by Scott or someone else from Century House. If Scott had already told them about Metzger's notebook, then even now I might still be bundled on to a flight at RAF Gutersloh and possibly not be seen again for a good few years.

Yes, the paranoia was there, and still is even today.

I never saw Scott again and, to this day, I don't know if that was his real name.

I returned to the UK in February 1992 and two months later, on 24 April, I was out of the army and started a somewhat troubled life based in Hereford. I knew that after twenty-two years' service my journey from soldier to civilian was not going to be an easy one. They say that two of the most stressful events in a person's life are moving house and losing their job. Well, at the stroke of a pen, the job I loved and the environment I had lived in for over twenty-two years totally vanished. Work was hard to find (there's not a lot of call in civilian life for someone who deals in death), and as a result my family's financial situation grew steadily worse and my personal stress levels were heading totally off the scale.

As I struggled to find a solution to our mounting debt problems, my past began to catch up with me. My days were becoming a melting pot of guilt, anger, remorse and feelings of personal failure. My nights were both sleepless and troubled as I relived events from my past, and I was fast approaching the point where I would do anything I could just to be alone.

It was early one morning in 1997 that I bumped into Thompson in Hereford city centre. I had not seen him since leaving the Regiment back in 1987. He was now a retired brigadier. Using my first name, as he had always done, he greeted me like an old friend, as opposed to just one of his men. Given what had gone on before, and was going on in my life at the time, the warmth of his handshake that morning was probably the most comforting feeling I had had in a long time. Given the straight-dealing type of man he was, I wasn't that surprised.

We agreed to meet the following week for coffee in Ascari's, an Italian café situated at the top of Hereford's West Street and, at the time, a regular haunt for both serving and former members of the Regiment.

I was still hanging on to Metzger's black book and, that morning, knowing that I was meeting Thompson, I had without really thinking about it removed it from its hiding place and slipped it into the hidden pocket of my Barbour jacket. I was toying with the idea of giving it to him. With his circle of contacts, he would have been able to get it to the right people but, as neither Scott's name nor either of my missions to Zinnwald came up, I didn't volunteer anything, telling myself that if he'd wanted to know he'd have asked. Well, sometimes it's better to let such events lie where they fall, buried in the past.

Thompson died unexpectedly the following year, on 19 August 1998, in Hereford. He was just fifty-five years old.

A month later, close to nine years from the day I had stolen it from the bar in Zinnwald – nine years spent waiting for a knock at the door from the authorities that never came – I came to the conclusion it was now too late. There was no way I could hand the notebook in, at least not without having to explain how I had come by it in the first place, and then having to face what I was convinced would be a massive backlash.

That was the main reason why I had kept quiet about the notebook's existence, and why I hadn't reported Scott for what he had done, or what had gone on during those final months of 1989. I would have had to justify my actions, the ones I had been forced to take while behind the Inner German Border. And it would have been my word against Scott's.

I'd like to say that I thought the powers that be would believe me rather than Scott. But I wasn't going to bet my livelihood, perhaps even my freedom, on it. So, assuming what Adler had told me in the stable block at Schwarzbachtal was true – that not even he knew about Metzger's book – I could assume that its existence was unknown to anybody but Scott and myself. Because, it was surely true to say that if Scott had been legitimate he would have told his bosses about the book's existence and they would have come straight to me and demanded I hand it over; the names in that book would have been of huge interest to Scott's agency. Instead, he had obviously felt unable to say anything to anybody.

What was to be done? My decision required some serious thought. Thompson was dead. We had not been close friends – he had been my commanding officer, a social chasm that was rarely crossed – but he had always been my fallback position: one of only two people on the planet who could verify some of what had taken place over a decade earlier. He could have verified that he had been present while I was briefed by Scott, and that it was at a meeting which had been arranged by him personally. Of course, the only other person who really knew what had happened back then was Scott – a man who I knew for a fact would rather kill me than help me. As a result, I was now feeling very alone and rapidly heading for a very dark place. I needed to get away. Somewhere I could think without interruption. Somewhere there would be no distractions. Nobody at my door, no phone calls.

I will never forget the look on my wife's face as I picked up my Bergen and told her that I needed time to think and would be back once I had sorted my head out. And, God bless her, she let me go without wanting to know why or where.

It was late afternoon the following day that I sat nursing a mug of tea on a remote part of the Brecon Beacons; a Selection check-point along the ridge that runs south from Pen y fan, past Corn Du; a favourite spot of mine overlooking the forestry block beside the Upper Neuadd Reservoir.

My ability to recall past events in great detail, especially when it came to sights, sounds, smells and what had been said, in some cases many years earlier, had in the past been something of a curse but now, with nothing but the sound of the wind whistling around me, I decided to cast my mind back to the events that had taken place close to a decade earlier.

It is the job of the security services to gather secret intelligence that is crucial to the security of the UK and its citizens, such as finding out the size and readiness of the target country's armed forces – the type of mission I had undertaken when breaking into the military base on the outskirts of Sarajevo. But that, of course, had been at the request of Thompson; a regimental matter and, as far as I knew at the time, nothing to do with Scott. Although, following our meeting in Covent Garden, I naturally began to harbour suspicions that he might have had a hand in it.

The work of an intelligence gatherer – whether it be a soldier working behind enemy lines prior to an invasion; an intelligence agent working undercover in a hostile country or a local asset, a foreign civilian working on behalf of the agency against his or her own government – is, to put it mildly, extremely dangerous. No one who takes on that sort of work should be under any delusion – whichever agency is behind it.

Whether it's the SIS, Hereford, some other secretive Ministry of Defence organisation, or a local asset, the operator's actions are always deniable. And if the mission goes wrong, if the operator is caught, then the agency will not only deny all knowledge but will have taken considerable care to cover its tracks. It is only by meticulously preserving secrecy that such agencies are able to continue to do the very valuable work they do.

That said, it is, I believe, a totally different story behind the scenes, back at agency HQ. All missions have to have been approved and sanctioned by the senior agency director and those in command because, should they go wrong, there will be a need for an official inquiry and, if fault is found, then someone's career path is likely to be drastically shortened.

Under normal circumstances, when Hereford got involved, the CO would be called down to SIS HQ in London – in those days to Century House on Westminster Bridge Road – where he would be briefed. On his return to the Regiment the team would be selected and an operational plan would be formulated. However, the details of the mission – who was taking part, the objective and time frame – were not divulged, nor were they ever discussed with anyone not directly involved. But this is not what had happened that long ago morning in London's Covent Garden.

On that occasion, the briefing had taken place in a public place, in an open-air café. Although you would have expected Thompson, as the commanding officer, to be there, the fact that I was also there should have indicated to me that what I was about to do might be somewhat irregular and maybe not your typical Regiment/agency-type mission. However, on this occasion Thompson, a man I trusted, had arranged it and, as he was also present at the meeting, I did not dwell on its irregular nature for long.

My mind kept drifting back to that first meeting with Scott. Again, I recalled how he had jumped in and told me his name before Thompson had had a chance to introduce him. And what's more if Scott had been his real name, then Thompson would have already been aware of that fact, but the look of surprise on his face told me he wasn't. I also remembered how as we had walked away, past the Royal Opera House, I had asked Thompson, *'How long have you known Scott, Boss?'*

'I've known him since childhood . . .' he had answered.

So Thompson's surprise at Scott calling himself by that name should have been a very clear warning that everything was not as it should have been.

You might wonder what made this so strange? Surely, you might assume, Scott would not use his real name? Well, that might be typical in a work of fiction, a book or a film, but in reality he would be highly unlikely to use a false name to me, his asset in this mission, as it would risk causing total confusion if I needed to contact him.

Then there was Scott's 'need to know' statement: *'Apart from the three of us sitting here this morning, you are not to talk to anyone back at the Regiment about your special task in Yugoslavia, or about this meeting. Is that clear?'*

Such a statement was unnecessary when dealing with an individual in my position. It was a given. It was automatically accepted that everything I was told on occasions such as this was not to be discussed back at the Regiment. So, why did Scott feel the need to reinforce the point? Taken on its own this was nothing to get anxious or excited about but, added to the other irregularities, I could see now it had been another warning flag.

Then there was the fact that, even twelve years later, I was still struggling to make sense of my first, strange non-mission in Sarajevo, Yugoslavia. Looking back now, I wondered if maybe it had been something organised behind the scenes by Scott, some sort of test.

And there was another pertinent fact: not only was the Covent Garden meeting held in a public place but also the two subsequent meetings I had with Scott, in Newington Butts and Victoria Park. They were all some distance away from Century House and there-fore carrying a low risk that someone he knew might spot him talking to Thompson and me and wondering what he was up to.

Thompson had explained the Covent Garden meeting away by telling me that '*Scott is slightly paranoid at the moment. He has long suspected that there is a mole within MI6.*' And, although I hadn't put too much weight on it at the time, I now recalled my closing statement to Thompson as we headed to Covent Garden tube station that day: '*And as far as everyone else is concerned I don't exist?*'

Thompson's response to my statement had been just one word: '*Exactly.*'

The first mission I performed for Scott, the one where I was tasked to find out what had happened to Littman, his missing East German agent, had only lasted a week and was basically a peacetime 'sneak and peak': get in, have a good nose around and get out again without being seen. A simple operation and one I had no reason to question. Then, during my second mission for Scott, the fact that I had no direct contact with him for close to three months meant I was denied any further red flags or warning signs regarding his intentions or motives. As a result, it was only when I had reached the Kassel Ost Raststätte on Route 7, and before Scott had arrived, that other warning signs had started to appear and I began to link them back to the anomalies at the beginning of the mission.

First off there was the emergency contact number, the one I was to use if the whole project turned to a bag of shit. '*My home phone number. Don't use it unless you have to, and never ever call me at Century House,*' Scott had told me.

Looking back now, alarm bells should have started ringing at that point. Of course, under normal circumstances, if I was still working for Hereford I wouldn't have needed Scott's home number. If I had a problem, needed additional information or an extraction, I would have contacted Thompson and, if need be, he would have contacted Scott. But I had left Hereford two years earlier, in 1987, and Thompson was no longer my CO.

It was nineteen hours after my phone call to Scott's home number that he turned up outside my motel room and, to my surprise, not only was he armed but the weapon was already in his hand, although concealed in his pocket and apparently ready for use if necessary. I have no idea what the protocol is now but, back then, it was not unusual for security service officers to be armed on active service in a hostile environment – as were MI5 officers operating in Ulster. But this was West Germany – a NATO country – and, as Scott was totally unaware of my intentions to head back East to find Huber, it should have been purely an admin exercise: a simple matter of chaperoning me and Metzger's little black book back to the UK. So, why was he carrying a pistol?

Then, later in Colditz, when I asked Scott if he had ever killed a man, he had answered, '*No*'. A statement I took at face value.

However, it wasn't until I was staring down at Schneider's body, lying flat on its back, eyes wide open but lifeless, with two bullet holes in his chest and a third in his forehead, that I thought: *Nice. Could have been a professional hit.*

It is true that all agency field operators receive weapons training, but back then you would have probably found that very few ever had to use one in a live situation or had been forced to kill someone. Given what I'd just seen, this was evidently not the case with Scott. He was obviously well experienced and had killed before – and, as a result, I knew he had lied to me.

Which brought me to the conversation we had later that morning in Colditz. The one where, after disposing of the two bodies, I returned to the castle and found myself staring down the barrel of a Makarov; wondering whether or not it was loaded.

As I watched the mist roll up the valley from Torpantau towards Cribyn and Pen y Fan, my world began to descend into darkness as I pictured Huber, still on her knees, face down on the floorboards, blood pooling around her head. As the image became clearer I felt my pulse rate rise and I recalled Scott's clinical statement.

'*Because it had to be done. They had served their purpose and no longer had a part to play in the game.*'

'*And what game would that be?*'

'*My game.*'

'*That still doesn't explain why they had to die.*'

Scott's response bordered on flippant. '*A secret is only a secret until somebody else knows. Once it's out in the open it's no longer a secret and therefore has no value to the holder.*'

It all started to fall into place. Scott obviously assumed that Huber was aware of Metzger's little black book and what it contained. I'd said, '*And you couldn't risk anybody else, specifically Huber, opening her mouth, revealing the existence of the book at some time in the future?*'

'*Smart lad.*'

'*And how exactly are you going to explain my death, or disappearance, to the powers that be back in Germany and London?*'

The look on Scott's face at the time had been one of pure malice.

'*Nobody knows that you're working for me, or that you're even here in East Germany.*'

'*What about Thompson and my current CO?*'

Scott had slowly shaken his head. '*Nobody. Thompson has no idea that this mission is even taking place. Your current colonel thinks you're working for the Luge Association who are currently in Austria, as an army observer.*'

I might have understood him murdering Huber and the young man if the two of them had been a threat to national security, but they weren't.

Now some of you will be thinking that surely *Scott* was just doing the sort of thing the agency does routinely, working outside the law, and answerable to no one.

Well, perhaps it's because we have been brought up reading books and watching films about the likes of James Bond, George Smiley and Jason Bourne that we now expect such agencies to be duplicitous, ruthless and murderous as a matter of course. But, in my experience, the sort of duplicity and murderous intention that Scott showed towards someone on the same side – me – was a complete outrage to all the codes and standards by which these organisations live and work. I can honestly say I have never come across or heard of anything similar.

The reality is that unless I bump into him again – which wouldn't end well – I'll probably never know what Scott's motives were. I can only guess. But all the evidence showed me that Scott had been working not in the interests of the agency that employed him, but in order to further his own private interests. I am far more cynical these days about what people in all walks of life will do in order to further their own careers, protect themselves, or to wield power or acquire wealth. It seems to me that wherever careers and money are involved, morals and common decency tend to fall by the wayside and, as a consequence, especially when we're talking about a military or intelligence environment, good men and women will suffer and die. The story of Metzger's black book was testimony to that. In all likelihood, it was full of information about operatives from a number of foreign agencies, both friendly and otherwise – men or women who were no doubt outwardly respectable – working 'for the greater good', but who were also prepared to talk to, or deal with, members of Baader-Meinhof, one of the most reviled terrorist organisations of its time, simply in order to get what they wanted. And whether Scott was actually a mole, which on the whole I now doubt, or simply acting on his own volition, trying to climb the career ladder, he was prepared to do whatever it took.

He had murdered three people in cold blood in order to ensure their silence. This was most certainly not the way Hereford operated, nor the way an officer of a national security agency should behave – nor in my experience do behave – and my firm conviction is that those in power back at Century House would never have authorised or condoned what he had done that morning.

As for killing me, an experienced and trusted SNCO who up until that point believed he had been working at the agency's behest, well, that was entirely beyond any code I have ever heard of.

Which brought me to something I had had trouble dealing with and still have trouble dealing with thirty years later – Huber. She wasn't the first dead women I'd ever seen. There had been many over the years, especially in Africa where we had found whole families, men, women and children murdered – butchered – but Kirstin was the first one with whom I had what, at the time, was turning into a deep personal attachment. The circumstances in which she died were nothing short of barbaric, and she died for no other reason than that Scott believed she knew more than she should and was a threat to him. I doubt she had even been aware of the existence of Metzger's little black book – well, not before hearing the conversation between Bonsack and myself that morning in Colditz. Even if she had been, I would be surprised if she had any idea of what it contained or its potential for causing trouble.

She was a beautiful young woman who had not only dreamed of a future for her country that was not controlled by the Stasi and the Kremlin, but she had risked her freedom and her life to achieve it by helping me. And now, with the Wall down and her dream about to be realised, she had had everything to live for. Instead, that morning Scott had executed her like a dog, without a moment's thought and, given the way he had dispatched Schneider, I suspect without any hint of emotion.

In truth, although it may appear to be a callous statement, I don't think it was the sight of her on her knees, face down on the floor-boards, with blood pooling around her head that was then, and even now, tearing me apart. It was knowing that I had totally underestimated Scott; misread the warning signs; been unaware of his potential for evil. As a result she had died alone. She had trusted me and I had failed her.

I told you earlier in the book that as a soldier, and especially a Special Forces soldier, we have to believe that what we are doing is 'for the greater good'. More importantly, we also have to believe that those in command, or in Scott's case in control, are operating in the same way; obeying the same rules. Otherwise there is no way we could do what we do. It may well not be until after you leave the Brotherhood that you realise that some of those you trusted with your life, those whose orders you followed without too many questions, those like Scott, were only out for themselves.

You rarely get to see the whole picture in this line of work and what Scott was really up to will no doubt remain a mystery. Sitting here today it is certainly still a mystery to me. All I can say with any certainty is that he was not what he seemed, and he was defi-nitely not working for the agency or in the national interest when he sent me into East Germany.

It was as I pushed these reminiscences safely back into their mental black box that I knew what I had to do and, as darkness began to fall over the Beacons, I turned up the blue flame on my

Calor gas stove. Tearing the pages out one by one, I burned Metzger's little black book.

But even as I watched the last page burst into flames, disintegrate and float to the ground, I realised that burning the book was not going to be the line in the sand that I had hoped it might be. It wasn't over, and it probably never would be – 'not in this lifetime'.

The sights, sounds and smell of that morning back in Colditz were now seared into my brain. What's more, the nightmares, memories and pain connected with that morning were not to be my only punishment. Back then, and even today, thirty years on . . . *everything was different. Now I was an angry, suspicious loner, one who would not only avoid forming relationships, but did his best to drive people away. Why?*

Because: 'One cannot be betrayed [again] if one has no people . . .'

Epilogue

W HAT TOOK PLACE in Leipzig during the autumn of 1989 tends to be overshadowed by the sudden collapse of the Berlin Wall, an event that was photographed and filmed by hundreds of journalists and then broadcast around the world. Leipzig was many miles from Berlin, out of the way, and today only a few grainy tapes of what became the huge Monday evening demonstrations remain. Outside of Germany, these events have mostly been forgotten.

Ninth of November 1989 is considered to be the date the Wall fell, but the structure itself was not taken down overnight. It was gradually smashed to pieces over the following weeks, with many ordinary people doing their bit to remove it, using hammers and chisels, keeping little pieces of history for themselves. The government finally stepped in and supervised its ultimate destruction in 1990. Some parts of it still remain in Berlin. Smaller pieces are in museums around the world.

However, one of the many challenges Germany had to overcome before full reunification could be achieved, even after Soviet approval had been assured, were the security concerns of its neighbours and allies – in particular, the resistance of Britain and France.

Moreover, Poland, which had obtained a large part of former German territory in 1945, following the end of the Second World War, expelling millions of Germans from their homes, was still in need of a legally binding agreement recognising its border with Germany. If this could be achieved, and with the help of the Americans, Britain's and France's fears for the consequences of the formation of a new, reunited Germany overcome, then reunification would be possible.

At midnight on 3 October 1990, only eleven months after the

Berlin Wall had fallen, 16.5 million East Germans officially joined 62 million West Germans and the country become one again.

Conversely, many of the East German negotiators who were present at the time felt that the talks had not gone far enough. A few years later, Matthias Platzeck, who at the time was Minister-President of Brandenburg said, 'There was an "Anschluss [joining, the term used to describe the annexation of Austria into Nazi Germany on 12 March 1938] mentality" at the unification negotiations. There is a lot that went wrong during those talks. We tried to explain to our West German negotiation partners that when a society takes on a new form, with a small group joining a much larger one, it's important to include some active elements or symbols from the smaller group for the sake of harmony. That way, the smaller group won't feel like they've been overwhelmed, steamrollered. But there was nothing left of the smaller group [East Germany] in the new united Germany.

'Such a thing would have been so easy to achieve, to save just a few symbols, a few structures – there are some aspects of the way East Germany handled medical care that are coming back now, seen as good ideas more than twenty years after being discarded. Some aspects of East Germany's education programme, like the twelve-year school system, and pre-school care from a very early age. All of these things were thrown out of the unification talks for ideological reasons. The rule was: what comes from the West is good, and what originates from the East is bad.'

In general terms the reunification of the two Germanys remains a somewhat shaky marriage. This may come as a surprise to those living outside of Germany, where the general picture seems to be of ever-increasing prosperity and harmony but, nearly three decades on, opinion polls inside Germany show widespread discontent, especially in the former communist East.

Chancellor Angela Merkel, who was born in Hamburg on 17 July 1954 (a former West German), has called German reunification a success, with many political leaders in Germany, Europe and beyond also singing its praises, and it's true that free speech and freedom of movement are now enjoyed by all Germans, but it has come at a hefty price.

In the years immediately following reunification millions of former

East Germans lost their jobs and homes, and were evicted from houses they had lived in for close to thirty years; homes once owned but abandoned by those who fled to the West during the Cold War and who had now returned to reclaim them.

As a result, many are still struggling to come to terms with life in a reunited Germany and are now, understandably, becoming nostalgic about their life in former East Germany – forgetting the bad and only remembering the good: the jobs for life, the guaranteed pensions, and housing. This is, of course, a great irritation to the West Germans who have helped pay the 1.6 trillion euros it has taken to help rebuild the East, and a reason for their disenchantment can be seen everywhere. The population of the former eastern territories has shrunk by over two million. Unemployment has soared, young people are moving away in their droves, and what was once one of the Eastern Bloc's leading industrial nations is now largely devoid of industry.

There are no ghost towns in the East as yet but some cities, those with dwindling populations, have torn down hundreds of high-rise blocks on their outskirts, allowing the forests to grow back around them.

It should, therefore, come as no surprise that in a recent opinion poll sixty-seven per cent of Easterners do not feel like they are part of a united country, and only twenty-five per cent said they felt like 'Ein Volk' (one people). More surprisingly, another poll found that one in thirteen Easterners would have preferred it if the Berlin Wall and the much larger Inner German Border were still standing, still separating the 'Two' Germanys.

Conversely, following German reunification in 1990 it was confirmed that the RAF had indeed received financial and logistic support from the Stasi, which had given members shelter and new identities.

In August 1991, as a direct result of what happened in East Germany, the Velvet Revolution in Czechoslovakia and the organised civil unrest in a number of other former Warsaw Pact states, a *coup d'état*, referred to as the August Putsch, began in Moscow. Its aim was to take control of the country from Soviet President Mikhail Gorbachev. The leaders of the coup included senior members of the KGB and hardliners within the Soviet Union's Communist Party, the CPSU – those who were opposed to Gorbachev's far-reaching reform programme. The coup was opposed, mainly in Moscow, by a short but effective campaign of civil resistance. It collapsed two days later, returning Gorbachev to government, but the event destabilised the Soviet Union.

Although the dissolution of the Soviet Union in December 1991 was a serious blow to all Leninist groups, attacks were still being committed under the RAF name well into the 1990s, including the killing of Ernst Zimmerman, CEO of MTU Aero Engines, the bombing at the US Air Force's Rhine-Main Air Base (near Frankfurt), and the shooting of Gerold von Braunmühl, a leading official at Germany's foreign ministry. Some of the assassins were never reliably identified and are still perhaps out there somewhere; giving me good reason to remain vigilant all these years later.

In February 1992, a week before the start of the Winter Olympic Games in Albertville in France, something happened that reminded me of my first mission to East Germany. German bobsledder Holger Czudaj confessed to the German news agency 'DPA' that he had worked for the former East German secret police, the Stasi. He said at the time, 'I am sorry to have worked for the Stasi, but I had no choice.' Czudaj was a member of the German four-man team, which had won the European title the previous weekend.

The paper also reported that Czudaj had worked for the Stasi from 1988 onwards and had written ten reports on fellow-bobsledders at his club, Dynamo Zinnwald, using the name Ralf Richter.

German sport was also rocked by other Stasi revelations at this time, with players and officials from two former East German soccer clubs, Dynamo Dresden and Hansa Rostock, admitting to working for the Stasi.

This made me remember not only how closely the Stasi had been interwoven with my life back then, but also all aspects of East German society.

By 1998 my mission into East Germany had been over for close to a decade, but the baggage – what had happened during those few traumatic months and the raft of unanswered questions – still weighed heavy on my soul. I was puzzled as to why Metzger's death had not been reported on the day that it happened. It's not as if the remains of a car bomb would have gone unnoticed. Then there was Bonsack and Schneider. Following their sudden disappearance, were they ever reported missing? Or was it just assumed by those in the know that, fearing reprisals from the authorities in the West, the two of them had taken the gap – disappeared – and were now living quietly below the radar like so many other fearful ex-terrorists who had once been the darlings of the former regime. Still, by that time, I had resigned myself to the fact that these questions would probably never be answered.

In the same year, although still in its infancy, the Internet, and the amount of information it made available to the ordinary person, was growing at an astonishing rate. As a result, those unanswered questions were beginning to raise their ugly heads once more. It always amazes me how, today, young children use a computer and trawl through the enormous amount of information the Internet provides with the same ease that they devour a sandwich but, back then, getting to grips with this new technology was a steep learning curve for a 46-year-old ex-soldier. On the other hand, what the Internet did provide was complete anonymity. Yes, I know it's different today, now that Big Brother (predominately the intelligence services) is capable of monitoring every key stroke we make, but back then I could ask my questions and trawl through the raft of possible answers without anyone being any the wiser. That said, I never did find any of the answers I was searching for. Maybe my assumptions at the time were correct? Maybe with the Wall down and the rapid changes that were being made to the German constitution and government, decisions were made by those still managing to cling to power not to rock the boat; to sweep such things under the carpet. Or, just maybe, it went much deeper than that.

On 20 April 1998, an eight-page typewritten letter in German was faxed to the Reuters news agency, signed 'RAF' and with the submachine-gun red star, declaring that the group had dissolved.

However, in 1999, following a robbery in Duisburg, Germany, forensics found traces of Staub and Klette, two leading members of the RAF, causing an official investigation into a refounding of the organisation. Again, in January 2016, German police identified three RAF members as being the perpetrators of an assault on an armoured truck transporting €1 million, thus fuelling suspicions that the RAF might be active once more. However, these robberies are seen as criminal and not terrorist acts.

The RAF has been held responsible for thirty-four deaths, including many secondary targets, such as chauffeurs and bodyguards, as well as many injuries throughout its almost thirty years of activity.

On 25 July 1998, eight years after the dissolution of the former Soviet Union, Boris Yeltsin, the then president of the Russian Federation, appointed Vladimir Putin head of the FSB (the successor agency to the KGB); a position Putin would hold until August 1999. On 9 August that year, Vladimir Putin was appointed one of three First Deputy Prime Ministers, a position which enabled him, later that day (as the previous government led by Sergei Stepashin had just been sacked), to be appointed acting Prime Minister of the Government of the Russian Federation by President Yeltsin. Yeltsin then announced that he wanted to see Putin as his successor. However, Yeltsin's main opponents and would-be successors, Moscow Mayor Yury Luzhkov and former Chairman of the Russian government Yevgeny Primakov, were already campaigning to replace the ailing president and fought hard to prevent Putin's emergence as Yeltsin's potential successor. To no avail.

On 31 December 1999, Boris Yeltsin unexpectedly resigned and, according to the Russian constitution, Vladimir Putin became Acting President of the Russian Federation.

The first Presidential Decree that Putin signed that day was a guarantee that corruption charges against the former President of the Russian Federation (Yeltsin) and members of his family would not be pursued. On 7 May 2000, Vladimir Putin was inaugurated president.

If you had told me back in 1989 that the KGB major standing on the other side of the road from me would, in ten short years, become arguably one of the three most powerful men on the planet, a man who would be hell-bent on resurrecting the former Soviet Union along with all its evils; someone capable of plunging the entire world into a war that could possibly spell the end of mankind, I would have probably laughed at you.

I often wonder what would have happened if Metzger, Bonsack and the Kremlin Old Guard had got their way – stopped the Wall falling, the Soviet Union disintegrating and, as a result, what Europe and indeed the world would look like today . . .